Microprocessor Design Using Verilog HDL

by Monte Dalrymple

Microprocessor Design Using Verilog HDL

by ~~Monte Dalrymple~~

Microprocessor Design Using Verilog HDL

Published by
Circuit Cellar, Inc.
4 Park Street
Vernon, CT 06066 USA

Notices
Knowledge and best practice in this field are constantly changing. As new research and experience broaden our understanding, changes in research methods, professional practices, or technologies may become necessary.

Practitioners and researchers must always rely on their own experience and knowledge in evaluating and using any information, methods, parts, electronics, designs, code, or experiments described herein. In using such information or methods they should be mindful of their own safety and the safety of others, including parties for whom they have a professional responsibility.

To the fullest extent of the law, neither the Publisher nor the authors, contributors, or editors, assume any liability for any injury and/or damage to persons or property as a matter of products liability, negligence or otherwise, or from any use or operation of any methods, products, instructions, or ideas contained in the material herein.

Many of the products and company names mentioned herein are the trademarks of their respective holders.

Library of Congress Control Number: 2011935355
ISBN 978-0-9630133-5-4

Prepress Production and cover Design: Jack Jamar Graphic Design, Maastricht
Printed by Wilco Amersfoort

119029-1/UK

Table of Contents

Preface

In 1978 I was starting my career as an Integrated Circuit (IC) designer, and one of the engineers I worked with told me that "CPU jocks get all the glory." At the time we were each responsible for the design of a peripheral controller to go with the Zilog Z8000 microprocessor, and even though I was a new engineer I could see the truth in his assertion. In many respects this statement is still true today.

I have now been on both sides of the fence, having designed a number of peripheral controllers as well as a number of microprocessors, and I can say the glory shouldn't be reserved for just the "CPU jocks." There are just as many challenges involved in designing an 802.11 Wi-Fi controller as there are in designing a microprocessor. One of the reasons that I am writing this book is to demystify the process of CPU design.

Designing a microprocessor is not really that difficult. After all, a CPU is just a collection of state machines. But the task can be almost unmanageable without the right tools, and the advent of hardware description languages (HDLs) has significantly reduced the amount of work required. Using an HDL such as Verilog gives a CPU designer (or any logic designer) more time to concentrate on the big picture rather than getting bogged down in implementation details.

The format of this book is not like any other that I have seen, and deliberately so. I want to take you, the reader, through the entire design process from start to finish. Along the way I'll discuss the various issues that I considered when making design decisions. I am cheating a little bit, because even though it looks like I never needed to go back and revisit a design decision, that is only because the book was written after much of the design was complete. There really were iterations involved in this project, but I did not want to confuse the narrative by including them.

IC design is my livelihood, so I am not going to just hand you a completed design. All of the information required is here, but you will still need to read the text, understand the figures, and go through the Verilog code yourself if you want to have your own working design by the end of the book. It is possible, and not even that difficult. Good luck!

I believe that there is a need for this type of book, and I am grateful to the staff at *Circuit Cellar* for giving me the opportunity to present this information. I wouldn't be the engineer that I am today without the mentoring that I received starting out from Bill Carter, Dan Hillman, and the late Ross Freeman. Thanks, guys. A special thank you is also owed to my children: Joseph, Kristy, Elizabeth and Lindsay. Without their cheerleading I don't know if this project would ever have been finished.

Monte Dalrymple
Livermore, California, USA

1. Introduction

Goals of This Book

My goal in writing this book is to share some of the techniques I have used over the course of my career designing microprocessors. During that time microprocessors have evolved from relatively simple 4- or 8-bit devices to today's multi-GHz behemoths. Design tools have changed radically over that time period, but many of the tasks required have not changed at all. No matter what the size, a microprocessor is just a combination of interconnected state machines, and a designer still has to worry about what each state machine is doing during each clock cycle.

To make the example in this book manageable, I'll use a well-known 8-bit instruction set architecture and implement this instruction set with bus timing that makes it suitable for implementation in either a modern field-programmable gate array (FPGA) or an application-specific integrated circuit (ASIC). The book has enough information for you to have a working design by the time you finish the book.

Target Audience

I hope that a wide variety of readers will find the information here useful. Electrical engineering and computer science students will benefit from a real-world design example, and the book can be used as the basis for a project targeting a different instruction set or different machine timing. Practicing engineers wanting to expand their horizons may find some of the techniques applicable in a current or future job. And sophisticated electronics hobbyists should be able to think about implementing that custom microprocessor they've always dreamed of.

I expect the reader to be at least familiar with logic design and to have a basic understanding of how a microprocessor works. Some familiarity with assembly language will also be required. I'll be using the Verilog hardware description language (HDL), but no previous knowledge of Verilog is required.

If you are going to implement this design in actual hardware, you will need to know how to use a logic synthesis tool to translate the Verilog code into logic gates. You will also need to know how to use the layout or routing tool for your target technology. All of the Verilog code provided in the book is completely independent of technology, but you may need to instantiate I/O buffers or clock drivers before final implementation.

What to Expect

This is not a book about computer architecture or instruction set design. Both of those subjects have been extensively covered in the literature. What I have not seen covered before is a nuts-and-bolts introduction on how to reduce a computer architecture and instruction set to practice, and that is what you'll learn here.

The first section of the book is a review of Verilog HDL, so if you are already familiar with the language you can probably skim through this section. Verilog HDL provides a number of features that are not understood by logic synthesis tools, and those features are not covered here.

Designing with Verilog can be very intimidating if you are used to working with Karnaugh maps, block diagrams and schematics. When I was first introduced to Verilog, it took several months for me to become comfortable with a text-only representation of a design. But Verilog allows a designer to be incredibly productive, and it really is just another way to represent a design. These days the only time I use a schematic is for a printed circuit board design, and even then that's only because there are no logic synthesis tools for board design. So there will only be a few block diagrams here, and no schematics. It is important that you become familiar with the Verilog representation of logic to understand this design.

The second section will cover the coding conventions used in the book. You may be tempted to skip this section, but it is very important to have a consistent coding style for a project. A consistent coding style makes it much easier to visualize the logic being described by the Verilog code. You are of course free to use whatever convention you like, but the one I present here has worked for me over the course of more than a dozen designs.

The next two sections cover the initial design work, and are probably the most important in the book. The temptation for any designer is to jump right into the design implementation to get something working quickly, and then iron out the bugs. In my experience this is exactly the wrong way to do things, as it often leads to putting band-aids over problems. Taking the time up front to think about special cases will usually pay off with a "cleaner" design in the end. Remember, it's the special cases that you never thought about that are not going to work correctly at some critical time.

Once the initial design work is done, I'll jump right into the implementation. If the initial design work has been done properly the actual Verilog coding is straightforward. I will cover much of the design in this section, but you're still going to have to do some of the coding yourself. But the initial design work sections will give you all of the information and tools required to do this coding.

Once the Verilog coding is done we're about half done with the project! This is because now the microprocessor has to be verified, and this will usually take as long as or longer than the design itself. In this section I'll show you how to develop a self-checking testbench and some tricks to make the debug and testing easier. I'll also mention some of the requirements to guarantee fault coverage. The actual testbench can be downloaded[1] from the Internet to verify your design.

In the last section I'll give a brief overview of logic synthesis and timing analysis, so that you can reduce your design to practice.

Typeface Conventions

Just like coding conventions for Verilog, typeface conventions are an important part of this kind of book. I'll use three different typefaces to distinguish something from normal text:

Normal typeface in bold will be used for important tips or tricks. These are the things you'll want to remember for future designs.

Normal typeface in italic will be used when referring to worksheets or mnemonics from the design spreadsheet. The design spreadsheet encapsulates all of the important aspects of the internal operation for the microprocessor in a single location. It is the equivalent of microcode for the design.

A `monospace font` will be used for all Verilog code. This type of font should always be used for Verilog code (or software in general) for code readability, because it keeps things lined up from line to line.

2. Verilog HDL

Overview

This is not a comprehensive introduction to Verilog HDL. The Verilog language has a number of features that you will never use in a design, either because logic synthesis tools don't support them or because their use is not advisable in the real world. If you want to learn Verilog HDL in all its glory, get a copy of the OVI Verilog HDL LRM[(2)] and be prepared to invest some serious time for study. What I present here is what you will really need to complete a design.

Verilog was originally used for simulation and modeling, and it was only later that logic synthesis tools became available to translate from a Verilog description directly to hardware. In some ways the requirements for simulation conflict with those for logic synthesis, and I will try to point out where these different requirements exist.

Verilog HDL has been standardized by the Institute of Electrical and Electronic Engineers (IEEE) and the standard continues to evolve. In this book I will only use features available in the 1995 version of the standard, mainly because many of the tools that I use only support this level of the language. The 2001 version of the standard adds a few features that reduce the amount of typing required, but I find that the reductions make it easier to not think about what I'm typing, which can lead to dumb conceptual mistakes.

Verilog code looks a lot like C code, so if you do much programming in C, you may find yourself accidentally including constructs from that language. Don't do it! Verilog describes hardware and operations occur in parallel, which is fundamentally different from sequential software operation.

Data Types and Their Use

Verilog HDL supports two basic data types, both of which represent signals, and these data types can take one of four distinct values: `0`, `1`, `Z` and `X`. Both upper case and lower case are valid for `X` and `Z`. Both data types can be either a scalar (one bit wide) or a vector (more than one bit wide).

The values 0 and 1 are the normal binary states used in logic design so there isn't much more to say about them.

The value Z, as you might suspect, is used to represent a high-impedance or floating node. Normally this value should never occur on an internal signal, because a floating node inside a chip will lead to all kinds of problems. This is why you should never use a bidirectional bus inside a chip. If you inadvertently forget to assign a value to a signal in the design the simulator will assign it a value of Z. This usually makes it really easy to find this kind of error, because a Z on the input to an expression will eventually cause the output to misbehave.

The value X represents "unknown." The output of a flip-flop or latch that is not initialized by reset will start out as unknown, and the output of a gate with a floating input will usually be unknown. Unknown values readily propagate through gates, latches and flip-flops, and this can be a blessing or a curse during simulation. Because they propagate so easily unknowns will often cause a simulation to blow up, where everything quickly goes unknown. It will often take several simulation runs to track down exactly which node started all the trouble. And if you're not careful about how state machines are initialized by reset, you may find that the design can never enter a rational state on start-up. But it is important to remember that the X value doesn't really exist in real hardware; it is a tool for helping you when simulating hardware.

Specifying a value for a scalar can be as simple as 0, 1, Z or X. Vectors are a little more complicated, requiring both a width and radix along with the values. For consistency I always specify the width and radix, even with a 1-bit value. I almost always use either a binary or hexadecimal. The reason is that the default radix for Verilog is decimal, which can be easy to forget and lead to problems if you're used to thinking in hexadecimal while designing. Here are some examples of values (note that it is not valid Verilog syntax to have numbers in isolation):

```
1'b0                                      /* a single 0                  */
8'bzzzzzzzz                               /* 8 bits floating             */
16'hab78                                  /* hexadecimal value AB78      */
```

The two Verilog data types are defined using the keywords wire and reg, and they are fundamentally different in how they work.

The wire data type is continuously assigned a value, so it works just like a physical wire. Verilog automatically assumes that any undeclared signal is a wire data type, but it's good form to always declare every signal explicitly rather than rely on an implicit declaration. Here are three examples of declaring a wire:

```
wire          ld_io_addr;                 /* update io address           */
wire          ld_mem_addr;                /* update memory address       */
wire    [7:0] io_data_out;                /* i/o output data bus         */
```

It is possible to use one `wire` keyword to declare multiple signals, but I prefer not to do that because I always like to include a short description of the signal function as a comment. It is also possible to assign a value to the `wire` at the same time as the declaration. I prefer to separate the declarations of all of the signals into one section of the Verilog code and keep the actual logic in a separate section because I find it makes it easier to find signals in the code.

Unlike the `wire` data type, the `reg` data type is assigned a value only when a specified condition is met. This means that the `reg` data type must be used for latches, flip-flops and memories, but it is also possible to use a `reg` to implement a regular logic function. Signals with the `reg` data type are declared as shown below:

```
reg         stk_tran;                    /* stack transaction              */
reg         t1;                          /* first clock of transaction     */
reg   [7:0] data_in;                     /* data input bus                 */
```

Memories are declared with a special syntax, as shown below. In general you will never use a memory declared like this in a design because the synthesis tool will implement the memory using flip-flops. Instead, you will almost always instantiate a dedicated memory block in the design. These two memory declarations are taken directly from the testbench, which is never compiled as logic but is only used for simulation. Note the different ordering for specifying the memory depth. It's specified this way because the `[0:65535]` is an index into the memory array that specifies the start and end of the index. This is the one place where I use a decimal number.

```
reg   [7:0] rdmem [0:65535];             /* inst/data read memory          */
reg   [7:0] wrmem [0:65535];             /* data write compare memory      */
```

Bit Widths and Labeling

In the examples above I used the indices `[7:0]` for byte-wide buses. Verilog does not impose any constraints on the indices used for vectors, so I could have just as easily used `[8:1]` or `[0:7]` in these examples. But it very rarely makes sense to use an oddball set of indices, and I don't recommend doing so unless absolutely necessary.

There are often cases where only one bit of a bus is needed, and the syntax for this case is just as you would expect, as shown below:

```
assign carry_bit  = af_reg_out[0];
assign par_bit    = af_reg_out[2];
assign sign_bit   = af_reg_out[7];
```

In cases where you need to use a sub-field of a bus, the syntax is almost the same. Here the 16-bit AF register is split into its two component 8-bit registers.

```
assign aa_reg_out = af_reg_out[15:8];
assign ff_reg_out = af_reg_out[7:0];
```

It is also possible to concatenate values, individual or otherwise, to assign a value to a bus. In the example below I create the sign-extend byte for an 8-bit value. It is important to note that the expression continues across input lines. Only the semicolon terminates the expression, and the advantage of a monospace font is evident in this example.

```
assign bsign_ext = {addb_in[7], addb_in[7], addb_in[7], addb_in[7],
                    addb_in[7], addb_in[7], addb_in[7], addb_in[7]};
```

There is an alternate way to do the replication of a bit to create a bus, as shown below. While this syntax does require less typing, I tend to use the example above just because it is more obvious to me what is going on.

```
assign bsign_ext = {8{addb_in[7]}};           /* sign-extend b bus in         */
```

Logical Operations

Verilog provides the usual complement of logical operators, namely AND, OR and Invert. It also provides identical bit-wise operations for multi-bit quantities. Verilog completely specifies operator precedence, but I don't want to have to remember exactly what the precedence is when writing code, so I always use parentheses to make my intentions explicit. Then there is never the possibility of an incorrect implementation. The only exception to this is the logical inversion operator, which I know is always the highest precedence. The operators for logical (single-bit) quantities are:

`!` is the logical inversion operator

`&&` is the logical AND operator

`||` is the logical OR operator

The code snippet below shows some examples of the use of these operators. Notice how the parentheses make the order of the operations explicit. Don't worry about the strange index for the `wr_addr` bus. I'll explain how that works later in this chapter.

```
assign ld_m_aa =   ld_regf && wr_addr[`WR_AA] && !alt_af_reg;
assign ld_m_ff = ((ld_regf && wr_addr[`WR_FF]) || ld_flag) && !alt_af_reg;
```

Bit-wise operations are very similar to the logical operations, and in fact I have seen some designers use the bit-wise operators for single-bit quantities. I strongly discourage this however, as the logical operators make it more readily apparent to a reader (which might be the original designer years in the future) that the operation is on individual signals. The only exception is for Exclusive-OR, because there is no equivalent logical operator. The operators for multi-bit quantities are:

~ is the bit-wise inversion operator.

& is the bit-wise AND operator

| is the bit-wise OR operator

^ is the bit-wise Exclusive-OR operator

Listing 2-1 shows some examples of the use of these operators in the logic portion of an arithmetic logic unit (ALU). Unlike the previous examples the `logic_out` bus is a `reg` data type. In this section of code the `logic_out` bus is continuously assigned a value, just like the `wire` data type. I'll cover why this is the case shortly.

```
always @ (aluop_reg or alua_in or alub_in) begin
  casex (aluop_reg)
    `AOP_BAND:  logic_out = {8'h00, alua_in[7:0] & alub_in[7:0]};
    `AOP_BOR:   logic_out = {8'h00, alua_in[7:0] | alub_in[7:0]};
    `AOP_BXOR:  logic_out = {8'h00, alua_in[7:0] ^ alub_in[7:0]};
    `AOP_RLD1:  logic_out = {8'h00, alub_in[3:0],  alua_in[3:0]};
    `AOP_RLD2:  logic_out = {8'h00, alua_in[7:4],  alub_in[7:4]};
    `AOP_RRD1:  logic_out = {8'h00, alua_in[3:0],  alub_in[7:4]};
    `AOP_RRD2:  logic_out = {8'h00, alua_in[7:4],  alub_in[3:0]};
    `AOP_APAS:  logic_out = alua_in;
    `AOP_PASS:  logic_out = alub_in;
    default:    logic_out = 16'h0000;
    endcase
  end
```

Listing 2-1. Using Verilog bit-wise operators.

Several of the previous examples have shown how to combine individual signals or smaller-width multi-bit signals into a wider multi-bit signal, but Verilog also provides a shorthand way to reduce multi-bit signals to an individual logical value. This is accomplished via the reduction operators, which are listed below:

`&` is the AND reduction operator.

`~&` is the NAND reduction operator

`|` is the OR reduction operator

`~|` is the NOR reduction operator

`^` is the Exclusive-OR reduction operator

`~^` is the Exclusive-NOR reduction operator

Each of these reduction operators returns the result of the corresponding logical function applied to all of the bits of the input multi-bit vector. Thus the `&` reduction operator returns a one if all of the input bits are one, and the `~|` reduction operator returns a one if all of the input bits are zero. The `^` reduction operator returns a one if an odd number of the input bits are one (odd parity). The code below shows a couple of examples of reduction operators in use. The first line tests for a value of 8'b01 on the least-significant byte of the ALU output, while the second line returns a one if the parity of this byte is even.

```
assign one_nxt  = ~|alu_result[7:1] && alu_result[0];
assign par_nxt  = ~^alu_result[7:0];
```

The example below shows the use of the conditional operator, which uses the `? :` construct. The way it works is that the value to the left of the `?` selects one of two values, just like a multiplexer would. If the control signal is one the value to the left of the `:` is selected, and if the control signal is zero the value to the right of the `:` is selected. Note that this operator has the lowest precedence of all of the operators, so all three expressions are evaluated before the selection is made. Although Verilog does not require it, I always put the select control in parentheses, especially when the select control is an expression. In this example the sign of the ALU output and the zero-detect for the ALU output are generated differently, depending on whether the operation is word or byte.

```
assign sign_nxt = (word_op) ?  alu_result[15]    :  alu_result[7];
assign zero_nxt = (word_op) ? ~|alu_result[15:0] : ~|alu_result[7:0];
```

The conditional operator makes it possible to specify priority trees. It also makes it possible to write code that is too confusing to figure out without drawing a truth tables, so I recommend being very careful with how you use conditionals. Listing 2-2 shows the implementation of a state machine. This is the only way that I cascade conditionals.

In this example, whenever the `ld_ctrl` signal is active the state will be updated. If the `dmar_reg` signal is active (along with the `ld_inta` signal) then the next state will always be the special `` `sDMA1`` state. If the `dmar_reg` signal is not active, but the `intr_reg` signal is active (again along with the `ld_inta` signal), then the next state will be the special `` `sINTA`` state. If neither of these conditions exist then the state merely transitions to the normal next state specified by the `state_nxt` variable.

```
always @ (posedge clkc or negedge resetb) begin
  if      (!resetb) state_reg <= `sRST;
  else if (ld_ctrl) state_reg <= (ld_inta && dmar_reg) ? `sDMA1 :
                                 (ld_inta && intr_reg) ? `sINTA : state_nxt;
  end
```

Listing 2-2. Implementing priority trees with a state machine.

I should note that the logic synthesis tool will implement this kind of Verilog description as a priority tree, which can lead to long signal paths if you get carried away with the depth of the tree. So use this type of construct carefully. The monospace type and alignment of the code makes it very easy to see the designer's intent for this priority tree.

The last logical operations that I use, although very rarely, are for testing logical equality. Usually I prefer to use an Exclusive-OR, possibly combined with a reduction operator to do a comparison. Both of these operators will return `X` if either operand contains an `X` or a `Z`, so they do behave just like other logical operations.

== is the "equal to" logical equality operator.

!= is the "not equal to" logical equality operator

Verilog has other relational operators available, but I never use them because I don't want to have to worry about unsigned versus twos-complement and so on.

Arithmetic Operations

Verilog defines all four basic arithmetic operations plus the modulus (remainder) operation, but I only use addition and subtraction. Even then, you need to think carefully about the bit widths of the two operands, the bit width of the result, and whether the operands are unsigned or twos-complement. Listing 2-3 shows the arithmetic portion of an ALU. This example uses two 4-bit operands plus the 1-bit carry-in to create a 5-bit result. The four least-significant bits of the result are the normal twos-complement result and the most-significant bit of the result is the carry-out.

```
always @ (aluop_reg or alua_in or alub_in or alu_cin) begin
  casex (aluop_reg) //synopsys parallel_case
    `AOP_SUB,
    `AOP_BSUB,
    `AOP_SBC,
    `AOP_BSBC: alu0_out = alua_in[3:0] - alub_in[3:0] - alu_cin;
    default:   alu0_out = alua_in[3:0] + alub_in[3:0] + alu_cin;
    endcase
  end
```

Listing 2-3. Example of Verilog arithmetic operations.

There are also shift operations defined in Verilog, but I never use them. I find it much easier to visualize the result of this type of operation when it is expressed directly using concatenation along with the necessary indices for the variables. Listing 2-4 shows the shifter portion of an ALU that supports seven different types of shift and rotate. Only two lines of this code could be replaced directly by the Verilog shift operators, which is another reason not to bother using them.

```
always @ (aluop_reg or alub_in or carry_bit) begin
  casex (aluop_reg) //synopsys parallel_case
    `AOP_RL,
    `AOP_RLA:   shft_out = {alub_in[6:0], carry_bit};      /* rotate left, thru carry     */
    `AOP_RLC,
    `AOP_RLCA:  shft_out = {alub_in[6:0], alub_in[7]};     /* rotate left                 */
    `AOP_RR,
    `AOP_RRA:   shft_out = {carry_bit, alub_in[7:1]};      /* rotate right, thru carry    */
    `AOP_RRC,
    `AOP_RRCA:  shft_out = {alub_in[0], alub_in[7:1]};     /* rotate right                */
    `AOP_SLA:   shft_out = {alub_in[6:0], 1'b0};           /* shift left                  */
    `AOP_SRA:   shft_out = {alub_in[7], alub_in[7:1]};     /* shift right arithmetic      */
    `AOP_SRL:   shft_out = {1'b0, alub_in[7:1]};           /* shift right logical         */
    default:    shft_out = 8'h00;                          /* not a shift operation       */
    endcase
  end
```

Listing 2-4. Implementing shift operations in Verilog.

Conditional Statements

Conditional statements using the `if-else` construct can only be used with `reg` data types, and the most common use of conditional statements will be when specifying flip-flops. Listing 2-5 shows two different uses of conditional statements, along with how to specify triggering conditions for a procedure. This procedure is triggered either by a rising edge on the `clkc` signal or a falling edge on the `resetb` signal. Once triggered, the outermost `if-else` specifies that the registers all be cleared if the `resetb` signal is zero. Otherwise, the individual conditional statements will determine which, if any, register will be loaded.

```
always @ (posedge clkc or negedge resetb) begin
  if (!resetb) begin
    ii_reg  <= 8'h00;
    pc_reg  <= 16'h0000;
    rr_reg  <= 8'h00;
    sp_reg  <= 16'h0000;
    tmp_reg <= 16'h0000;
    end
  else begin
```

```
    if (ld_ii)  ii_reg  <= data_bus[15:8];
    if (ld_pc)  pc_reg  <= data_bus;
    if (ld_rr)  rr_reg  <= data_bus[15:8];
    if (ld_sp)  sp_reg  <= data_bus;
    if (ld_tmp) tmp_reg <= (inta_reg) ? {ii_reg, data_in} : data_bus;
    end
  end
```

Listing 2-5. Using conditional statements.

The outermost `if-else` uses the `begin-end` construct to group statements together for simultaneous evaluation, because otherwise the conditional operation would terminate with the first semicolon. Similarly, the entire body of the procedure is surrounded be a `begin-end` construct to encapsulate the operation. The individual conditional statements don't need a `begin-end` construct because each statement stands alone.

Conditional statements are also used to define priority trees for `reg` data types. Listing 2-6 shows a counter that can be loaded from two different sources. The `refclk_pls` signal has the highest priority when loading the counter, followed by the `prescale_pls` signal. If neither of these signals is active the counter decrements if the `refclk_reg` signal is active (it is an individual signal).

```
always @ (posedge clkc or negedge clearb) begin
  if       (!clearb)       prescale_reg <= 7'h00;
  else if (refclk_pls)    prescale_reg <= rti_divisor;
  else if (prescale_pls) prescale_reg <= divisor_reg;
  else                    prescale_reg <= (prescale_reg - refclk_reg);
  end
```

Listing 2-6. Using conditional statements to implement a priority tree.

Personally, I prefer to code this type of operation using multiplexers on the right-hand side of an expression, as shown in Listing 2-7. It takes a little less typing and is just how I am used to coding.

```
always @ (posedge clkc or negedge clearb) begin
  if (!clearb) prescale_reg <= 7'h00;
  else         prescale_reg <= (refclk_pls)   ? rti_divisor :
                               (prescale_pls) ? divisor_reg : (prescale_reg - refclk_reg);
  end
```

Listing 2-7. Implementing a priority tree using multiplexers.

Case Statements

Conditional statements using the `case-endcase` construct provide a powerful way to specify complex pieces of logic, but there are a few subtleties involved that you need to be careful of. Like the `if-else` construct, the `case-endcase` construct can only be used with `reg` data types.

The first subtlety is that the `case-endcase` construct does not automatically include a `default` case. In fact, if you don't include a `default` case or otherwise specify every possible case, the simulator will hold the previous value. What's worse is that the logic synthesis tool will use a latch to mimic this behavior! So always either specify every possible case or include the `default` case. Listing 2-8 shows the use of the `default` case:

```
always @ (iack_tran or io_tran or io_data_in or ivec_data_in or mem_data_in) begin
  case ({iack_tran, io_tran})
    2'b01:    data_in = io_data_in;                 /* i/o transaction             */
    2'b10:    data_in = ivec_data_in;               /* interrupt ack transaction   */
    default:  data_in = mem_data_in;                /* memory transaction          */
    endcase
  end
```

Listing 2-8. Using the default case statement.

It would obviously be nice to be able to use don't-care states in a `case-endcase` construct, and Verilog provides a way to do this, using either `casez` or `casex` in the place of the `case`. The difference between the two is fairly subtle, and I won't even attempt to clarify it here. I always just use `casex`. Listing 2-9 shows an example.

```
always @ (nmi_reg or imd2_reg or imd1_reg or din0_reg or din1_reg) begin
  casex ({nmi_reg, imd2_reg, imd1_reg})
    3'b00x:  int_addr = 16'h0038;                   /* mode 0/1 interrupt          */
    3'b010:  int_addr = {din1_reg, din0_reg};       /* mode 2 interrupt            */
    3'b1xx:  int_addr = 16'h0066;                   /* non-maskable interrupt      */
    default: int_addr = 16'h0000;                   /* trap, reset                 */
    endcase
  end
```

Listing 2-9. Don't-cares and casex statements.

Once you include don't-cares in the `case` decision, there is the possibility of overlap between the various cases. Verilog specifies a priority-tree implementation in these circumstances, which is not always what you want. There is no way to override this operation for the simulation, but if you include a "magic comment" in exactly the right spot, the synthesis tool will implement the overlapping cases using parallel logic. Be very careful doing this, because it can lead to a difference between the simulation and the actual hardware. I will only include this special synthesis tool override when I have analyzed the overlap to make sure that I want parallel logic rather than a decision tree.

An example of a forced parallel case is shown in Listing 2-10. In this example the `state_reg` variable is encoded one-hot (only one bit is high at once in the state), so there will always be a theoretical overlap between the cases. But I want the logic as fast as possible, so a priority-tree implementation should not be used. This example also shows the nesting of `case-endcase` constructs and the use of `begin-end` constructs with a case entry. Neither of the `begin-end` constructs are strictly necessary in this example, but I always include them as a matter of course when the code goes over to the next line.

```
always @ (state_reg) begin
  casex (state_reg) //synopsys parallel_case
    `OF1B:                tflg_ctl = `TFLG_Z;
    `RD1A,
    `RD2A: begin
      casex ({page_reg, inst_reg})
        12'b1xxx10100011,
        12'b1xxx10101011,
        12'b1xxx10110011,
        12'b1xxx10111011: tflg_ctl = `TFLG_1;
        default:          tflg_ctl = `TFLG_Z;
        endcase
      end
    `BLK1:                tflg_ctl = `TFLG_B;
    default:              tflg_ctl = `TFLG_NUL;
    endcase
  end
```

Listing 2-10. Forcing a parallel case implementation.

Procedural Statements

Procedural statements are used to assign values to `reg` data types, as has been illustrated in several of the preceding examples. Verilog provides two keywords for starting a procedural statement, namely `initial` and `always`, but logic synthesis tools only recognize the `always` keyword. I only mention the `initial` keyword here because it is useful when writing testbenches, for setting up conditions at the start of a simulation.

A procedural statement started with the `initial` keyword is executed exactly one time, at startup. This type of behavior doesn't really have an analog for most circuitry, which is why logic synthesis tools do not recognize this keyword. Some FPGA technologies allow the initial state of latches and flip-flops to be specified with the configuration, but they do not use the `initial` keyword to implement this feature.

The `always` keyword is followed by an `@` symbol and a list of triggering conditions enclosed in parenthesis. This is called the sensitivity list, and how you specify the sensitivity list determines the type of circuitry that the logic synthesis tool will implement. The rules are fairly simple, and are best illustrated by example.

If you don't want the logic synthesis tool to implement latches or flip-flops, the sensitivity list must include every signal that contributes to the `reg` variable controlled by the procedural statement. Going back to the example used for the `casex` statement, shown again in Listing 2-11, you'll see that the sensitivity list includes all three signals used by the `casex` statement, as well as every signal that occurs on the right-hand side of the assignment statements. However, this is still not enough to prevent the logic synthesis tool from implementing a latch. You also need to make sure that the `casex` statement covers all possibilities, and this is why I always include a `default` case for all `case` statements.

```
always @ (nmi_reg or imd2_reg or imd1_reg or din0_reg or din1_reg) begin
  casex ({nmi_reg, imd2_reg, imd1_reg})
    3'b00x:  int_addr = 16'h0038;                /* mode 0/1 interrupt         */
    3'b010:  int_addr = {din1_reg, din0_reg};    /* mode 2 interrupt           */
    3'b1xx:  int_addr = 16'h0066;                /* non-maskable interrupt     */
    default: int_addr = 16'h0000;                /* trap, reset                */
    endcase
  end
```

Listing 2-11. The sensitivity list for procedural statements.

It is fairly common during code debugging to have to go back and add signals to the right-hand side of these types of assignment statements. But if you do that always remember to also add the signal to the sensitivity list! Otherwise you're going to end up with some kind of a latch.

If you really want a latch, there is a specific way to do it. In Listing 2-12 the conditional update of the `data_lat` variable creates the latch. The latch is level-sensitive because the `ld_bit` enable signal is used directly rather than being conditioned by a `posedge` or `negedge` Verilog keyword.

```
always @ (ld_bit or data_in) begin
  if (ld_bit) data_lat <= data_in;
  end
```

Listing 2-12. Implementing a simple latch.

If you need a latch that also has a reset, use the example in Listing 2-13. The order of the assignment statements is important here. Since the assignment statement conditioned with the `resetb` signal occurs first this is a reset-override latch function.

```
always @ (ld_bit or resetb or data_in) begin
  if      (!resetb) data_lat <= 1'b0;
  else if (ld_bit) data_lat <= data_in;
  end
```

Listing 2-13. Implementing a latch with an asynchronous reset.

Using latches in a design is an excellent way to save power, but you need to be very careful with the potential race between the enable and data input signals. Just because the design works in the simulation doesn't mean that it will work in the real world, and vice-versa.

The example I used for the `if-else` construct, shown again in Listing 2-14, introduced the syntax for flip-flops. The sensitivity list contains only the clock and the optional asynchronous reset signal. Both of these signals must be conditioned by either the `posedge` or `negedge` keyword. The logic synthesis tool recognizes this specific format for the sensitivity list to create flip-flops. In this example the flip-flops are clocked by the rising edge of the `clkc` signal and have an active-low asynchronous reset. A flip-flop will use the falling edge of the clock if the clock is conditioned by the `negedge` keyword, and you can specify an active-high reset by conditioning the reset signal with a `posedge` keyword.

```
always @ (posedge clkc or negedge resetb) begin
  if (!resetb) begin
    ii_reg  <= 8'h00;
    pc_reg  <= 16'h0000;
    rr_reg  <= 8'h00;
    sp_reg  <= 16'h0000;
    tmp_reg <= 16'h0000;
    end
  else begin
    if (ld_ii)  ii_reg  <= data_bus[15:8];
    if (ld_pc)  pc_reg  <= data_bus;
    if (ld_rr)  rr_reg  <= data_bus[15:8];
    if (ld_sp)  sp_reg  <= data_bus;
    if (ld_tmp) tmp_reg <= (inta_reg) ? {ii_reg, data_in} : data_bus;
    end
  end
```

Listing 2-14. The logic synthesis tool recognizes this format for flip-flops.

It is possible to specify both an asynchronous reset and an asynchronous set for a flip-flop, but be extremely careful doing this. If the target technology does not provide such a flip-flop primitive, the logic synthesis tool will try to create one out of the logic primitives available. This will almost always yield disastrous results that may simulate properly but will not work when implemented. If you absolutely have to have both an asynchronous reset and an asynchronous set, make sure that you code the priority between them to properly match what the technology provides. Even then, always check the output of the logic synthesis tool to make sure that it actually used the special flip-flops.

All of the examples so far have used basic D-type flip-flops. The logic synthesis tool makes it unnecessary to worry about exactly what type of flip-flop to use, because it will almost always make the best choice from the available technology. So all you, as a designer, need to worry about is properly describing how you what the logic to function. For example, if you need a set-reset function here is an 8-bit set-override register:

```
always @ (posedge clkc or negedge resetb) begin
  if (!resetb) dma_ack_reg <= 8'h00;
  else         dma_ack_reg <= dack_set | (~dack_res & dma_ack_reg);
  end
```

Listing 2-15. Implementing a set-reset flip-flop.

Listing 2-16 shows a simple toggle register. I should note that the `resetb` signal is critical here. If it is not included the logic will work fine in the real world, but the `div2_reg` signal will remain unknown forever in the simulation.

```
always @ (posedge clkc or negedge resetb) begin
  if (!resetb) div2_reg <= 1'b0;
  else         div2_reg <= !div2_reg;
  end
```

Listing 2-16. Implementing a toggle flip-flop.

If you have been looking closely at the examples for the `reg` data type so far, you're probably wondering why sometimes the assignment operator is = while at other times <= is used for the assignment operator. The = symbol is used for a "blocking" assignment, while the <= symbol is used for a "non-blocking" assignment, and the difference between the two is critical for the proper simulation of your logic.

The blocking = assignment operator tells the simulator to evaluate the expression before continuing to the next line of Verilog code. The non-blocking <= assignment operator tells the simulator to queue all of the expressions triggered by the same condition in a sensitivity list for evaluation in parallel. Choosing the wrong type of operator will almost always result in a difference between simulation and the actual logic, because logic synthesis tools do not make a distinction between these two operators.

The bottom line is that you should always use the non-blocking <= assignment operator for flip-flops and latches, because this is how real logic elements work. Real flip-flops clocked by a common clock will evaluate at the same time. Using a blocking = assignment operator for flip-flops will lead to the simulator evaluating flip-flops sequentially, in the order that they exist in the Verilog code. This will clearly lead to problems if the output of one flip-flop is used for the input of another flip-flop described later in the code.

Using the blocking = assignment operator is appropriate when describing combinational logic using `if-else` or `case-endcase` constructs, because this matches how real non-sequential logic works. Once you have written Verilog code for a while choosing the correct assignment operator will become automatic. Until the choice becomes automatic I recommend using the copy-paste-modify method of writing code. Even after all my years of designing using Verilog I find it quicker to use this method.

Design Hierarchy

All of the preceding examples were just isolated pieces of Verilog code, but a real design needs some kind of structure or hierarchy. The `module-endmodule` construct allows you to encapsulate anything from a single gate function to the entire design. In fact, at least one module is always required for Verilog code to be compiled for simulation or logic synthesis.

Listing 2-17 illustrates a small but complete module definition. All of the Verilog code is contained between the `module` and `endmodule` keywords. The `module` keyword is followed by the name of the module, which is in turn followed by a list of the ports (input, output, or bidirectional) of the module. All of the module ports must be declared as either an `input`, an `output` or an `inout`, using syntax similar to that used for declaring variables. Only these port signals will be visible outside the module, but the port names themselves and any internal variables really are local to the module.

```
module reg_byte (data_reg, clk, data_bus, ld_byte, rep_high, rep_low, resetb);

  input        clk;           /* main clock                                          */
  input        ld_byte;       /* load register                                       */
  input        rep_high;      /* replicate high nibble                               */
  input        rep_low;       /* replicate low nibble                                */
  input        resetb;        /* internal reset                                      */
  input  [7:0] data_bus;      /* input bus                                           */
  output [7:0] data_reg;      /* registered data                                     */

  /*****************************************************************************/
  /*                                                                           */
  /* signal declarations                                                       */
  /*                                                                           */
  /*****************************************************************************/
  wire   [7:0] data_nxt;                               /* data mux out           */

  reg    [7:0] data_out;                               /* registered data        */

  /*****************************************************************************/
  /*                                                                           */
  /* byte register with nibble swap/replicate                                  */
  /*                                                                           */
  /*****************************************************************************/
  assign data_nxt = (rep_high) ? {data_bus[7:4], data_bus[7:4]} :
                    (rep_low)  ? {data_bus[3:0], data_bus[3:0]} : data_bus;
```

```
always @ (posedge clk or negedge resetb) begin
  if      (!resetb) data_out <= 8'h00;
  else if (ld_byte) data_out <= (swap_nibl) ? {data_nxt[3:0], data_nxt[7:4]} : data_nxt;
  end

endmodule
```

Listing 2-17. Defining a module.

Modules may be instantiated (placed) inside other modules to any depth and any number of times as long as each instance is given a unique name, but no recursion or circular references are allowed. Listing 2-18 shows two instances of the above `reg_byte` module with names `REG_1` and `REG_2`. This example uses the "dot notation" to connect signals to the ports of the modules. Signals can also be connected automatically in the order defined in the module definition, but I find that the dot notation results in fewer connection errors even though it means more typing. The order of the ports doesn't matter when instantiated using dot notation.

```
reg_byte REG_1 ( .data_reg(reg_1_reg), .clk(clk), .data_bus(data_bus), .ld_byte(ld_reg1),
                 .rep_high(rep_high), .rep_low(rep_low), .resetb(resetb),
                 .swap_nibl(swap_nibl) );

reg_byte REG_2 ( .data_reg(reg_2_reg), .clk(clk), .data_bus(data_bus), .ld_byte(ld_reg2),
                 .rep_high(rep_high), .rep_low(rep_low), .resetb(resetb),
                 .swap_nibl(swap_nibl) );
```

Listing 2-18. Instantiating modules.

You'll notice that the signal names do not need to be the same across the module boundary, and this is what makes it easy to use multiple instances of a module as in this example. It is also possible to leave a module port unconnected. This is accomplished either by leaving the port off of the list when the module is instantiated or by leaving the port connection blank using empty parentheses. Inputs should never be left unconnected because that results in a value of `Z` being passed into the module. It is quite common to leave unused outputs unconnected.

The top level module of a design is the input to a logic synthesis tool, but simulating a design will require that it be instantiated in a testbench module that provides the stimulus and response for the simulation.

The Power of `define

One of the most useful features that is not part of the Verilog language but that is supported by virtually every Verilog simulator and logic synthesis tool is the `define compiler directive. This directive creates macros for text substitution, which can make the Verilog code much more readable. Whenever an ` character (the accent grave, not the single quote) followed immediately by a macro name is encountered, the text from the macro definition is substituted before any processing of the Verilog code is done. Because this is a compiler directive, as opposed to Verilog code, the `define statements should be outside of any Verilog module.

Listing 2-19 shows how to use the `define directive to set up a substitution for a bus that is two bits wide.

```
`define TFLG_IDX    1
`define TFLG_NUL    2'b00          //No load
`define TFLG_Z      2'b01          //Load result of test for zero
`define TFLG_1      2'b10          //Load result of test for one
`define TFLG_B      2'b11          //Load result of compare
```

Listing 2-19. Using `define statements.

Only the non-white text on the same line following the macro name is substituted for the `name in the Verilog code, and any comments are automatically excluded from the substitution. So, in this example you would use the `TFLG_IDX macro to declare the width of the bus:

```
reg    [`TFLG_IDX:0] tflg_ctl;                    /* temp flag control          */
```

After the macro substitution this line looks like this as far as the simulator or logic synthesis tool is concerned:

```
reg    [1:0] tflg_ctl;                            /* temp flag control          */
```

Using the remainder of these macro substitutions when specifying the operation of this bus is shown in Listing 2-20. Note how much more readable the code is.

```
always @ (state_reg) begin
  casex (state_reg) //synopsys parallel_case
    `OF1B:                tflg_ctl = `TFLG_Z;
    `RD1A,
    `RD2A: begin
      casex ({page_reg, inst_reg})
        12'b1xxx10100011,
        12'b1xxx10101011,
        12'b1xxx10110011,
        12'b1xxx10111011: tflg_ctl = `TFLG_1;
        default:          tflg_ctl = `TFLG_Z;
        endcase
      end
    `BLK1:                tflg_ctl = `TFLG_B;
    default:              tflg_ctl = `TFLG_NUL;
    endcase
  end
```

Listing 2-20. Macro substitutions make code more readable.

One of the major advantages of writing code using macro substitutions is that you can easily change the width of the bus or the encoding on the bus just by changing the `` `define `` statements. There is no need to change multiple locations in the Verilog code to experiment with different encodings.

Macro substitutions created with a `` `define `` are valid from the point where they are defined until the end of the Verilog code or until the macro is redefined. This means that they will be applied throughout the hierarchy of the design. Note that even though redefinitions are possible, you should never do it unless you are deliberately trying to obfuscate how the Verilog code is supposed to work or you really are trying to shoot yourself in the foot.

Listing 2-21 shows the receiving end of this bus, where these macro substitutions are used exactly the same way:

```
always @ (tflg_ctl or alu_one or alu_zero or ff_reg_out) begin
  case (tflg_ctl)
    `TFLG_1:  tflg_nxt = alu_one;                      /* blk set if done (next xfr)   */
    `TFLG_Z:  tflg_nxt = alu_zero;                     /* blk set if done (this xfr)   */
    `TFLG_B:  tflg_nxt = alu_zero || !ff_reg_out[2];   /* blk cp set if done or match  */
    default:  tflg_nxt = 1'b0;
    endcase
  end
```

Listing 2-21. Macro substitutions in case statements.

I almost always use macro substitutions for control buses and state machine states. I have seen some people use the example below, but I find this to be overkill, because it just means more typing without really adding to the readability of the code.

```
`define TRUE        1'b1             //alias for a '1'
`define FALSE       1'b0             //alias for a '0'
```

Using the `define directive with one-hot encoding is a little more complicated. If you will be decoding the signal using individual bit selects you will need to do something like Listing 2-22 to use the individual bit selects at the receiving end of the bus:

```
`define ADCTL_IDX   3
`define ADD_RSTVAL  4'b0000          //Pipeline register reset value
`define ADD_PC      4'b0001          //Select address register from PC
`define ADD_HL      4'b0010          //Select address register from HL
`define ADD_SP      4'b0100          //Select address register from SP
`define ADD_ALU     4'b1000          //Select address register from ALU

`define AD_PC       0                //Address from PC
`define AD_HL       1                //Address from HL
`define AD_SP       2                //Address from SP
`define AD_ALU      3                //Address from ALU
```

Listing 2-22. One-hot macro substitutions.

Using the `` `define`` directive when there are don't-cares involved is also a little more complicated. This is because normally you should never specify an `X` when assigning values to a signal. In Listing 2-23 the last macro substitution can only be used for decoding the bus with a `casex` construct, while the remainder are used for either encoding or decoding of the bus.

```
`define MAIN_PG     4'b0000     //no instruction prefix byte(s)
`define INTR_PG     4'b0001     //interrupt acknowledge
`define CB_PAGE     4'b0010     //CB instruction prefix
`define DMA_PG      4'b0011     //dma acknowledge
`define DD_PAGE     4'b0100     //DD instruction prefix
`define FD_PAGE     4'b0101     //FD instruction prefix
`define DDCB_PG     4'b0110     //DD-CB instruction prefix
`define FDCB_PG     4'b0111     //FD-CB instruction prefix
`define ED_PAGE     4'b1000     //ED instruction prefix
`define DEC_ED      4'b1xxx     //ED page
```

Listing 2-23. Macro substitutions when there are don't-cares.

I should note that the Verilog language provides a feature somewhat similar to the `` `define`` compiler directive, using the `parameter` keyword. I never use this feature, mainly because it has a local scope and more restrictions on its use. The local scope (that is, within a module) means that there is always the possibility of accidentally having different definitions in different modules

Conditional Compilation

The `` `define`` compiler directive has one other use, in conjunction with the `` `ifdef-`else-`endif`` compiler directives. These compiler directives allow you to include sections of Verilog code, exclude sections of Verilog code, or to choose between two sections of Verilog code. This allows a designer to create a single file that can still contain any technology-specific primitives or connections that might be required. These compiler directives can be used outside of Verilog modules to select between different modules to include, or inside of modules to select specific Verilog code to include.

The way the `` `ifdef`` works is that it tests whether or not the accompanying macro has been previously defined. If this test is true then all subsequent lines, up until either an `` `else`` or an `` `endif`` will be included in the Verilog source. Otherwise all subsequent lines until either an `` `else`` or `` `endif`` are excluded from the Verilog source. If the test is false and there is an `` `else`` present then all of the lines after the `` `else`` and up until the `` `endif`` are included in the Verilog source.

For example, the three lines below allow me to select between three different versions of a design. Two of the choices must always be commented out, leaving just one of the macros defined. There is no substitution text specified for the macros, because the `` `ifdef `` test is only whether or not the macro has been defined, not what the value is.

```
// `define ASIC_VERSION
// `define FPGA_VERSION
`define SIM_VERSION
```

For example, in Listing 2-24, using these definitions I can choose between two different top level clocking options. In an FPGA I might need to have a direct clock input, while in an Application-Specific Integrated Circuit (ASIC) version or in the simulation I will be using an on-chip oscillator. Of course, this is just the top level connections, and there will be similar `` `ifdef `` sections to instantiate an oscillator or dedicated input buffer.

```
`ifdef FPGA_VERSION

  input        CLK_IN;        /* master clock input                    */

`else //ASIC_VERSION or SIM_VERSION

  input        CLK_20MI;      /* 20MHz oscillator input                */
  inout        CLK_20MO;      /* 20MHz oscillator output               */

`endif
```

Listing 2-24. Conditional compilation.

The `` `ifdef-`else-`endif `` construct by itself only allows a two-way decision, but these constructs can be nested if necessary. Be very careful when doing this because it is easy to lose track of the conditions being applied. This is why I always include a comment on the `` `else `` line to indicate exactly which case applies. Listing 2-25 is an example of a three-way decision using nested `` `ifdef `` directives. One of the advantages of nested directives over individual directives is that you can guarantee a default case.

```
`ifdef FPGA_VERSION

  CLKBUF     DRVOSC   ( .Y(osc_hs), .PAD(CLK_IN) );

`else //ASIC_VERSION or SIM_VERSION

`ifdef ASIC_VERSION

  INPAD      CLKPAD   ( .O(osc_hs_out), .I(CLK_IN) );
  BUFCKRLX1 DRVOSC   ( .O(osc_hs),     .I(hs_osc_out) );

`else //SIM_VERSION or none defined

  assign osc_hs = CLK_IN;

`endif

`endif
```

Listing 2-25. Multi-way conditional compilation.

The previous example showed `` `ifdef `` selecting between different implementation options, but it is also possible to use this compiler directive to control details of the functionality of the design. For example, I have used conditional compilation to add optional instructions to a CPU design, to select between a single-clock multiply instruction implementation and a one-clock-per-bit multiply implementation, and to select between two different cases for the operation of a status flag, all within a single design. Having all of the design options present in a single file makes keeping track of different source versions much easier.

Aggregating Files With `` `include ``

The last compiler directive that I use during the design phase is `` `include ``. This directive makes it easy to organize all of the design files into a list in one file. Then I only need to load this file into the simulator or the logic synthesis tool. Listing 2-26 shows is an example of such a file, which I traditionally call hierarchy.v, for obvious reasons.

```
/*************************************************************************************/
/**                                                                                 **/
/** COPYRIGHT (C) 2011, SYSTEMYDE INTERNATIONAL CORPORATION, ALL RIGHTS RESERVED    **/
/**                                                                                 **/
/** chip design file include list                          Rev 0.0  05/27/2011      **/
/**                                                                                 **/
/*************************************************************************************/
  `include "defines.v"                               /* control signal mnemonics   */
  `include "control.v"                               /* processor control          */
  `include "datapath.v"                              /* processor data path        */
    `include "alu_log.v"                             /* alu logic unit             */
    `include "alu_math.v"                            /* alu math unit              */
    `include "alu_shft.v"                            /* alu shifter unit           */
    `include "aluamux.v"                             /* alu a input multiplexer    */
    `include "alubmux.v"                             /* alu b input multiplexer    */
    `include "aluout.v"                              /* alu output multiplexer     */
  `include "extint.v"                                /* processor external interface */
  `include "machine.v"                               /* processor state machine    */
  `include "y80_top.v"                               /* cpu top level              */
```

Listing 2-26. The `include compiler directive.

No particular order for the files is necessary when using `` `include ``, because Verilog allows forward module references. But the file that includes all of the `` `define `` directives needs to be first so that the compiler can properly use the macros defined there. It is convenient to show the overall hierarchy of the design using indentation, as shown in the example above.

3. Verilog Coding Style

Importance of Coding Style

Now that you are familiar with Verilog HDL, it's important to talk about coding style. Just as a consistent set of drawing rules makes understanding schematic diagrams easier, a consistent coding style makes understanding Verilog code easier.

No standard for a Verilog coding style will satisfy everyone, and just about every designer will have their own take on what is best. What I present here works for me, but you are free to use whatever rules you like. But whatever style you choose the most important thing is to be consistent throughout the project. This is just as true for one-person projects as it is for huge projects involving teams in many different physical locations.

Even if your project is one-off, I guarantee that at some point in the future you, or someone else, will try to go through the Verilog code and figure out how it is supposed to work. If the Verilog is clean and well-organized this process will be much less painful.

In all fairness, I should note that I have seen some Verilog code that seems to have been written with obfuscation in mind. If you are in the business of selling Intellectual Property (IP) in the form of Verilog source code it could be argued that making the code difficult to understand makes good business sense. Personally, I don't agree with this philosophy.

Files Versus Modules

Any reasonably sized project will have multiple Verilog modules, which immediately raises the question of how to partition modules among files. Nothing is more frustrating than encountering a module instantiation and then trying to find the module if it is buried somewhere in a project file. So the rule here is simple:

- **One Verilog HDL module per file.**

It will be just as frustrating trying to find the Verilog code for a module if the file names in the project are different from the Verilog module names.

- **File name is the same as the Verilog module name.**

Modern operating systems allow file names longer than the eight characters that used to be the norm. But just because the computer understands long file names doesn't mean that all of the tools you might be using will understand long file names. So I always limit Verilog module names to eight characters or less and make the module names as descriptive as possible.

- **Keep Verilog module names short (ideally eight characters or less) but descriptive.**

Indentation

The subject of indentation often invokes arguments with almost religious fervor, and I have seen more different indentation styles than I can count. One thing just about everyone agrees on is that indentation should use spaces rather than tab characters. The problem with tab characters is that they may display differently between applications, as well as print differently on different printers.

- **Use a monospace font.**
- **Use spaces, not tabs, for indentation.**

Indentation provides important visual cues about the relationship between lines of Verilog code. At the same time, too much white space can make it hard to read the code, so it's a delicate balance. I prefer to use a consistent two-character space for indentation. One character isn't enough to be a visual cue, and three or more spaces seem to be a waste of space.

- **Use two-character spaces for indentation.**

Lining up similar items in columns makes it much easier to scan through the code when looking for something, especially on paper. When debugging Verilog code or reading through code trying to understand the operation I prefer a printed copy that I can mark up with notes.

- **Line up variable names in declarations.**
- **Line up comment blocks.**
- **Line up variables in assignment statements.**

Nothing makes Verilog code more difficult to follow than lines that wrap around onto the next line. So I always use a fixed width for all code. Verilog doesn't care about white space, including carriage returns, so break up long lines yourself and line up the right-hand side of expressions in the same column.

- **Use fixed width pages.**
- **Break up long statements across multiple lines and indent the continuation lines to line things up by column.**

Indentation is used to group Verilog statements, using constructs like `begin-end` or `case-endcase`, and I have seen several different methods used for this grouping. The style I prefer is shown in Listing 3-1. I like to keep the `begin` keyword on the line that is invoking the group of statements. All of the grouped statements, including the `end` that goes with the `begin`, then use the same indentation. Some designers prefer to have the `begin` on a separate indented line, with the grouped statement indented yet again, but I find that method to be a waste of white space. The `case-endcase` construct is done the same way.

```
always @ (nmi_reg or imd2_reg or imd1_reg or din0_reg or din1_reg) begin
  casex ({nmi_reg, imd2_reg, imd1_reg})
    3'b00x:  int_addr = 16'h0038;                 /* mode 0/1 interrupt         */
    3'b010:  int_addr = {din1_reg, din0_reg};     /* mode 2 interrupt           */
    3'b1xx:  int_addr = 16'h0066;                 /* non-maskable interrupt     */
    default: int_addr = 16'h0000;                 /* trap, reset                */
    endcase
  end
```

Listing 3-1. Using indentation to make the code more readable.

The bottom line is that you should pick whatever style makes the most sense to you, but then use it consistently.

- **Use one indentation style for begin-end, module-endmodule, case-endcase, etc.**

Naming Conventions

Verilog HDL is case-sensitive, so the signal names `clk`, `Clk` and `CLK` refer to different signals. However, many times I have encountered specialized vendor tools that are not case-sensitive, and this creates a huge problem when trying to use a netlist created from Verilog with a logic synthesis tool. As a result I never rely on case differences to distinguish signals. In fact, the only time that I use upper case is to denote macro names and top-level module port names.

- **Use lower case for all internal signals and module names.**
- **Use upper case for top-level module port names.**
- **Use upper case for `` `define `` macro definitions.**
- **Never use an identical name for a lower-case name and an upper-case name.**

There are no restrictions on the length of signal names in Verilog, but as soon as you start typing a lot of expressions you will find that shorter names are easier to use than long names. So I always try to make the names descriptive, but I rarely use names longer than about a dozen characters.

- **Use descriptive signal names, but try for less than twelve characters in length.**

It is often convenient to know the type of logic that is generating a signal without having to trace back through the source code. So I always try to identify register and latch outputs. In cases where there are multiple clock domains in the design, I always try to tag signals that cross clock domain boundaries with an identifier of the source clock domain.

- **Whenever possible, name flip-flop outputs with a `_reg` suffix.**
- **Whenever possible, name latch outputs with a `_lat` suffix.**
- **When a signal will cross a clock domain boundary, include a tag in the signal name identifying the source clock domain.**

Using logic synthesis tools greatly reduces the need for active-low signals, but it still does happen. Since the most common logic design error is an inverted signal, active-low signals should always be named so that it is obvious that they are active-low. This naming can get messy when the signal is a register or latch output, so decide up front how you're going to handle that case.

Many designers use a `_n` suffix to denote an active-low signal. This has the advantage of being completely unambiguous, but requires two extra characters in the name. The alternative I use appends a `b` (short for bar) to the name to denote active-low. This can obviously be ambiguous if the name would normally end with a `b`. This is fairly rare, but if it happens I append a `t` (short for true) after the `b` in the name to indicate active-high.

- **Name all active-low signals with an identifiable suffix.**

Inputs, Outputs and Variables

As I mentioned previously, when instantiating a module using dot notation the order of the ports does not matter. But there is no reason not to use the same port order for the instantiation that is used in the module definition.

- **Use the same port order for module definition and module instantiation.**

The port order for a module might not seem important, but using a logical and consistent port ordering makes finding connections between modules much easier. A fairly common way to order the ports is bidirectionals, followed by outputs, followed by inputs. Within each of these groups the ports are arranged alphabetically. Grouping the ports like this makes it easy to determine if a port is an input to the module or an output generated by the module.

- **Use a consistent port ordering algorithm for modules.**

Another place where ordering can help with finding signals in a module is the ordering for the input/output declarations and the `wire` and `reg` declarations. Unfortunately there doesn't seem to be a consensus on the best way to do this. Clearly, it is better to keep input and output declarations separate. The same is true of `wire` and `reg` declarations. I prefer to declare names grouped by width and alphabetically within each group with a common width. This makes it easy to scan for a specific signal name when you know the width. The easiest way to illustrate this is with in Listing 3-2 below.

```
/*******************************************************************************************/
/*                                                                                         */
/* signal declarations                                                                     */
/*                                                                                         */
/*******************************************************************************************/
wire          ld_io_addr;                                /* update io address              */
wire          ld_mem_addr;                               /* update memory address          */
wire    [7:0] io_data_out;                               /* i/o output data bus            */
wire    [7:0] mem_data_out;                              /* memory output data bus         */

reg           dma_ack;                                   /* dma acknowledge                */
reg           ftch_tran;                                 /* inst fetch transaction         */
reg           halt_tran;                                 /* halt transaction               */
reg           iack_tran;                                 /* int ack transaction            */
reg           io_read;                                   /* i/o read enable                */
reg           io_tran;                                   /* i/o transaction                */
reg           io_strobe;                                 /* i/o data strobe                */
reg           ivec_rd;                                   /* interrupt vector enable        */
reg           mem_rd;                                    /* memory read enable             */
reg           mem_tran;                                  /* memory transaction             */
reg           mem_wr;                                    /* memory write enable            */
reg           mwr_tran;                                  /* memory write transaction       */
reg           reti_tran;                                 /* reti transaction               */
```

```
reg          t1;                    /* first clock of transaction   */
reg    [7:0] data_in;               /* data input bus               */
reg   [15:0] io_addr_out;           /* i/o address bus              */
reg   [15:0] mem_addr_out;          /* memory address bus           */
```

Listing 3-2. Ordering input and output declarations.

This example also illustrates some of the indentation guidelines mentioned previously. The exact algorithm you use for organizing declarations isn't important as long as you are consistent throughout the design.

- **Declare all ports and variables at the beginning of the module.**
- **Use a consistent ordering algorithm for declaring ports and variables.**

Comments and More Comments

Several of the examples so far have shown how I prefer to use comments to aid the readability of the Verilog code. But there are a few other ways that comments can make the Verilog much easier to understand. But first of all, every file should start with a header comment. Listing 3-3 shows a typical header comment block:

```
/*******************************************************************************************/
/**                                                                                       **/
/**                      DO NOT DELETE OR MODIFY THIS COMMENT BLOCK                       **/
/**                                                                                       **/
/** THE MATERIAL CONTAINED IN THIS FILE IS SUBJECT TO A NON-DISCLOSURE AGREEMENT, AND MAY **/
/** NOT BE DISCLOSED TO ANY PERSON OR PERSONS OUTSIDE THE RECEIVING PARTY'S ORGANIZATION. **/
/**                                                                                       **/
/** COPYRIGHT (C) 2011, Systemyde International Corporation, ALL RIGHTS RESERVED          **/
/**                                                                                       **/
/** y80 top level                                                   Rev 0.0  05/27/2011 **/
/**                                                                                       **/
/*******************************************************************************************/
```

Listing 3-3. File headers and the copyright notice.

If you work in a large organization or otherwise get lawyers involved the verbiage in this comment block can get rather long, but I have found that this works for me. The most important part of this comment block is the copyright notice. If you don't include anything else in your header comment block, at least retain the copyright to your work.

Even though the file and module name should be descriptive, it never hurts to include a little more information about what is in the file/module. Some designers like to include information about where the module is used in the design hierarchy and which modules are placed within a module, but I prefer to use a separate file that shows the entire design hierarchy in one location.

Large projects will probably use some kind of version control system, but I still like to keep the version and date modified information in the file itself. This information is very useful when working with a printed copy of the file.

- **Include a header comment block in every file, containing at least a copyright notice.**

I like to use comment blocks to break a module into easily identifiable sections. Using a standard style for these types of comment blocks makes it easy to scan though the Verilog code when looking for some specific information. For example, the signal declarations section would start with a comment block as shown in Listing 3-4:

```
/*********************************************************************************************/
/*                                                                                           */
/* signal declarations                                                                       */
/*                                                                                           */
/*********************************************************************************************/
```

Listing 3-4. Start the signal declarations section with a comment block.

I prefer to organize the code in modules by function. This is very useful when debugging because it allows me to isolate the specific section of code that I am interested in. Each functional block starts with a header that provides a basic description of the function. Listing 3-5 shows an example:

```
/*********************************************************************************************/
/*                                                                                           */
/* processor state machine                                                                   */
/*                                                                                           */
/*********************************************************************************************/
```

Listing 3-5. Start each functional block with a comment block.

The choice of how large or how small to make function blocks is a matter of personal preference, but I like to break the design into pieces that need no more than a couple of pages to describe. Of course there are always exceptions to this rule, and you'll have to decide what works best for you.

- **Use comment blocks to separate code into functional blocks within a module.**

Comment blocks can also be very useful to document the operation of state machines or other complex logic. Listing 3-6 shows a comment block taken from an actual design. This state machine controls the operation of a gated clock that runs at different frequencies under software control. Including the state sequence and a rudimentary timing diagram means that I don't have to go back and generate a new one by hand every time I revisit the design.

```
/*****************************************************************************************/
/*                                                                                     */
/* clock control                                                                       */
/*                                                                                     */
/*****************************************************************************************/
/*                                                                                     */
/*   ckdivm_reg    00000111112222233333444445555566666777778888899999                  */
/*   ckdivl_reg    01234012340123401234012340123401234012340123401234                  */
/*   ckdivm_rst    .................................................1                  */
/*   ph1           ................................111111111111......                  */
/*   ph2           111111111111......................................                  */
/*   ph2c (1x)     .................................................1                  */
/*   ph2c (2x)     ........................1........................1                  */
/*   ph2c (5x)     .........1.........1.........1.........1.........1                  */
/*   ph2c (10x)    ....1....1....1....1....1....1....1....1....1....1                  */
/*   ph2c (20x)    ..1.1..1.1..1.1..1.1..1.1..1.1..1.1..1.1..1.1..1.1                  */
/*   ph2c (50x)    11111111111111111111111111111111111111111111111111                  */
/*                                                                                     */
/*****************************************************************************************/
```

Listing 3-6. Document state machine operation with a comment block.

I have seen some Verilog code that included exactly zero comments. Worse still, there was no organization to the code. All of the `assign` statements were grouped together and all of the flip-flops were contained in a single large `always` block. Variables were declared without any apparent order and without regard to type or width. Needless to say, this code was extremely difficult to decipher.

If you don't like the coding style that I have presented here, come up with your own and use it. Remember that poor coding practices do not guarantee job security.

- **Use comment blocks to document state machines or other complex logic.**

Overall Design Organization

There is no one-size-fits-all guideline for organizing a design into modules, and usually a design will naturally partition itself into manageable pieces. In most projects that I have worked on the average file size is well below 100,000 characters or about 25 pages.

Some commercial IP that I have seen carries the design partitioning to an extreme, perhaps to make reverse-engineering painful. I consider this approach to be counter-productive. After all, every module that is instantiated needs to be wired up in the next level of the hierarchy, which is just more typing.

- **Partition the design into manageable pieces, but don't get carried away.**

As an example, consider the case of the simple 8-bit register shown in Listing 3-7. This module, along with 16-bit and 32-bit versions, was used in an ASIC design I did when I first started designing using Verilog.

```
module reg_byte (data_reg, clk, data_bus, ld_byte, resetb);

  input         clk;            /* main clock                                    */
  input         ld_byte;        /* load register                                 */
  input         resetb;         /* internal reset                                */
  input   [7:0] data_bus;       /* input bus                                     */
  output  [7:0] data_reg;       /* registered data                               */

  /******************************************************************************/
  /*                                                                            */
  /* signal declarations                                                        */
  /*                                                                            */
  /******************************************************************************/
  reg     [7:0] data_out;                              /* registered data       */

  /******************************************************************************/
  /*                                                                            */
  /* byte register                                                              */
```

```
/*                                                                              */
/******************************************************************************/
always @ (posedge clk or negedge resetb) begin
  if      (!resetb) data_out <= 8'h00;
  else if (ld_byte) data_out <= data_bus;
  end

endmodule
```

Listing 3-7. An entire module.

To instantiate this 8-bit register three times requires the code shown in Listing 3-8:

```
reg_byte REG_1 ( .data_reg(reg_1_reg), .clk(clk), .data_bus(data_bus), .ld_byte(ld_reg_1),
                 .resetb(resetb) );
reg_byte REG_2 ( .data_reg(reg_2_reg), .clk(clk), .data_bus(data_bus), .ld_byte(ld_reg_2),
                 .resetb(resetb) );
reg_byte REG_2 ( .data_reg(reg_3_reg), .clk(clk), .data_bus(data_bus), .ld_byte(ld_reg_3),
                 .resetb(resetb) );
```

Listing 3-8. Instantiating the 8-bit register module.

While just implementing the registers directly without the extra level of hierarchy requires the code shown in Listing 3-9:

```
always @ (posedge clk or negedge resetb) begin
  if (!resetb) begin
    reg_1_reg <= 8'h00;
    reg_2_reg <= 8'h00;
    reg_3_reg <= 8'h00;
    end
  else begin
    if (ld_reg_1) reg_1_reg <= data_bus;
    if (ld_reg_2) reg_2_reg <= data_bus;
    if (ld_reg_3) reg_3_reg <= data_bus;
    end
  end
```

Listing 3-9. Directly implementing three 8-bit registers.

Clearly there isn't much of a difference in the amount of coding required, regardless of the number of registers involved, so I prefer to implement the registers directly and remove a level of hierarchy. Implementing the registers directly also allows for different reset values.

But there will be cases where the extra hierarchy might be required. In this specific example, the logic synthesis tool was not taking advantage of the different types of flip-flops available in the ASIC library, so the actual module used a `` `define `` to directly instantiate the correct flip-flops to use.

4. Initial Design Work

Introduction

Now that we have the preliminaries out of the way it's time to decide exactly what we're going to design. There are three basic characteristics of a CPU that constrain everything you do in the design: the instruction set architecture (ISA), the external bus interface, and the basic machine cycle timing.

These three characteristics are not completely independent. In some cases the choice of ISA will influence the choice for the basic machine cycle timing. At the same time certain combinations of external bus interface and basic machine cycle timing either do not make sense or require significant hardware support. For example, a very slow bus interface with a single-clock basic machine cycle means that a cache memory will probably be required to take advantage of the machine speed. Conversely, a single-clock bus interface with a multi-clock basic machine cycle means that the bus interface will not be running at full speed.

If you are incredibly lucky you may be able to influence or choose all three of these characteristics. But in the real world that seldom happens, and you might have some measure of control over the definition of just one of these aspects of the design. So that's how I will present the design here. I'll use an existing ISA and define the external bus interface and basic machine cycle timing.

Instruction Set Architecture

To make this example realistic I'm going to use a mature, well-known 8-bit ISA. The Z80-CPU was introduced by Zilog in 1976, and is a derivative of the original Intel 8080. Even though the Z80 architecture is over 35 years old, both the original design (now in a vastly different technology) and derivatives of the design are still being produced. In fact the Rabbit series of microprocessors trace their roots directly back to the Z80.

The Z80 uses a Complex Instruction Set Computer (CISC) architecture. This makes the design more interesting (i.e., complex), because there are numerous special cases to consider. This kind of design complexity was the impetus behind the move to Reduced Instruction Set Computer (RISC) machines, but using a CISC machine here will more clearly demonstrate how to manage design complexity and make the design trade-offs that occur in most real-world designs.

What follows here is not a definitive description of the Z80 architecture. When we get to the actual design implementation, each instruction will be described in excruciating detail. But if you want to understand the Z80 architecture in more detail before then, refer to the original Zilog documentation[3] or get one of the many books[4],[5] written on the subject.

The register set for the Z80 is shown in Figure 4-1. The Z80 is an accumulator-based machine (the register labeled A is the accumulator), and uses the accumulator as the destination for most operations. However, instructions are also available that operate on other registers as well as directly on memory locations. The direct memory operations affect the choice of external bus timing, as we'll see shortly.

Most registers are eight bits wide, and many can be paired to form 16-bit registers. The HL register pair is used as a 16-bit accumulator for the 16-bit operations that are available. There are two banks of registers, with only one bank available at a time. The original reason for including an alternate bank of registers was for fast context-switching in the case of an interrupt. This context-switching works well with a single interrupt, but the alternate register bank is also useful for programs requiring more register resources.

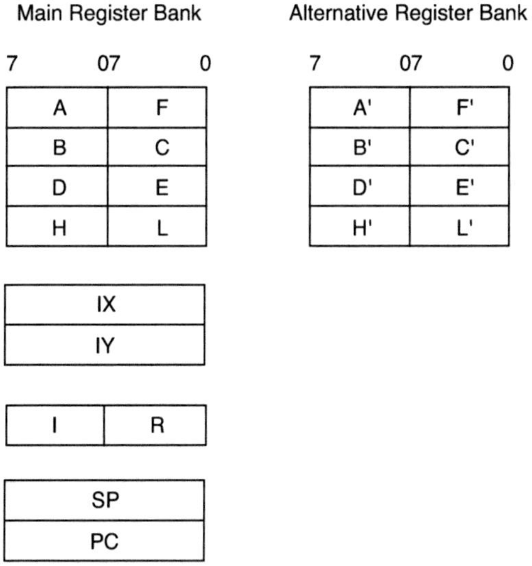

Figure 4-1. The Z80 register architecture.

The two index registers, IX and IY, are used almost exclusively as address pointers using indexed addressing mode.

The Flag register (F) holds the status flags for the CPU, arranged in the register as shown in Figure 4-2. Two of the bits (U5 and U3) are not really flags but can still be read and written.

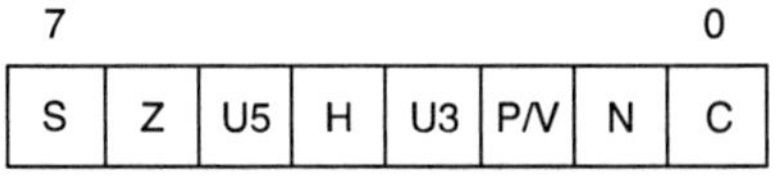

Figure 4-2. The Z80 Flag register.

The Sign flag (S) stores the most significant bit of the result. This is used with signed (2's complement) arithmetic, where the MSB is zero for positive numbers and one for negative numbers.

The Zero flag (Z) is set to one if the result of an operation is zero.

The Half-Carry flag (H) is the carry out of bit 3 of the result. This flag is necessary to adjust an arithmetic result when using BCD numbers.

The Parity/Overflow flag (PV) reports the parity of the result for logical operations, with the flag set to one if the result has even parity and zero if the result has odd parity. This bit reports the overflow status of arithmetic operations. Overflow occurs when the two operands have the same sign but the sign of the result is different. This means that the actual result cannot be represented in the eight or sixteen bits allocated for the result.

The Negative flag (N) records the type of the last arithmetic operation (add or subtract) for use when adjusting an arithmetic result when using BCD numbers. The bit is set to one for subtract operations and set to zero for add operations.

The Carry flag (C) is set to one whenever there is a carry or borrow from the most significant bit of the result of an arithmetic operation. This is useful for implementing multiple precision arithmetic in software.

The Interrupt register (I) holds the upper eight bits of the address of an interrupt vector table. The Z80 provides a vectored interrupt capability, where the interrupting peripheral device returns an 8-bit identifier to the processor during an interrupt acknowledge cycle. This vector, concatenated with the contents of the I register, makes a memory address that selects an entry in the table in memory. Each entry in this table in turn points to the start of an interrupt service routine. This vectored interrupt capability is a significant feature of the Z80 and we'll want to keep it for this implementation.

The Refresh register (R) was used by the original Z80 as a refresh counter for dynamic memories (DRAM). This counter incremented with each instruction and the processor performed special bus cycles to refresh DRAM with each instruction fetch. The technology of dynamic memory has advanced significantly since 1976, and this type of refresh mechanism is no longer appropriate, so I won't include it in this design. But I'll keep the R register and the associated instructions for programming compatibility.

The Stack Pointer (SP) and Program Counter (PC) are both sixteen bits wide and operate as you would expect. The stack grows downward in memory, from higher memory address to lower memory addresses. Stack operation are always sixteen bits, so the SP will always increment and decrement by two. But the SP does not need to be aligned to an even address. When pushing data to the stack the SP register is decremented before the memory write occurs. When popping data from the stack the SP register is incremented after the memory read occurs.

The Z80 instruction set isn't even close to being orthogonal, although a number of opcodes use common fields for register encoding. This complicates the instruction decode somewhat, as we'll see later. Although all Z80 opcodes are a single byte, there are four byte values used as "escape" opcodes to select a different meaning for the actual opcode. This leads to instructions that range in length from one byte to four bytes.

The following tables show the opcode maps for the Z80 instruction set. The first two tables show the mapping for the first (and in many cases only) byte of the opcode. The arrangement of the instructions in these two tables is fairly regular, which helps with the instruction decoding, as we'll see shortly.

If the first byte of the opcode is 0xCB, 0xDD, 0xED or 0xFD then at least one more byte is required to decode the instruction. This a common technique for expanding the number of instructions available beyond the 256 possible with a single-byte opcode.

LSB-> MSBv	0	1	2	3	4	5	6	7
0	NOP	LD BC,mn	LD (BC),A	INC BC	INC B	DEC B	LD B,n	RLCA
1	DJNZ e	LD DE,mn	LD (DE),A	INC DE	INC D	DEC D	LD D,n	RLA
2	JR NZ,e	LD HL,mn	LD (mn),HL	INC HL	INC H	DEC H	LD H,n	DAA
3	JR NC,e	LD SP,mn	LD (mn),A	INC SP	INC (HL)	DEC (HL)	LD (HL),n	SCF
4	LD B,B	LD B,C	LD B,D	LD B,E	LD B,H	LD B,L	LD B,(HL)	LD B,A
5	LD D,B	LD D,C	LD D,D	LD D,E	LD D,H	LD D,L	LD D,(HL)	LD D,A
6	LD H,B	LD H,C	LD H,D	LD H,E	LD H,H	LD H,L	LD H,(HL)	LD H,A
7	LD (HL),B	LD (HL),C	LD (HL),D	LD (HL),E	LD (HL),H	LD (HL),L	HALT	LD (HL),A
8	ADD A,B	ADD A,C	ADD A,D	ADD A,E	ADD A,H	ADD A,L	ADD A,(HL)	ADD A,A
9	SUB B	SUB C	SUB D	SUB E	SUB H	SUB L	SUB (HL)	SUB A
A	AND B	AND C	AND D	AND E	AND H	AND L	AND (HL)	AND A
B	OR B	OR C	OR D	OR E	OR H	OR L	OR (HL)	OR A
C	RET NZ	POP BC	JP NZ,mn	JP mn	CALL NZ,mn	PUSH BC	ADD A,n	RST 00
D	RET NC	POP DE	JP NC,mn	OUT (n),A	CALL NC,mn	PUSH DE	SUB n	RST 10
E	RET PO	POP HL	JP PO,mn	EX (SP),HL	CALL PO,mn	PUSH HL	AND n	RST 20
F	RET P	POP AF	JP P,mn	DI	CALL P,mn	PUSH AF	OR n	RST 30

Table 4-1. First half of the opcode table for 1-byte opcodes.

LSB-> MSBv	8	9	A	B	C	D	E	F
0	EX AF,AF'	ADD HL,BC	LD A,(BC)	DEC BC	INC C	DEC C	LD C,n	RRCA
1	JR e	ADD HL,DE	LD A,(DE)	DEC DE	INC E	DEC E	LD E,n	RRA
2	JR Z,e	ADD HL,HL	LD HL,(mn)	DEC HL	INC L	DEC L	LD L,n	CPL
3	JR C,e	ADD HL,SP	LD A,(mn)	DEC SP	INC A	DEC A	LD A,n	CCF
4	LD C,B	LD C,C	LD C,D	LD C,E	LD C,H	LD C,L	LD C,(HL)	LD C,A
5	LD E,B	LD E,C	LD E,D	LD E,E	LD E,H	LD E,L	LD E,(HL)	LD E,A
6	LD L,B	LD L,C	LD L,D	LD L,E	LD L,H	LD L,L	LD L,(HL)	LD L,A
7	LD A,B	LD A,C	LD A,D	LD A,E	LD A,H	LD A,L	LD A,(HL)	LD A,A
8	ADC A,B	ADC A,C	ADC A,D	ADC A,E	ADC A,H	ADC A,L	ADC A,(HL)	ADC A,A
9	SBC A,B	SBC A,C	SBC A,D	SBC A,E	SBC A,H	SBC A,L	SBC A,(HL)	SBC A,A
A	XOR B	XOR C	XOR D	XOR E	XOR H	XOR L	XOR (HL)	XOR A
B	CP B	CP C	CP D	CP E	CP H	CP L	CP (HL)	CP A
C	RET Z	RET	JP Z,mn	**Page CB**	CALL Z,mn	CALL nn	ADC A,n	RST 08
D	RET C	EXX	JP C,mn	IN A,(n)	CALL C,mn	**Page DD**	SBC A,n	RST 18
E	RET PE	JP (HL)	JP PE,mn	EX DE,HL	CALL PE,mn	**Page ED**	XOR n	RST 28
F	RET M	LD SP,HL	JP M,mn	EI	CALL M,mn	**Page FD**	CP n	RST 38

Table 4-2. Second half of the opcode table for 1-byte opcodes.

If the first byte of the opcode is 0xDD then the following two tables are used. In most cases the instruction is identical to the corresponding 1-byte instruction, with indexed addressing using the IX register substituted for indirect addressing using the HL register.

LSB-> MSBv	0	1	2	3	4	5	6	7
0								
1								
2		LD IX,mn	LD (mn),IX	INC IX				
3					INC (IX+d)	DEC (IX+d)	LD (IX+d),n	
4							LD B,(IX+d)	
5							LD D,(IX+d)	
6							LD H,(IX+d)	
7	LD (IX+d),B	LD (IX+d),C	LD (IX+d),D	LD (IX+d),E	LD (IX+d),H	LD (IX+d),L		LD (IX+d),A
8							ADD A,(IX+d)	
9							SUB (IX+d)	
A							AND (IX+d)	
B							OR (IX+d)	
C								
D								
E		POP IX		EX (SP),IX		PUSH IX		
F								

Table 4-3. First half of the opcode table for 0xDD-prefixed opcodes.

LSB-> MSBv	8	9	A	B	C	D	E	F
0		ADD IX,BC						
1		ADD IX,DE						
2		ADD IX,IX	LD IX,(mn)	DEC IX				
3		ADD IX,SP						
4							LD C,(IX+d)	
5							LD E,(IX+d)	
6							LD L,(IX+d)	
7							LD A,(IX+d)	
8							ADC A,(IX+d)	
9							SBC A,(IX+d)	
A							XOR (IX+d)	
B							CP (IX+d)	
C				**Page DD-CB**				
D								
E		JP (IX)						
F		LD SP,IX						

Table 4-4. Second half of the opcode table for 0xDD-prefixed opcodes.

If the first byte of the opcode is 0xFD then the following two tables are used. In most cases the instruction is identical to the corresponding 1-byte instruction, with indexed addressing using the IY register substituted for indirect addressing using the HL register.

LSB-> MSBv	0	1	2	3	4	5	6	7
0								
1								
2		LD IX,mn	LD (mn),IX	INC IX				
3					INC (IX+d)	DEC (IX+d)	LD (IX+d),n	
4							LD B,(IX+d)	
5							LD D,(IX+d)	
6							LD H,(IX+d)	
7	LD (IX+d),B	LD (IX+d),C	LD (IX+d),D	LD (IX+d),E	LD (IX+d),H	LD (IX+d),L		LD (IX+d),A
8							ADD A,(IX+d)	
9							SUB (IX+d)	
A							AND (IX+d)	
B							OR (IX+d)	
C								
D								
E		POP IX		EX (SP),IX		PUSH IX		
F								

Table 4-5. First half of the opcode table for 0xFD-prefixed opcodes.

LSB-> MSBv	8	9	A	B	C	D	E	F
0		ADD IX,BC						
1		ADD IX,DE						
2		ADD IX,IX	LD IX,(mn)	DEC IX				
3		ADD IX,SP						
4							LD C,(IX+d)	
5							LD E,(IX+d)	
6							LD L,(IX+d)	
7							LD A,(IX+d)	
8							ADC A,(IX+d)	
9							SBC A,(IX+d)	
A							XOR (IX+d)	
B							CP (IX+d)	
C				**Page DD-CB**				
D								
E		JP (IX)						
F		LD SP,IX						

Table 4-6. Second half of the opcode table for 0xFD-prefixed opcodes.

If the first byte of the opcode is 0xED then the following two tables are used. As you can see, this page is kind of the "kitchen sink" for Z80 instructions.

LSB-> MSBv	0	1	2	3	4	5	6	7
0								
1								
2								
3								
4	IN B,(C)	OUT (C),B	SBC HL,BC	LD (mn),BC	NEG	RETN	IM 0	LD I,A
5	IN D,(C)	OUT (C),D	SBC HL,DE	LD (mn),DE			IM 1	LD A,I
6	IN H,(C)	OUT (C),H	SBC HL,HL	LD (mn),HL				RRD
7			SBC HL,SP	LD (mn),SP				
8								
9								
A	LDI	CPI	INI	OUTI				
B	LDIR	CPIR	INIR	OTIR				
C								
D								
E								
F								

Table 4-7. First half of the opcode table for 0xED-prefixed opcodes.

LSB-> MSBv	8	9	A	B	C	D	E	F
0								
1								
2								
3								
4	IN C,(C)	OUT (C),C	ADC HL,BC	LD BC,(mn)		RETI		LD R,A
5	IN E,(C)	OUT (C),E	ADC HL,DE	LD DE,(mn)			IM 2	LD A,R
6	IN L,(C)	OUT (C),L	ADC HL,HL	LD HL,(mn)				RLD
7	IN A,(C)	OUT (C),A	ADC HL,SP	LD SP,(mn)				
8								
9								
A	LDD	CPD	IND	OUTD				
B	LDDR	CPDR	INDR	OTDR				
C								
D								
E								
F								

Table 4-8. Second half of the opcode table for 0xED-prefixed opcodes.

If the first byte of the opcode is 0xCB then the following two tables are used. Even though it looks complicated, these opcode are really only ten unique instructions.

LSB-> MSBv	0	1	2	3	4	5	6	7
0	RLC B	RLC C	RLC D	RLC E	RLC H	RLC L	RLC (HL)	RLC A
1	RL B	RL C	RL D	RL E	RL H	RL L	RL (HL)	RL A
2	SLA B	SLA C	SLA D	SLA E	SLA H	SLA L	SLA (HL)	SLA A
3								
4	BIT 0,B	BIT 0,C	BIT 0,D	BIT 0,E	BIT 0,H	BIT 0,L	BIT 0,(HL)	BIT 0,A
5	BIT 2,B	BIT 2,C	BIT 2,D	BIT 2,E	BIT 2,H	BIT 2,L	BIT 2,(HL)	BIT 2,A
6	BIT 4,B	BIT 4,C	BIT 4,D	BIT 4,E	BIT 4,H	BIT 4,L	BIT 4,(HL)	BIT 4,A
7	BIT 6,B	BIT 6,C	BIT 6,D	BIT 6,E	BIT 6,H	BIT 6,L	BIT 6,(HL)	BIT 6,A
8	RES 0,B	RES 0,C	RES 0,D	RES 0,E	RES 0,H	RES 0,L	RES 0,(HL)	RES 0,A
9	RES 2,B	RES 2,C	RES 2,D	RES 2,E	RES 2,H	RES 2,L	RES 2,(HL)	RES 2,A
A	RES 4,B	RES 4,C	RES 4,D	RES 4,E	RES 4,H	RES 4,L	RES 4,(HL)	RES 4,A
B	RES 6,B	RES 6,C	RES 6,D	RES 6,E	RES 6,H	RES 6,L	RES 6,(HL)	RES 6,A
C	SET 0,B	SET 0,C	SET 0,D	SET 0,E	SET 0,H	SET 0,L	SET 0,(HL)	SET 0,A
D	SET 2,B	SET 2,C	SET 2,D	SET 2,E	SET 2,H	SET 2,L	SET 2,(HL)	SET 2,A
E	SET 4,B	SET 4,C	SET 4,D	SET 4,E	SET 4,H	SET 4,L	SET 4,(HL)	SET 4,A
F	SET 6,B	SET 6,C	SET 6,D	SET 6,E	SET 6,H	SET 6,L	SET 6,(HL)	SET 6,A

Table 4-9. First half of the opcode table for 0xCB-prefixed opcodes.

LSB-> MSBv	8	9	A	B	C	D	E	F
0	RRC B	RRC C	RRC D	RRC E	RRC H	RRC L	RRC (HL)	RRC A
1	RR B	RR C	RR D	RR E	RR H	RR L	RR (HL)	RR A
2	SRA B	SRA C	SRA D	SRA E	SRA H	SRA L	SRA (HL)	SRA A
3	SRL B	SRL C	SRL D	SRL E	SRL H	SRL L	SRL (HL)	SRL A
4	BIT 1,B	BIT 1,C	BIT 1,D	BIT 1,E	BIT 1,H	BIT 1,L	BIT 1,(HL)	BIT 1,A
5	BIT 3,B	BIT 3,C	BIT 3,D	BIT 3,E	BIT 3,H	BIT 3,L	BIT 3,(HL)	BIT 3,A
6	BIT 5,B	BIT 5,C	BIT 5,D	BIT 5,E	BIT 5,H	BIT 5,L	BIT 5,(HL)	BIT 5,A
7	BIT 7,B	BIT 7,C	BIT 7,D	BIT 7,E	BIT 7,H	BIT 7,L	BIT 7,(HL)	BIT 7,A
8	RES 1,B	RES 1,C	RES 1,D	RES 1,E	RES 1,H	RES 1,L	RES 1,(HL)	RES 1,A
9	RES 3,B	RES 3,C	RES 3,D	RES 3,E	RES 3,H	RES 3,L	RES 3,(HL)	RES 3,A
A	RES 5,B	RES 5,C	RES 5,D	RES 5,E	RES 5,H	RES 5,L	RES 5,(HL)	RES 5,A
B	RES 7,B	RES 7,C	RES 7,D	RES 7,E	RES 7,H	RES 7,L	RES 7,(HL)	RES 7,A
C	SET 1,B	SET 1,C	SET 1,D	SET 1,E	SET 1,H	SET 1,L	SET 1,(HL)	SET 1,A
D	SET 3,B	SET 3,C	SET 3,D	SET 3,E	SET 3,H	SET 3,L	SET 3,(HL)	SET 3,A
E	SET 5,B	SET 5,C	SET 5,D	SET 5,E	SET 5,H	SET 5,L	SET 5,(HL)	SET 5,A
F	SET 7,B	SET 7,C	SET 7,D	SET 7,E	SET 7,H	SET 7,L	SET 7,(HL)	SET 7,A

Table 4-10. Second half of the opcode table for 0xCB-prefixed opcodes.

Two prefix bytes, 0xDD followed by 0xCB select these two tables. The 0xDD prefix modifies the 0xCB page of opcodes to use the IX register with indexed addressing. These instructions are unique in that the index offset is fetched before the final opcode byte is fetched.

LSB-> MSBv	0	1	2	3	4	5	6	7
0							RLC (IX+d)	
1							RL (IX+d)	
2							SLA (IX+d)	
3								
4							BIT 0,(IX+d)	
5							BIT 2,(IX+d)	
6							BIT 4,(IX+d)	
7							BIT 6,(IX+d)	
8							RES 0,(IX+d)	
9							RES 2,(IX+d)	
A							RES 4,(IX+d)	
B							RES 6,(IX+d)	
C							SET 0,(IX+d)	
D							SET 2,(IX+d)	
E							SET 4,(IX+d)	
F							SET 6,(IX+d)	

Table 4-11. First half of the opcode table for 0xDD-0xCB-prefixed opcodes.

LSB-> MSBv	8	9	A	B	C	D	E	F
0							RRC (IY+d)	
1							RR (IY+d)	
2							SRA (IY+d)	
3							SRL (IY+d)	
4							BIT 1,(IY+d)	
5							BIT 3,(IY+d)	
6							BIT 5,(IY+d)	
7							BIT 7,(IY+d)	
8							RES 1,(IY+d)	
9							RES 3,(IY+d)	
A							RES 5,(IY+d)	
B							RES 7,(IY+d)	
C							SET 1,(IY+d)	
D							SET 3,(IY+d)	
E							SET 5,(IY+d)	
F							SET 7,(IY+d)	

Table 4-12. Second half of the opcode table for 0xDD-0xCB-prefixed opcodes.

Two prefix bytes, 0xFD followed by 0xCB select these two tables. The 0xFD prefix modifies the 0xCB page of opcodes to use the IY register with indexed addressing. These instructions are unique in that the index offset is fetched before the final opcode byte is fetched.

LSB-> MSBv	0	1	2	3	4	5	6	7
0							RLC (IX+d)	
1							RL (IX+d)	
2							SLA (IX+d)	
3								
4							BIT 0,(IX+d)	
5							BIT 2,(IX+d)	
6							BIT 4,(IX+d)	
7							BIT 6,(IX+d)	
8							RES 0,(IX+d)	
9							RES 2,(IX+d)	
A							RES 4,(IX+d)	
B							RES 6,(IX+d)	
C							SET 0,(IX+d)	
D							SET 2,(IX+d)	
E							SET 4,(IX+d)	
F							SET 6,(IX+d)	

Table 4-13. First half of the opcode table for 0xFD-0xCB-prefixed opcodes

LSB-> MSBv	8	9	A	B	C	D	E	F
0							RRC (IY+d)	
1							RR (IY+d)	
2							SRA (IY+d)	
3							SRL (IY+d)	
4							BIT 1,(IY+d)	
5							BIT 3,(IY+d)	
6							BIT 5,(IY+d)	
7							BIT 7,(IY+d)	
8							RES 1,(IY+d)	
9							RES 3,(IY+d)	
A							RES 5,(IY+d)	
B							RES 7,(IY+d)	
C							SET 1,(IY+d)	
D							SET 3,(IY+d)	
E							SET 5,(IY+d)	
F							SET 7,(IY+d)	

Table 4-14. Second half of the opcode table for 0xFD-0xCB-prefixed opcodes.

The original Z80 was designed at the transistor level, with incomplete decoding of the opcodes to minimize the transistor count. This resulted in numerous unused opcodes (the shaded entries in the tables above) that actually performed valid operations. Even though these operations have been documented by users, for the most part they have never been officially acknowledged by Zilog. For this project I will only implement the instructions in the Zilog documentation. Feel free to research the undocumented operations and add them to your version of the design. You can also add your own custom instructions using any of these unused opcodes.

It is important to note that the Z80 is a little-endian machine, where the address of a multi-byte quantity is the address of the least-significant byte, which is also the lowest memory address. Normally all 16-bit quantities are read and written least-significant-byte first, at the lower memory address, followed by the most-significant byte to the next higher memory address. The only exception to this order occurs during a stack write, because the stack grows downward in memory. We'll have to remember this special case later during the implementation phase.

External Bus Interface

The original Z80 used an external bus interface that was suitable for the memory technology of the time, but since I am targeting this design towards either an FPGA or part of a larger ASIC it makes sense to tailor the bus interface to that type of environment.

The timing diagrams in Figure 4-3 show the operation that is typical for FPGA or ASIC memories. The important thing to note is that these memories operate synchronously, sampling the address, write data and write enable on the rising edge of the clock. Read data, which is on a separate bus from the write data, is valid on the next rising edge of the clock after the address is sampled.

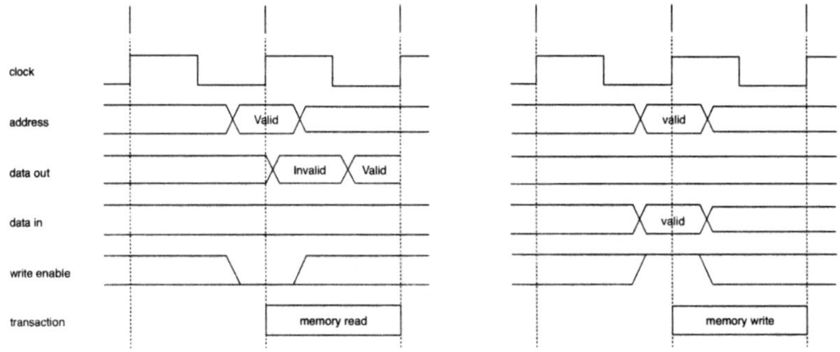

Figure 4-3. FPGA or ASIC memory timing.

Looking at these timing diagrams, the first thought is to use a single-clock bus interface and deal with the delayed read data with pipelining in the CPU. One problem with this approach is that external memories typically don't use this type of interface, and what happens if we want to be able to connect to external memories? Also, pipelining will necessarily add complexity (more hardware) to the design.

This is an example of the type of trade-off that designers have to make with every design. In this case, I'll deliberately choose to compromise the performance and go with a two-clock bus cycle. This will make it easier to possibly connect to external memories while at the same time reducing the complexity of the design. The timing I'll use is shown in the timing diagrams in Figure 4-4.

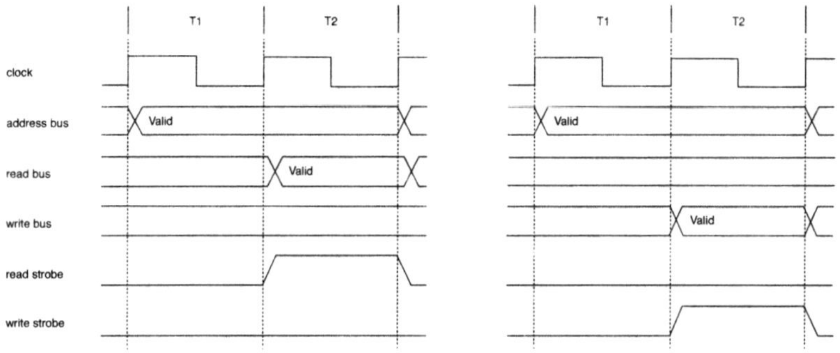

Figure 4-4. Bus interface timing for this CPU.

Why isn't the timing for the write data the same as that for the address in the write cycle? As I mentioned previously, the Z80 instruction set includes read-modify-write operations. If we try to drive the write data at the start of the write transaction there won't be any time to do any operation on the read data that is being sampled by the same clock edge! Driving the write data during the second clock cycle of the transaction will allow us to operate on the data during the first clock of the write transaction.

Clearly this timing is compatible with the timing of on-chip memories, but it will also work well with external memory devices if necessary. One thing to note about this bus timing is that the extra memory bandwidth available with on-chip memories doesn't have to be wasted. This is because memory reads and writes from a Direct Memory Access (DMA) controller or video controller can be interleaved with the CPU accesses. The timing diagrams in Figure 4-5 show the clock cycles available for use with an internal single-clock memory.

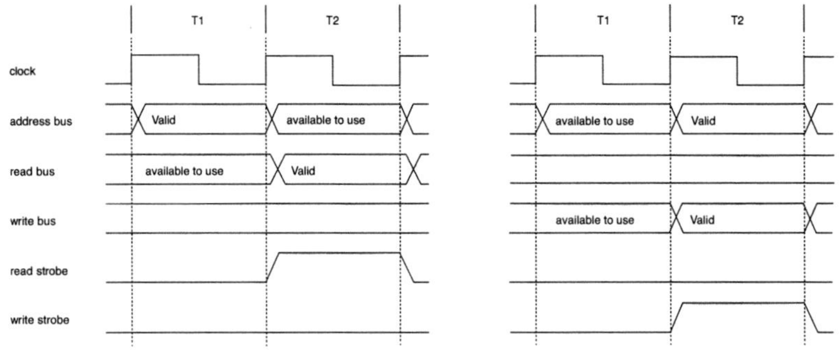

Figure 4-5. One clock is available for other use during bus transactions.

The original Z80 included a Wait input, to allow interfacing to slow memory or peripheral devices. Since this design will be implemented in either an FPGA or as part of a larger ASIC, it could be argued that a Wait input will not be necessary. In my experience it is better to design this type of feature in at the beginning and not use it rather than try to add it in later. I have encountered a number of peripheral functions in ASICs that had peculiar timing requirements that led to the use of wait states, mainly to guarantee a certain cycle time for transactions. The timing diagrams in Figure 4-6 show the operation with a Wait state. The two-clock bus cycle is much easier to stretch with Wait states than a single-clock bus cycle would be.

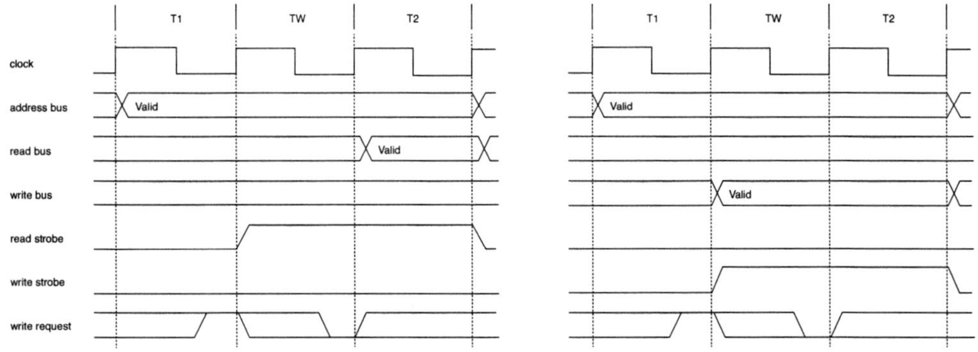

Figure 4-6. Inserting Wait states into bus transactions.

Similarly, the original Z80 included a bus request function that allowed an external bus master like a DMA controller to take control of the bus from the CPU. In the Z80 the external bus could be released between any bus transaction, even in the middle of an instruction. This type of operation is probably not necessary for this design, particularly if the interleaved transfers mentioned above are implemented. But we'll decide this later, when we start implementing the instructions.

On-chip memories use separate read and write data busses, so it makes sense to keep them separate out of the CPU. The original Z80 used a single data bus for memory transactions, I/O transactions and the interrupt vector during interrupt acknowledge transactions. Since we will be using separate read and write data busses for the memory, it's reasonable to think about how to implement I/O data transfers and the interrupt vector transfer.

For several reasons, including bus loading and ease of routing, I will separate the busses for each of these functions. So the CPU will have separate unidirectional 8-bit busses for memory read, memory write, I/O read, I/O write, and interrupt vector read. For the same reasons, let's separate the memory address bus from the I/O address bus. So the design top level interface signals include those shown in Listing 4-1:

```
input   [7:0] IO_DATA_IN;      /* i/o input data bus                      */
input   [7:0] IVEC_DATA_IN;    /* interrupt vector bus                    */
input   [7:0] MEM_DATA_IN;     /* memory input bus                        */
output        IACK_TRAN;       /* interrupt acknowledge transaction       */
output        IO_READ;         /* i/o read enable                         */
output        IO_TRAN;         /* i/o transaction                         */
output        IO_STROBE;       /* i/o data strobe                         */
output        IVEC_RD;         /* interrupt vector enable                 */
output        MEM_RD;          /* memory read enable                      */
output        MEM_TRAN;        /* memory transaction                      */
output        MEM_WR;          /* memory write enable                     */
output  [7:0] IO_DATA_OUT;     /* i/o output data bus                     */
output  [7:0] MEM_DATA_OUT;    /* memory output data bus                  */
output [15:0] IO_ADDR_OUT;     /* i/o address bus                         */
output [15:0] MEM_ADDR_OUT;    /* memory address bus                      */
```

Listing 4-1. Top level design interface signals.

The IACK_TRAN, IO_TRAN and MEM_TRAN signals will be necessary if we need to create Wait states based on the type of transaction. The MEM_RD and MEM_WR signals are as shown in the previous timing diagrams. On-chip memories really only need the MEM_WR signal because they are always either doing a read or a write, but external memories will also require a MEM_RD signal.

For the I/O bus there is an industry standard, the AMBA Peripheral Bus (APB), that uses a direction control signal (IO_READ) and single strobe (IO_STROBE), as shown in the timing diagrams in Figure 4-7. The APB is really a single-clock bus, but our two-clock transactions will still be compatible.

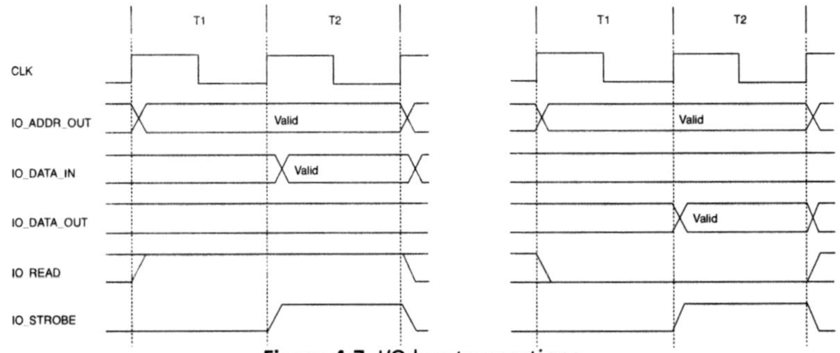

Figure 4-7. I/O bus transactions.

The only remaining transaction that we need to define is the interrupt acknowledge, shown in Figure 4-8. The easiest thing to do is to make it look just like a normal read transaction. This has the added advantage of providing at least one clock cycle to resolve external interrupt priorities, during the first clock of the transaction.

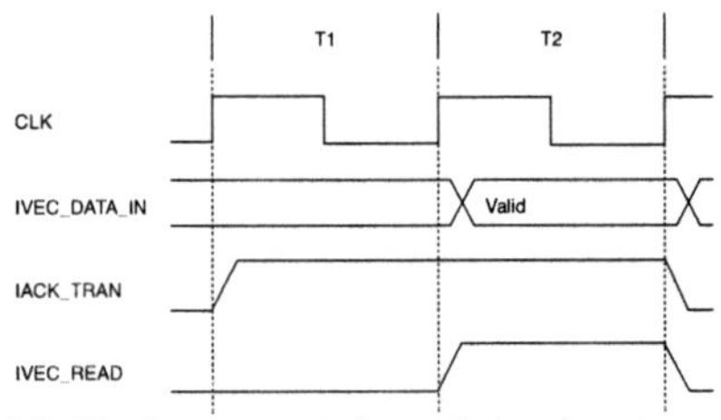

Figure 4-8. The Interrupt Acknowledge bus transactions.

I'll leave the remainder of the external bus interface until we get deeper into the design, but this is the core of what is required.

Machine Cycle

Once the external bus interface timing has been defined, it's time to decide on the timing for machine cycles. The obvious choice is two clocks, to match the bus timing, and that should be fine for instruction fetches, data reads and data writes. But what about the other operations that the CPU does? Things like address calculations, cycles necessary to update the PC for Jump, Call and Return instructions, cycles necessary to set up for an Interrupt Acknowledge, and so on. The choices here are single clock cycles or an enforced two-clock-cycle machine cycle.

Single clock clearly gives better performance, but there may be system-level advantages to having a uniform two-clock machine cycle. For example, this may make a state machine controlling interleaved accesses easier to design. If we want to add address translation logic, via a Memory Management Unit (MMU), address calculation cycles might need to be two clocks anyway. If we go with a uniform two-clock machine cycle we can output a bus clock that cycles once per machine cycle to fool the marketing folks into thinking that we have single-cycle execution. (I have seen this done.)

Perhaps the most compelling reason for going with a uniform two-clock machine cycle is the fact that this will provide the opportunity to use these machine cycles to prefetch instructions in parallel. I will not implement this operation in this design, but it is a useful feature for you to attempt to add.

Before we jump into the details of the micro-architecture, we need to work out the timing for machine cycles. The way to do this is to work backwards from when the address and data need to be available. This is often an iterative process, particularly when pipelining is involved. As a first pass, look at the timing diagram in Figure 4-9 for an instruction fetch.

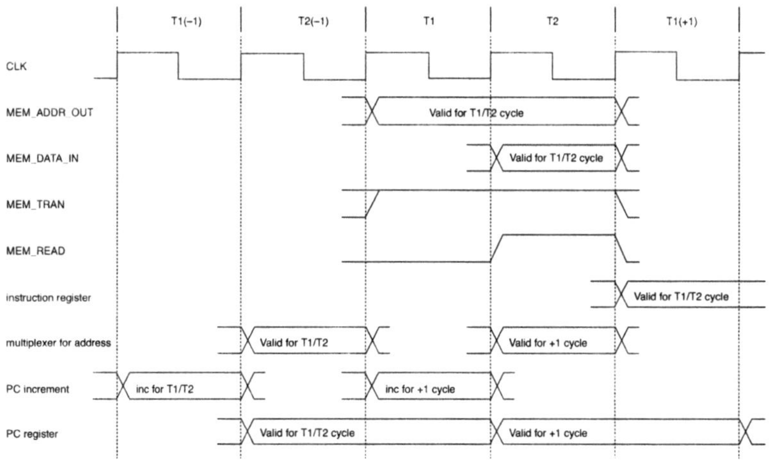

Figure 4-9. Determining the internal timing.

It is good design practice to have output signals come directly from the outputs of flip-flops. Not only does this give the maximum time for outputs to propagate to their destination, it simplifies the timing constraints for the logic synthesis and routing tools. If we do this for the address outputs it means the multiplexer that selects the source for the address must stabilize during the clock cycle just before the T1 cycle of a read transaction. Trying to increment the PC during the same clock cycle will probably lead to long signal paths and limit the maximum clock frequency. This means that the PC increment should occur during the T1 cycle of the previous bus transaction. This same timing must also be used for the indexed addressing case, or a PC-relative jump, validating the utility of the two-clock machine cycle.

With this timing the instruction register does not become available until after the current machine cycle is complete. What this really means is that the fetch of the next instruction must start while the current instruction is being executed, which is the simplest form of pipelining. We need to keep this in mind when working on the microarchitecture.

5. Microarchitecture

Introduction

The microarchitecture of a CPU consists of the details of how the ISA is implemented. In other words, the details of how the various functional elements of the design operate, clock cycle by clock cycle, for the entire instruction set. There are obviously a number of ways that this information can be presented, ranging from a huge set of timing diagrams to a microcode listing.

A set of timing diagrams might be practical if every instruction had exactly the same timing or if there were a very limited number of instructions. But for most designs using timing diagrams exclusively to present the microarchitecture is just not practical. But like the example in the previous section, a certain number of timing diagrams will always be required.

At the other end of the spectrum is microcode, which presents the architecture in what looks like software. I have worked on microcoded designs, and quite frankly found myself drawing a lot of timing diagrams to try to figure out what was really going on. Another thing that I don't like about microcode is that it is usually inconvenient to try to compare the details of the operations between different instructions.

The technique that I have used for many designs, that I will present here, uses a spreadsheet program to combine the best features of timing diagrams with the best features of microcode.

Organizing the Design Spreadsheet

Designing a system this complex can only be done by starting with a top level view and progressively adding more detail. Once the design is completely specified the implementation is done from the bottom up, one section of Verilog at a time. In the technique presented here the individual worksheets in the spreadsheet contain the details of the design, and the individual worksheets become progressively more detailed as I compete them.

The design spreadsheet[(6)] does not use any of the normal calculation features of a spreadsheet program. Instead, the rows and columns are used to organize the various operations that occur within the CPU for each instruction.

Each row in the spreadsheet is used for a separate instruction, but not necessarily for individual opcodes. To make the size of the spreadsheet manageable I use a single row for instructions that differ only in a common bit field. For example, an instruction that is identical except for the source register will use a single row. Bit fields shared this way do not have to be complete. In the Z80 instruction set seven possible bit combinations in a 3-bit field select one of the seven CPU registers to use. The remaining bit combination for this field selects indirect register addressing, so this opcode uses a separate row in the spreadsheet because the instruction timing is different for this case.

Columns in the spreadsheet represent different clock cycles. Each possible clock cycle for each possible machine cycle has a separate column. Clearly not every instruction will use every possible machine cycle, so unused cycles are shaded to indicate this.

Organized like this, the rows in the spreadsheet contain essentially the same information as a timing diagram. Short mnemonics in each column act much the same as microcode. A separate worksheet is used for each function in the CPU, like the ALU inputs, ALU operation, etc. The sort function of the spreadsheet program allows grouping of instructions in a variety of ways. Groups of opcodes can the be copied directly from the spreadsheet into the word processor used to create the Verilog code.

Since the spreadsheet contents flow directly into the Verilog code, it is critical that the contents of the spreadsheet start with the correct information. There are two important worksheets that I always place at the start of the design spreadsheet, called *Operation* and *Internal Code*.

The *Operation* Worksheet

The *Operation* worksheet provides a concise description of the operation of every instruction in a single location. Creating this worksheet is a convenient way to identify unique cases in the instruction set, and it forces the designer to start to become familiar with the instruction set. The *Operation* worksheet excerpt in Figure 5-1 shows the various add instructions.

Num	Instruction	Opcode byte 1	Opcode byte 2	Opcode byte 3	Opcode byte 4	Mach State	S	Z	H	PV	N	C	Operation
1	ADC A,(HL)	10001110				3	S	Z	H	V	0	C	A = A + (HL) + CF
2	ADC A,(IX+d)	11011101	10001110	----d---		5	S	Z	H	V	0	C	A = A + (IX+d) + CF
3	ADC A,(IY+d)	11111101	10001110	----d---		5	S	Z	H	V	0	C	A = A + (IY+d) + CF
4	ADC A,n	11001110	----n---			2	S	Z	H	V	0	C	A = A + n + CF
5	ADC A,r	10001rrr				1	S	Z	H	V	0	C	A = A + r + CF
6	ADC HL,ss	11101101	01ss1010			2	S	Z	H	V	0	C	HL = HL + ss + CF
7	ADD A,(HL)	10000110				3	S	Z	H	V	0	C	A = A + (HL)
8	ADD A,(IX+d)	11011101	10000110	----d---		5	S	Z	H	V	0	C	A = A + (IX+d)
9	ADD A,(IY+d)	11111101	10000110	----d---		5	S	Z	H	V	0	C	A = A + (IY+d)
10	ADD A,n	11000110	----n---			2	S	Z	H	V	0	C	A = A + n
11	ADD A,r	10000rrr				1	S	Z	H	V	0	C	A = A + r
12	ADD HL,ss	00ss1001				1			H		0	C	HL = HL + ss
13	ADD IX,xx	11011101	00xx1001			2			H		0	C	IX = IX + xx
14	ADD IY,yy	11111101	00yy1001			2			H		0	C	IY = IY + yy

Figure 5-1. Operation worksheet for Add instructions.

The *num* column is present in every worksheet, and provides a convenient way to return the worksheet to a defined order. While working on a worksheet you will constantly be sorting the rows into a different order and there has to be a way to get things back to a common starting point.

The *Instruction* column lists every instruction for the design. I prefer to use alphabetical order, because it makes finding a specific instruction easy, but feel free to choose any order that works for you. Choose carefully though, because this will be the default row order for the rest of the design spreadsheet. This column is also present in every worksheet.

Next come the *opcode* columns. For the Z80 opcodes can be up to four bytes in length, so there are four *opcode* columns. Unused columns are shaded to make the opcode length obvious. When you enter this information for the first time, double-, triple- and quadruple-check it, because a mistake here will propagate throughout the design spreadsheet, with disastrous results.

The *Mach State* column is included in this worksheet primarily for documentation purposes. When first filling out this worksheet it is a best guess as to the number of machine cycles that are going to be required. Clearly one machine cycle will be needed for each byte of opcode, one for an address computation, one for an operand fetch, and so on. With only a couple of exceptions, the number of machine cycles required by an instruction can be completely determined by counting the required memory accesses and address calculation operations.

This column is not cast in stone at this point, and may need to be updated to reflect the final implementation. I should note that the numbers presented here implicitly assume a 16-bit data path in the design.

You might be tempted to gloss over the *Mach State* column, but that would be a mistake. Understanding the number of machine cycles required for each instruction is critical to understanding the internal structure of the design. I'll go over the machine states in detail after discussing the instruction set, but you should try to figure out where the number in the *Mach State* column comes from while going through this worksheet.

The next six columns show the effect of each instruction on the Flags. This is just a high-level indication that a particular flag is affected, rather than a detailed description of how the flag is affected. For example, most of the flags will have a different source for a byte operation and a word operation. A blank entry means that the flag is not affected by the instruction.

The *operation* column holds a detailed description of the operation for each instruction. I use an intuitive pseudo-code to describe the operations. The intent here is just to include enough detail so that nothing is forgotten when we get to filling out the remainder of the spreadsheet. Feel free to use a more formal description if necessary.

Going through the *Operation* worksheet is the easiest way to become familiar with the instruction set, so I'll discuss the entire worksheet detailing the bit fields in the opcodes and highlighting special cases. I can't stress enough how important it is to understand the contents of this worksheet.

The excerpt from the *Operation* worksheet in Figure 5-1 shows all of the instructions available to add two numbers together. Addition with and without a carry-in are available, for both 8-bit and 16-bit operands. Note that three of the add instructions don't affect all of the flags. This is deliberate, as these instructions were intended to be used for address calculations.

There are several bit fields in the *opcode* columns that need explaining. The ----*d*--- byte is a two's-complement number that will be sign-extended to sixteen bits and added to an index register to form an address for the operand. In a similar fashion, the ----*n*--- byte is an immediate data value that is one of the operands for the instruction. When fetched, these bytes will be loaded into temporary registers for use.

There are a number of examples of bit fields in the opcodes shown in Table 5-1. The 2-bit *ss*, *xx* and *yy* fields have the meanings shown below. Notice how the prefix bytes modify the operand to select either the IX register or the IY register instead of the HL register.

Value	*ss*	*xx*	*yy*
00	BC	BC	BC
01	DE	DE	DE
10	HL	IX	IY
11	SP	SP	SP

Table 5-1. Word register select bit fields.

The 3-bit *rrr* field selects an 8-bit register for the operand as shown in Table 5-2. Only seven bit combinations are valid for this bit field, with the remaining bit combination selecting a different addressing mode with different instruction timing. We'll need to keep this in mind while filling out the remainder of the spreadsheet and when generating the Verilog code.

Value	*rrr*
000	B
001	C
010	D
011	E
100	H
101	L
111	A

Table 5-2. Byte register select bit field.

The *Operand* worksheet excerpt in Figure 5-2 shows the subtract and compare instructions. There are no address-only versions of subtract, but otherwise this group is similar to the add instructions.

Num	Instruction	Opcode byte 1	Opcode byte 2	Opcode byte 3	Opcode byte 4	Mach State	S	Z	H	PV	N	C	Operation
27	CP (HL)	10111110				3	S	Z	H	V	1	C	A - (HL)
28	CP (IX+d)	11011101	10111110	----d---		5	S	Z	H	V	1	C	A - (IX+d)
29	CP (IY+d)	11111101	10111110	----d---		5	S	Z	H	V	1	C	A - (IY+d)
30	CP n	11111110	----n---			2	S	Z	H	V	1	C	A - n
31	CP r	10111rrr				1	S	Z	H	V	1	C	A - r
167	SBC (IX+d)	11011101	10011110	----d---		5	S	Z	H	V	1	C	A = A - (IX+d) - CY
168	SBC (IY+d)	11111101	10011110	----d---		5	S	Z	H	V	1	C	A = A - (IY+d) - CY
169	SBC A,(HL)	10011110				3	S	Z	H	V	1	C	A = A - (HL) - CY
170	SBC A,n	11011110	----n---			2	S	Z	H	V	1	C	A = A - n - CY
171	SBC A,r	10011rrr				1	S	Z	H	V	1	C	A = A - r - CY
172	SBC HL,ss	11101101	01ss0010			2	S	Z	H	V	1	C	HL = HL - ss - CF
190	SUB (HL)	10010110				3	S	Z	H	V	1	C	A = A - (HL)
191	SUB (IX+d)	11011101	10010110	----d---		5	S	Z	H	V	1	C	A = A - (IX+d)
192	SUB (IY+d)	11111101	10010110	----d---		5	S	Z	H	V	1	C	A = A - (IY+d)
193	SUB n	11010110	----n---			2	S	Z	H	V	1	C	A = A - n
194	SUB r	10010rrr				1	S	Z	H	V	1	C	A = A - r

Figure 5-2. *Operation* worksheet for Subtract and Compare instructions.

The excerpt in Figure 5-3 contains the Increment and Decrement instructions. All of the 8-bit versions operate like Add and Subtract, but do not affect the Carry flag. This is probably because these instructions were intended to be used for things like loop counters. Preserving the Carry flag allows tests inside of a loop to communicate outside the loop. The 16-bit versions do not affect any flags, because they are usually used with addresses.

Num	Instruction	Opcode byte 1	Opcode byte 2	Opcode byte 3	Opcode byte 4	Mach State	S	Z	H	PV	N	C	Operation
38	DEC (HL)	00110101				4	S	Z	H	V	1		(HL) = (HL) - 1
39	DEC (IX+d)	11011101	00110101	----d---		6	S	Z	H	V	1		(IX+d) = (IX+d) -1
40	DEC (IY+d)	11111101	00110101	----d---		6	S	Z	H	V	1		(IY+d) = (IY+d) -1
41	DEC IX	11011101	00101011			2							IX = IX - 1
42	DEC IY	11111101	00101011			2							IY = IY - 1
43	DEC r	00rrr101				1	S	Z	H	V	1		r = r - 1
44	DEC ss	00ss1011				1							ss = ss - 1
60	INC (HL)	00110100				4	S	Z	H	V	0		(HL) = (HL) + 1
61	INC (IX+d)	11011101	00110100	----d---		6	S	Z	H	V	0		(IX+d) = (IX+d) + 1
62	INC (IY+d)	11111101	00110100	----d---		6	S	Z	H	V	0		(IY+d) = (IY+d) + 1
63	INC IX	11011101	00100011			2							IX = IX + 1
64	INC IY	11111101	00100011			2							IY = IY + 1
65	INC r	00rrr100				1	S	Z	H	V	0		r = r + 1
66	INC ss	00ss0011				1							ss = ss + 1

Figure 5-3. Operation worksheet for Increment and Decrement instructions.

The *Operation* worksheet excerpt with the logical operations is shown in Figure 5-4. Only 8-bit logical operations are available, and they treat most of the flags differently than arithmetic instructions. The H, N and C flags are all forced to specific values and the PV flag reflects the parity of the result instead of signaling overflow.

Num	Instruction	Opcode byte 1	Opcode byte 2	Opcode byte 3	Opcode byte 4	Mach State	S	Z	H	PV	N	C	Operation
15	AND (HL)	10100110				3	S	Z	1	P	0	0	A = A & (HL)
16	AND (IX+d)	11011101	10100110	----d---		5	S	Z	1	P	0	0	A = A & (IX+d)
17	AND (IY+d)	11111101	10100110	----d---		5	S	Z	1	P	0	0	A = A & (IY+d)
18	AND n	11100110	----n---			2	S	Z	1	P	0	0	A = A & n
19	AND r	10100rrr				1	S	Z	1	P	0	0	A = A & r
119	OR (HL)	10110110				3	S	Z	0	P	0	0	A = A | (HL)
120	OR (IX+d)	11011101	10110110	----d---		5	S	Z	0	P	0	0	A = A | (IX+d)
121	OR (IY+d)	11111101	10110110	----d---		5	S	Z	0	P	0	0	A = A | (IY+d)
122	OR n	11110110	----n---			2	S	Z	0	P	0	0	A = A | n
123	OR r	10110rrr				1	S	Z	0	P	0	0	A = A | r
195	XOR (HL)	10101110				3	S	Z	0	P	0	0	A = A ^ (HL)
196	XOR (IX+d)	11011101	10101110	----d---		5	S	Z	0	P	0	0	A = A ^ (IX+d)
197	XOR (IY+d)	11111101	10101110	----d---		5	S	Z	0	P	0	0	A = A ^ (IY+d)
198	XOR n	11101110	----n---			2	S	Z	0	P	0	0	A = A ^ n
199	XOR r	10101rrr				1	S	Z	0	P	0	0	A = A ^ r

Figure 5-4. *Operation* worksheet for logical instructions.

Rounding out the arithmetic and logical instructions are five special cases, shown in Figure 5-5. These instructions are all unique in one way or another. The Decimal Adjust instruction is particularly messy to implement, using the state of the H, N and C flags, along with the contents of the accumulator, to determine how the accumulator is modified. Interestingly, the PV flag reports the parity of the result for this instruction.

Num	Instruction	Opcode byte 1	Opcode byte 2	Opcode byte 3	Opcode byte 4	Mach State	S	Z	H	PV	N	C	Operation
26	CCF	00111111				1			C		0	C	CF = ~CF
36	CPL	00101111				1			1		1		A = ~A
37	DAA	00100111				1	S	Z	H	P		C	Decimal Adjust Accumulator
117	NEG	11101101	01000100			2	S	Z	H	V	1	C	A = 0 - A
173	SCF	00110111				1			0		0	1	CF = 1

Figure 5-5. *Operation* worksheet for the special arithmetic instructions.

The exact algorithm for the Decimal Adjust instruction is shown in Table 5-3. The two right-most columns show the constant to be added to the accumulator and the resulting value for the Carry flag.

prior to DAA instruction					after DAA instruction	
N flag	C flag	A[7:4]	H flag	A[3:0]	add to A	C flag
0	0	0-9	0	0-9	8'h00	0
0	0	0-8	0	A-F	8'h06	0
0	0	0-9	1	0-3	8'h06	0
0	0	A-F	0	0-9	8'h60	1
0	0	9-F	0	A-F	8'h66	1
0	0	A-F	1	0-3	8'h66	1
0	1	0-2	0	0-9	8'h60	1
0	1	0-2	0	A-F	8'h66	1
0	1	0-3	1	0-3	8'h66	1
1	0	0-9	0	0-9	8'h00	0
1	0	0-8	1	6-F	8'hFA	0
1	1	7-F	0	0-9	8'hA0	1
1	1	6-F	1	6-F	8'h9A	1

Table 5-3. Decimal Adjust instruction operation.

The Z80 instruction set includes Bit Test, Bit Set and Bit Reset instructions, for both registers and memory operands. Table 5-4 shows the encoding for the 3-bit *bbb* field in the opcode for these instructions.

Value	bbb
000	0
001	1
010	2
011	3
100	4
101	5
110	6
111	7

Table 5-4. Bit select encoding for bit operation instructions.

If you look closely at the Bit Test/Set/Reset excerpt from the *Operation* worksheet in Figure 5-6, you'll notice an apparent anomaly in the number of machine cycles required for the indexed addressing mode. The count shown doesn't seem to account for the required address calculation. But if you look at the opcode maps with a two byte prefix, you'll see that all of the instructions on these two pages have exactly the same format. So I should be able to use the time during the fetch of the fourth byte of the opcode to do the address calculation.

Num	Instruction	Opcode byte 1	Opcode byte 2	Opcode byte 3	Opcode byte 4	Mach State	S	Z	H	PV	N	C	Operation
20	BIT b,(HL)	11001011	01bbb110			4		Z	1		0		(HL) & bit
21	BIT b,(IX+d))	11011101	11001011	----d---	01bbb110	5		Z	1		0		(IX+d) & bit
22	BIT b,(IY+d))	11111101	11001011	----d---	01bbb110	5		Z	1		0		(IY+d) & bit
23	BIT b,r	11001011	01bbbrrr			2		Z	1		0		r & bit
136	RES b,(HL)	11001011	10bbb110			5							(HL) = (HL) & ~bit
137	RES b,(IX+d)	11011101	11001011	----d---	10bbb110	6							(IX+d) = (IX+d) & ~bit
138	RES b,(IY+d)	11111101	11001011	----d---	10bbb110	6							(IY+d) = (IY+d) & ~bit
139	RES b,r	11001011	10bbbrrr			2							r = r & ~bit
174	SET b,(HL)	11001011	11bbb110			5							(HL) = (HL) | bit
175	SET b,(IX+d)	11011101	11001011	----d---	11bbb110	6							(IX+d) = (IX+d) | bit
176	SET b,(IY+d)	11111101	11001011	----d---	11bbb110	6							(IY+d) = (IY+d) | bit
177	SET b,r	11001011	11bbbrrr			2							r = r | bit

Figure 5-6. *Operation* worksheet for the Bit Test/Set/Reset instructions.

There are six special rotate instructions, shown in the excerpt in Figure 5-7. The 1-byte opcodes are actually left over from the 8080 instruction set. They are unique in their treatment of the flags, which is why they are listed here. The Rotate Digit instructions are for use with BCD numbers. As in the case of the Decimal Adjust instruction, these two rotate instructions report the parity of the result in the PV flag.

Num	Instruction	Opcode byte 1	Opcode byte 2	Opcode byte 3	Opcode byte 4	Mach State	S	Z	H	PV	N	C	Operation
148	RLA	00010111				1			0		0	C	{CY,A} = {A,CY}
153	RLCA	00000111				1			0		0	C	A = {A[6,0],A[7]}; CY = A[7]
154	RLD	11101101	01101111			5	S	Z	0	P	0		A = {A[7:4],(HL)[7:4]}; (HL) = {(HL)[3:0],A[3:0]}
159	RRA	00011111				1			0		0	C	{A,CY} = {CY,A}
164	RRCA	00001111				1			0		0	C	A = {A[0],A[7,1]}; CY = A[0]
165	RRD	11101101	01100111			5	S	Z	0	P	0		A = {A[7:4],(HL)[3:0]}; (HL) = {A[3:0],(HL)[7:4]}

Figure 5-7. *Operation* worksheet for the special rotate instructions.

The seven different types of shift and rotate instructions are shown in the excerpt from the *Operation* worksheet in Figure 5-8. Shift and rotate instructions with the indexed addressing mode should be able to do the address calculation during the fetch of the fourth byte of the opcode just like the bit test/set/reset instructions.

It might appear that there is a missing shift instruction. After all, there are two arithmetic shift instructions but only one logical shift instruction. If you think about it, you'll realize that a shift left logical is the same as a shift left arithmetic.

Num	Instruction	Opcode byte 1	Opcode byte 2	Opcode byte 3	Opcode byte 4	Mach State	S	Z	H	PV	N	C	Operation
144	RL (HL)	11001011	00010110			5	S	Z	0	P	0	C	{CY,(HL)} = {(HL),CY}
145	RL (IX+d)	11011101	11001011	----d---	00010110	6	S	Z	0	P	0	C	{CY,(IX+d)} = {(IX+d),CY}
146	RL (IY+d)	11111101	11001011	----d---	00010110	6	S	Z	0	P	0	C	{CY,(IY+d)} = {(IY+d),CY}
147	RL r	11001011	00010rrr			2	S	Z	0	P	0	C	{CY,r} = {r,CY}
149	RLC (HL)	11001011	00000110			5	S	Z	0	P	0	C	(HL) = {(HL)[6,0],(HL)[7]}; CY = (HL)[7]
150	RLC (IX+d)	11011101	11001011	----d---	00000110	6	S	Z	0	P	0	C	(IX+d) = {(IX+d)[6,0],(IX+d)[7]}; CY = (IX+d)[7]
151	RLC (IY+d)	11111101	11001011	----d---	00000110	6	S	Z	0	P	0	C	(IY+d) = {(IY+d)[6,0],(IY+d)[7]}; CY = (IY+d)[7]
152	RLC r	11001011	00000rrr			2	S	Z	0	P	0	C	r = {r[6,0],r[7]}; CY = r[7]
155	RR (HL)	11001011	00011110			5	S	Z	0	P	0	C	{(HL),CY} = {CY,(HL)}
156	RR (IX+d)	11011101	11001011	----d---	00011110	6	S	Z	0	P	0	C	{(IX+d),CY} = {CY,(IX+d)}
157	RR (IY+d)	11111101	11001011	----d---	00011110	6	S	Z	0	P	0	C	{(IY+d),CY} = {CY,(IY+d)}
158	RR r	11001011	00011rrr			2	S	Z	0	P	0	C	{r,CY} = {CY,r}
160	RRC (HL)	11001011	00001110			5	S	Z	0	P	0	C	(HL) = {(HL)[0],(HL)[7,1]}; CY = (HL)[0]
161	RRC (IX+d)	11011101	11001011	----d---	00001110	6	S	Z	0	P	0	C	(IX+d) = {(IX+d)[0],(IX+d)[7,1]}; CY = (IX+d)[0]
162	RRC (IY+d)	11111101	11001011	----d---	00001110	6	S	Z	0	P	0	C	(IY+d) = {(IY+d)[0],(IY+d)[7,1]}; CY = (IY+d)[0]
163	RRC r	11001011	00001rrr			2	S	Z	0	P	0	C	r = {r[0],r[7,1]}; CY = r[0]
178	SLA (HL)	11001011	00100110			5	S	Z	0	P	0	C	(HL) = {(HL)[6,0],0}; CY = (HL)[7]
179	SLA (IX+d)	11011101	11001011	----d---	00100110	6	S	Z	0	P	0	C	(IX+d) = {(IX+d)[6,0],0}; CY = (IX+d)[7]
180	SLA (IY+d)	11111101	11001011	----d---	00100110	6	S	Z	0	P	0	C	(IY+d) = {(IY+d)[6,0],0}; CY = (IY+d)[7]
181	SLA r	11001011	00100rrr			2	S	Z	0	P	0	C	r = {r[6,0],0}; CY = r[7]
182	SRA (HL)	11001011	00101110			5	S	Z	0	P	0	C	(HL) = {(HL)[7],(HL)[7,1]}; CY = (HL)[0]
183	SRA (IX+d)	11011101	11001011	----d---	00101110	6	S	Z	0	P	0	C	(IX+d) = {(IX+d)[7],(IX+d)[7,1]}; CY = (IX+d)[0]
184	SRA (IY+d)	11111101	11001011	----d---	00101110	6	S	Z	0	P	0	C	(IY+d) = {(IY+d)[7],(IY+d)[7,1]}; CY = (IY+d)[0]
185	SRA r	11001011	00101rrr			2	S	Z	0	P	0	C	r = {r[7],r[7,1]}; CY = r[0]
186	SRL (HL)	11001011	00111110			5	S	Z	0	P	0	C	(HL) = {0,(HL)[7,1]}; CY = (HL)[0]
187	SRL (IX+d)	11011101	11001011	----d---	00111110	6	S	Z	0	P	0	C	(IX+d) = {0,(IX+d)[7,1]}; CY = (IX+d)[0]
188	SRL (IY+d)	11111101	11001011	----d---	00111110	6	S	Z	0	P	0	C	(IY+d) = {0,(IY+d)[7,1]}; CY = (IY+d)[0]
189	SRL r	11001011	00111rrr			2	S	Z	0	P	0	C	r = {0,r[7,1]}; CY = r[0]

Figure 5-8. *Operation* worksheet for the shift and rotate instructions.

The next excerpt from the *Operation* worksheet, in Figure 5-9, shows the 8-bit load instructions. There are three new bit field symbols introduced in this excerpt. The ----*m*--- byte is the upper eights bits of a 16-bit immediate address. The 3-bit *rdr* and *rsr* fields use the same encoding that is used for the *rrr* field. I use them here to make it obvious that there are two separate register select bit fields in the opcode.

The load instructions with immediate data and indexed addressing are probably going to require some special handling, because these are the only cases where the fourth opcode byte is immediate 8-bit data. All other cases where the fourth byte is immediate data have that byte as the most-significant byte of a 16-bit quantity.

Two of the load instructions here affect the flags, which is very unusual. Both instructions load the state of the interrupt enable into the PV flag.

Num	Instruction	Opcode byte 1	Opcode byte 2	Opcode byte 3	Opcode byte 4	Mach State	S	Z	H	PV	N	C	Operation
78	LD (BC),A	00000010				3							(BC) = A
79	LD (DE),A	00010010				3							(DE) = A
80	LD (HL),n	00110110	----n---			3							(HL) = n
81	LD (HL),r	01110rrr				3							(HL) = r
82	LD (IX+d),n	11011101	00110110	----d---	----n---	5							(IX+d) = n
83	LD (IX+d),r	11011101	01110rrr	----d---		5							(IX+d) = r
84	LD (IY+d),n	11111101	00110110	----d---	----n---	5							(IY+d) = n
85	LD (IY+d),r	11111101	01110rrr	----d---		5							(Iy+d) = r
86	LD (mn),A	00110010	----n---	----m---		5							(mn) = A
91	LD A,(BC)	00001010				3							A = (BC)
92	LD A,(DE)	00011010				3							A = (DE)
93	LD A,(mn)	00111010	----n---	----m---		5							A = (mn)
94	LD A,I	11101101	01010111			2	S	Z	0	F	0		A = I
95	LD A,R	11101101	01011111			2	S	Z	0	F	0		A = R
99	LD I,A	11101101	01000111			2							I = A
104	LD r,(HL)	01rrr110				3							r = (HL)
105	LD r,(IX+d)	11011101	01rrr110	----d---		5							r = (IX+d)
106	LD r,(IY+d)	11111101	01rrr110	----d---		5							r = (IY+d)
107	LD R,A	11101101	01001111			2							R = A
108	LD r,n	00rrr110	----n---			2							r = n
109	LD rd,rs	01rdrrsr				1							rd = rs

Figure 5-9. *Operation* worksheet for the byte load instructions.

The next *Operation* worksheet excerpt, in Figure 5-10, shows the 16-bit load instructions. The 2-bit *dd* field uses the same encoding as the *ss* field shown previously. The ----*n*--- and ----*m*--- bytes are used for both 16-bit immediate address and 16-bit immediate data.

Num	Instruction	Opcode byte 1	Opcode byte 2	Opcode byte 3	Opcode byte 4	Mach State	S	Z	H	PV	N	C	Operation
87	LD (mn),HL	00100010	----n---	----m---		6							(mn) = L; (mn+1) = H
88	LD (mn),IX	11011101	00100010	----n---	----m---	7							(mn) = IXL; (mn+1) = IXH
89	LD (mn),IY	11111101	00100010	----n---	----m---	7							(mn) = IYL; (mn+1) = IYH
90	LD (mn),ss	11101101	01ss0011	----n---	----m---	7							(mn) = ssl; (mn+1) = ssh
96	LD dd,(mn)	11101101	01dd1011	----n---	----m---	7							ddl = (mn); ddh = (mn+1)
97	LD dd,mn	00dd0001	----n---	----m---		3							dd = mn
98	LD HL,(mn)	00101010	----n---	----m---		6							L = (mn); H = (mn+1)
100	LD IX,(mn)	11011101	00101010	----n---	----m---	7							IXL = (mn); IXH = (mn+1)
101	LD IX,mn	11011101	00100001	----n---	----m---	4							IX = mn
102	LD IY,(mn)	11111101	00101010	----n---	----m---	7							IYL = (mn); IYH = (mn+1)
103	LD IY,mn	11111101	00100001	----n---	----m---	4							IY = mn
110	LD SP,HL	11111001				1							SP = HL
111	LD SP,IX	11011101	11111001			2							SP = IX
112	LD SP,IY	11111101	11111001			2							SP = IY

Figure 5-10. *Operation* worksheet for the word load instructions.

The exchange instructions are shown in the *Operation* worksheet excerpt in Figure 5-11. The machine cycles for the exchanges with the top of the stack are exactly as you would expect, although when we get to the implementation we'll need to decide whether to do read-read-write-write or read-write-read-write.

But the other three exchange instructions require some thought. In the original Z80 all three of these instructions execute in one machine cycle, and we certainly don't want to do worse than that. For the exchange between the DE and HL registers a dedicated alternate path, in parallel with the normal data path, will allow one machine cycle operation. For the bank exchanges the solution is even simpler. Rather than actually moving the data, we only need to toggle a control bit which selects the active bank.

Num	Instruction	Opcode byte 1	Opcode byte 2	Opcode byte 3	Opcode byte 4	Mach State	S	Z	H	PV	N	C	Operation
48	EX (SP),HL	11100011				6							H <-> (SP+1); L <-> (SP)
49	EX (SP),IX	11011101	11100011			7							IXH <-> (SP+1); IXL <-> (SP)
50	EX (SP),IY	11111101	11100011			7							IYH <-> (SP+1); IYL <-> (SP)
51	EX AF,AF'	00001000				1							AF <-> AF'
52	EX DE,HL	11101011				1							DE <-> HL
53	EXX	11011001				1							BC <-> BC'; DE <-> DE'; HL <-> HL'

Figure 5-11. *Operation* worksheet for the exchange instructions.

The next excerpt from the *Operation* worksheet, in Figure 5-12, shows the stack read and write instructions. The 2-bit *tt* field uses the encoding shown in Table 5-5.

Value	*tt*
00	BC
01	DE
10	HL
11	AF

Table 5-5. Word register select bit field for Push and Pop.

As I mentioned previously, the instructions that write to the stack write data in the reverse order from every other memory write instruction, and this will require special handling during the implementation of the design.

Num	Instruction	Opcode byte 1	Opcode byte 2	Opcode byte 3	Opcode byte 4	Mach State	S	Z	H	PV	N	C	Operation
130	POP IX	11011101	11100001			5							IXL = (SP); IXH = (SP+1); SP = SP+2
131	POP IY	11111101	11100001			5							IYL = (SP); IYH = (SP+1); SP = SP+2
132	POP tt	11tt0001				4							ttl = (SP); tth = (SP+1); SP = SP+2
133	PUSH IX	11011101	11100101			5							(SP-1) = IXH; (SP-2) = IXL; SP = SP-2
134	PUSH IY	11111101	11100101			5							(SP-1) = IYH; (SP-2) = IYL; SP = SP-2
135	PUSH tt	11tt0101				4							(SP-1) = tth; (SP-2) = ttl; SP = SP-2

Figure 5-12. *Operation* worksheet for the Push and Pop instructions.

The program branch instructions are shown in the *Operation* worksheet excerpt in Figure 5-13. A number of new bit fields are introduced here. The *--(e-2)-* byte is a two's-complement number that will be sign-extended to sixteen bits and added to the PC to jump to another program location. Both of the jump-relative instructions use the PC of the next instruction to perform the calculation. This saves us from having to keep a version of the PC that has not been incremented just for these cases.

The 2-bit *cc* field uses the encoding shown in Table 5-6 to select one of four conditions for the PC-relative jump:

Value	*cc*	condition
00	NZ	Z = 0
01	Z	Z = 1
10	NC	C = 0
11	C	C = 1

Table 5-6. Condition code bit field for the Jump Relative instruction.

The 3-bit *fff* field uses the encoding shown in Table 5-7 to select one of eight flag conditions for Jump, Call and Return instructions.

Value	fff	condition
000	NZ	Z = 0
001	Z	Z = 1
010	NC	C = 0
011	C	C = 1
100	PO	PV = 0
101	PE	PV = 1
110	P	S = 0
111	M	S = 1

Table 5-7. Condition code bit field for the Jump, Call and Return instructions.

The 3-bit *vvv* field selects a dedicated address so that only no address operands are needed. The instructions that use this field obviously require much less code space than regular call instructions, in addition to executing faster. Table 5-8 shows the encoding for the address select bit field.

Value	vvv	address
000	0	16'h0000
001	8	16'h0008
010	10	16'h0010
011	18	16'h0018
100	20	16'h0020
101	28	16'h0028
110	30	16'h0030
111	38	16'h0038

Table 5-8. Address select bit field for the Restart instruction.

With conditional branches it is possible to execute in fewer machine cycles if the branch is not taken. It is obvious and easy to skip the stack operations for Call instructions, but it is also possible to skip the fetch of the address operand. Skipping a 2-byte address operand really only saves one machine cycle because the PC needs to be adjusted, so I won't implement this option here. Feel free to implement this option in your version of the design.

Even if the address operands are always fetched it is also possible to either skip or nullify the machine cycle that loads the new PC. Skipping a machine cycle adds to the complexity of the design and only saves one machine cycle, but Jumps are so common in software that it's probably worth the extra effort. I won't implement this option with the DJNZ instruction, because it almost always branches with normal use.

Num	Instruction	Opcode byte 1	Opcode byte 2	Opcode byte 3	Opcode byte 4	Mach State	S	Z	H	PV	N	C	Operation
24	CALL f,mn	11fff100	----n---	----m---		5/3							if (f) then (SP-1) = PCH; (SP-2) = PCL; PC = mn; SP = SP-2
25	CALL mn	11001101	----n---	----m---		5							(SP-1) = PCH; (SP-2) = PCL; PC = mn; SP = SP-2
46	DJNZ e	00010000	--(e-2)-			3							B = B-1; if {B != 0} PC = PC + j
71	JP (HL)	11101001				2							PC = HL
72	JP (IX)	11011101	11101001			3							PC = IX
73	JP (IY)	11111101	11101001			3							PC = IY
74	JP f,mn	11fff010	----n---	----m---		4/3							if {f} PC = mn
75	JP mn	11000011	----n---	----m---		4							PC = mn
76	JR cc,e	001cc000	--(e-2)-			3							if {cc} PC = PC + e
77	JR e	00011000	--(e-2)-			3							PC = PC + e
140	RET	11001001				5							PCL = (SP); PCH = (SP+1); SP = SP+2
141	RET f	11fff000				5/1							if {f} PCL = (SP); PCH = (SP+1); SP = SP+2
166	RST v	11vvv111				4							(SP-1) = PCH; (SP-2) = PCL; SP = SP-2; PC = {R, 0, v, 0000}

Figure 5-13. *Operation* worksheet for the program branch instructions.

Instead of memory-mapped I/O, the Z80 instruction set provides a separate I/O address space, with dedicated I/O instructions. These are shown in the next excerpt from the *Operation* worksheet, in Figure 5-14. Setting the flags based on the input data is handy, because this is where parity is most often used.

Num	Instruction	Opcode byte 1	Opcode byte 2	Opcode byte 3	Opcode byte 4	Mach State	S	Z	H	PV	N	C	Operation
58	IN A,(n)	11011011	----n---			4							A = (n)
59	IN r,(C)	11101101	01rrr000			4	S	Z	0	P	0		r = (C)
126	OUT (C),r	11101101	01rrr001			4							(C) = r
127	OUT (n),A	11010011	----n---			4							(n) = A

Figure 5-14. *Operation* worksheet for the I/O instructions.

The block compare, load and I/O instructions are examples of the type of CISC instructions that were cited as the reason that RISC machines were superior, performing multiple operations with just one instruction. This complexity complicates the design in a number of ways that are not immediately obvious from the *Operation* worksheet excerpt in Figure 5-15.

The first complication is that some of the flags have unique uses with these instructions. In addition, different flags are set based on different operations within the instruction, which complicates their implementation. In several cases the setting of a flag by one operation controls whether or not the instruction is complete.

The second complication has to do with interrupts. Because these instructions can take a significant number of machine cycles to complete, they sample interrupts during every iteration. This is different from normal instructions where the interrupts are sampled once at the end of the instruction.

The final complication also has to do with interrupts. If a block instruction is interrupted, it must resume where it left off after the interrupt is serviced. This means rewinding the PC so that the instruction is re-fetched after the interrupt.

Num	Instruction	Opcode byte 1	Opcode byte 2	Opcode byte 3	Opcode byte 4	Mach State	S	Z	H	PV	N	C	Operation
32	CPD	11101101	10101001			5	S	Z	H	Z	1		A - (HL); BC = BC-1; HL = HL-1
33	CPDR	11101101	10111001			4+2i	S	Z	H	Z	1		A - (HL); BC = BC-1; HL = HL-1; repeat while {BC != 0}
34	CPI	11101101	10100001			5	S	Z	H	Z	1		A - (HL); BC = BC-1; HL = HL+1
35	CPIR	11101101	10110001			4+2i	S	Z	H	Z	1		A - (HL); BC = BC-1; HL = HL+1; repeat while {BC != 0}
67	IND	11101101	10101010			5		Z			1		(HL) = I/O(BC); B = B-1; HL = HL-1
68	INDR	11101101	10111010			4+2i		Z			1		(HL) = I/O(BC); B = B-1; HL = HL-1; repeat while {B != 0}
69	INI	11101101	10100010			5		Z			1		(HL) = I/O(BC); B = B-1; HL = HL+1
70	INIR	11101101	10110010			4+2i		Z			1		(HL) = I/O(BC); B = B-1; HL = HL+1; repeat while {B != 0}
113	LDD	11101101	10101000			5			0	Z	0		(DE) = (HL); BC = BC-1; DE = DE-1; HL = HL-1
114	LDDR	11101101	10111000			4+2i			0	Z	0		(DE) = (HL); BC = BC-1; DE = DE-1; HL = HL-1; repeat while {BC != 0}
115	LDI	11101101	10100000			5			0	Z	0		(DE) = (HL); BC = BC-1; DE = DE+1; HL = HL+1
116	LDIR	11101101	10110000			4+2i			0	Z	0		(DE) = (HL); BC = BC-1; DE = DE+1; HL = HL+1; repeat while {BC != 0}
124	OTDR	11101101	10111011			4+2i		Z			1		I/O(BC) = (HL); B = B-1; HL = HL-1; repeat while {B != 0}
125	OTIR	11101101	10110011			4+2i		Z			1		I/O(BC) = (HL); B = B-1; HL = HL+1; repeat while {B != 0}
128	OUTD	11101101	10101011			5		Z			1		I/O(BC) = (HL); B = B-1; HL = HL-1
129	OUTI	11101101	10100011			5		Z			1		I/O(BC) = (HL); B = B-1; HL = HL+1

Figure 5-15. *Operation* worksheet for the block instructions.

The excerpt from the *Operation* worksheet shown in Figure 5-16 relates to interrupts. This is one place where I won't keep strict compatibility with the Z80. In Interrupt Mode 0 the interrupt acknowledge cycle fetches an instruction to execute. This mode is very rarely used and not worth the effort to implement.

I always like to include interrupt acknowledge operation in the *Operation* worksheet, because it will use many of the same states that are used for normal instruction execution.

Num	Instruction	Opcode byte 1	Opcode byte 2	Opcode byte 3	Opcode byte 4	Mach State	S	Z	H	PV	N	C	Operation
45	DI	11110011				1							IFF1 = 0; IFF2 = 0
47	EI	11111011				1							IFF1 = 1; IFF2 = 1
54	HALT	01110110				3							PC = PC - 1
55	IM 0	11101101	01000110			2							IM = 0
56	IM 1	11101101	01010110			2							IM = 1
57	IM 2	11101101	01011110			2							IM = 2
142	RETI	11101101	01001101			6							PCL = (SP); PCH = (SP+1); SP = SP+2
143	RETN	11101101	01000101			6							PCL = (SP); PCH = (SP+1); SP = SP+2; IFF1 = IFF2
200	ZINTACK					5							(SP-1) = PCH; (SP-2) = PCL; SP = SP-2; PC = (vector table); IFF2 = IFF1; IFF1 = 0

Figure 5-16. *Operation* worksheet for the interrupt-related instructions.

The vector table value used during the interrupt acknowledge depends on the type of interrupt as well as the interrupt mode. For a Non-maskable interrupt the value is 16'h0066. For a Maskable interrupt in Interrupt Mode 1 the value is 16'h0038. For a Maskable interrupt in Interrupt Mode 2 the value is the concatenation of the I register with the vector returned during the interrupt acknowledge transaction.

Last but not least, is the "No Operation" instruction in Figure 5-17, which doesn't fit anywhere else. This should be the easiest instruction to implement.

Num	Instruction	Opcode byte 1	Opcode byte 2	Opcode byte 3	Opcode byte 4	Mach State	S	Z	H	PV	N	C	Operation
118	NOP	00000000				1							No operation

Figure 5-17. *Operation* worksheet for the No Operation instructions.

While I am on the subject of the instruction set, this is the right time to think about how I am going to use the opcode information in the design.

The *Internal Code* Worksheet

The main function of the *Internal Code* worksheet is to create the Verilog instruction code identifiers for each instruction. These identifiers will be used in Verilog `case` statements to generate control signals. The issue here is how to encode the page information. You've already seen the encoding that I have chosen, but I'll repeat it here in Listing 5-1 and explain how I settled on this particular encoding.

```
`define MAIN_PG     4'b0000     //no instruction prefix byte(s)
`define INTR_PG     4'b0001     //interrupt acknowledge
`define CB_PAGE     4'b0010     //CB instruction prefix
`define DMA_PG      4'b0011     //dma acknowledge
`define DD_PAGE     4'b0100     //DD instruction prefix
`define FD_PAGE     4'b0101     //FD instruction prefix
`define DDCB_PG     4'b0110     //DD-CB instruction prefix
`define FDCB_PG     4'b0111     //FD-CB instruction prefix
`define ED_PAGE     4'b1000     //ED instruction prefix
`define DEC_ED      4'b1xxx     //ED page
```

Listing 5-1. The encoding for the page information.

I'll be the first to admit that this encoding may not be optimal, so feel free to use your own version. The exact encoding isn't really important until you start generating the Verilog code. But once the Verilog is started modifying this encoding can become painful, because at that point it's more than just entries in a spreadsheet column. If you really want to avoid this limitation, it is always possible to treat the page bits symbolically and use concatenation. Then the code would look something like Listing 5-2.

```
always @ (state_reg) begin
  casex (state_reg) //synopsys parallel_case
    `OF1B:                      tflg_ctl = `TFLG_Z;
    `RD1A,
    `RD2A: begin
      casex ({page_reg, inst_reg})
        {`DEC_ED,  8'b10100011},
        {`DEC_ED,  8'b10101011},
        {`DEC_ED,  8'b10110011},
        {`DEC_ED,  8'b10111011}: tflg_ctl = `TFLG_1;
        default:                 tflg_ctl = `TFLG_Z;
        endcase
```

```
      end
    `BLK1:                         tflg_ctl = `TFLG_B;
    default:                       tflg_ctl = `TFLG_NUL;
    endcase
  end
```

Listing 5-2. Using the page information symbolically.

I don't like to treat the opcode itself symbolically because that makes it easy to forget that there are bit fields embedded within it. And I prefer not to mix a symbolic value and an explicit value in the same expression, which is why I don't use the above example in the actual design.

As far as the encoding, it is usually best to use the default value for the most common case, so that's why I use `4'b0000` for no prefix byte. The DD and FD prefixes are identical except for the index register selected, so they should differ by just one bit to make the decoding logic simpler. The same is true of the DD-CB and FD-CB prefix cases. The ED prefix selects a page that is completely unrelated to any other page and includes all of the complex block instructions, so I use a single bit for it. The CB prefix encoding isn't really important because most of those instructions are very similar.

Using a prefix identifier to mark an interrupt or DMA acknowledge is very convenient, because it will allow us to automatically inhibit control signals that might otherwise cause problems. It's very easy to forget to inhibit an operation when using dedicated signals for interrupt or DMA acknowledge.

The *Internal Code* worksheet is about the only place where the calculation features of a spreadsheet are used. Even then it's really only the concatenation function that comes in handy. Shown in Figure 5-18 is an excerpt from that worksheet.

Creating the *page_reg* and *inst_reg* columns requires sorting the *Opcode byte* columns. Sorting the *Opcode byte 1* column alphabetically groups all of the opcodes that use a prefix byte together, which allows all of the actual opcodes to be copied to the *inst_reg* column. This also makes it easy to set up the *page_reg* column with the proper values. Then it's just a question of concatenating these columns to create the required pseudo-Verilog format in the remaining column.

	Instruction	Opcode byte 1	Opcode byte 2	Opcode byte 3	Opcode byte 4	page_reg	inst_reg	internal code (binary)
1	ADC A,(HL)	10001110				12'b0000	10001110	12'b000010001110,
2	ADC A,(IX+d)	11011101	10001110	----d---		12'b0100	10001110	12'b010010001110,
3	ADC A,(IY+d)	11111101	10001110	----d---		12'b0101	10001110	12'b010110001110,
4	ADC A,n	11001110	----n---			12'b0000	11001110	12'b000011001110,
5	ADC A,r	10001rrr				12'b0000	10001rrr	12'b000010001rrr,
6	ADC HL,ss	11101101	01ss1010			12'b1xxx	01ss1010	12'b1xxx01xx1010,
7	ADD A,(HL)	10000110				12'b0000	10000110	12'b000010000110,
8	ADD A,(IX+d)	11011101	10000110	----d---		12'b0100	10000110	12'b010010000110,
9	ADD A,(IY+d)	11111101	10000110	----d---		12'b0101	10000110	12'b010110000110,
10	ADD A,n	11000110	----n---			12'b0000	11000110	12'b000011000110,
11	ADD A,r	10000rrr				12'b0000	10000rrr	12'b000010000rrr,
12	ADD HL,ss	00ss1001				12'b0000	00ss1001	12'b000000xx1001,
13	ADD IX,xx	11011101	00xx1001			12'b0100	00xx1001	12'b010000xx1001,
14	ADD IY,yy	11111101	00yy1001			12'b0101	00yy1001	12'b010100xx1001,

Figure 5-18. *Internal Code* worksheet with binary *internal code* information.

Notice that I keep some of the bit field identifiers from the opcodes in the Verilog format column. I do this is to remind myself when there is a special set of encoding to use. Then I can manually substitute the appropriate values for the identifier. This may seem like a lot on manual work, but I haven't found a better way to do it.

Shown in Figure 5-19 is another excerpt from the *Internal Code* worksheet, this one using the symbolic version for the page identifier. It is created in exactly the same way as before, although it is just as easy to generate using a few global replacement commands. The full worksheet contains both sets of this information.

	Instruction	Opcode byte 1	Opcode byte 2	Opcode byte 3	Opcode byte 4	page_reg	inst_reg	internal code (symbolic)
1	ADC A,(HL)	10001110				{`MAIN_PG,	10001110	{`MAIN_PG, 10001110},
2	ADC A,(IX+d)	11011101	10001110	----d---		{`DD_PAGE,	10001110	{`DD_PAGE, 10001110},
3	ADC A,(IY+d)	11111101	10001110	----d---		{`FD_PAGE,	10001110	{`FD_PAGE, 10001110},
4	ADC A,n	11001110	----n---			{`MAIN_PG,	11001110	{`MAIN_PG, 11001110},
5	ADC A,r	10001rrr				{`MAIN_PG,	10001rrr	{`MAIN_PG, 10001rrr},
6	ADC HL,ss	11101101	01ss1010			{`DEC_ED,	01ss1010	{`DEC_ED, 01xx1010},
7	ADD A,(HL)	10000110				{`MAIN_PG,	10000110	{`MAIN_PG, 10000110},
8	ADD A,(IX+d)	11011101	10000110	----d---		{`DD_PAGE,	10000110	{`DD_PAGE, 10000110},
9	ADD A,(IY+d)	11111101	10000110	----d---		{`FD_PAGE,	10000110	{`FD_PAGE, 10000110},
10	ADD A,n	11000110	----n---			{`MAIN_PG,	11000110	{`MAIN_PG, 11000110},
11	ADD A,r	10000rrr				{`MAIN_PG,	10000rrr	{`MAIN_PG, 10000rrr},
12	ADD HL,ss	00ss1001				{`MAIN_PG,	00ss1001	{`MAIN_PG, 00xx1001},
13	ADD IX,xx	11011101	00xx1001			{`DD_PAGE,	00xx1001	{`DD_PAGE, 00xx1001},
14	ADD IY,yy	11111101	00yy1001			{`FD_PAGE,	00yy1001	{`FD_PAGE, 00xx1001},

Figure 5-19. *Internal Code* worksheet with symbolic *internal code* information.

The *internal code* column from this worksheet, along with the *Instruction* and *Opcode* columns, is used in all subsequent worksheets. As the information in these worksheets is sorted into groups the instruction identifier values in the *internal code* column can then be transferred directly into the Verilog code for generating control signals.

The Big Picture

Now that I know exactly what each instruction is supposed to do, how each instruction is encoded, and have made my best guess about to how many machine cycles will be required for each instruction, it's time to think about how the design will be structured. Normally I do this by assigning Verilog module names and creating a design hierarchy for these modules. If fact, you have already seen the hierarchy for this design, in Figure 2-26. But since you may not yet be comfortable using Verilog for this type of information, a top level block diagram is shown in Figure 5-20.

At the top level, I'll partition the design into just four functional modules. The machine.v module is the main state machine, and this state feeds into the control logic in the control.v module. All of the internal control signals are generated in the control.v module. The datapath.v module will contain the ALU, the visible registers, the program counter and instruction register. The extint.v module is the external interface, and is responsible for all of the external signals for the design. The timing for all of the external signals is created in this module. This partitioning may seem coarse, but I usually don't like to have more than half a dozen modules instantiated in any given level of the design hierarchy.

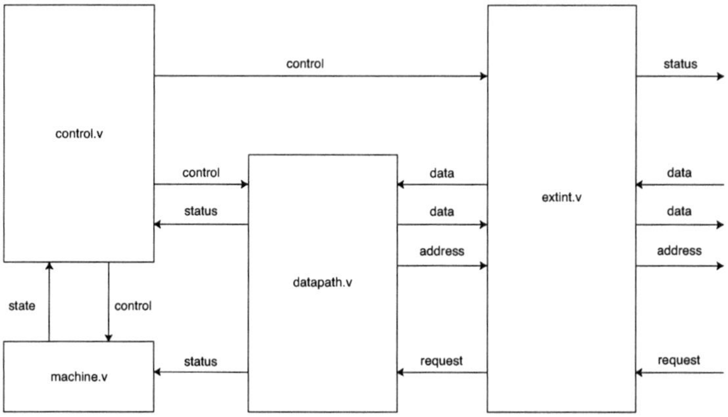

Figure 5-20. Block diagram of the top level.

Only the datapath.v module is complex enough to warrant its own block diagram, shown in Figure 5-21. There is nothing particularly complicated about this design, so this block diagram is straightforward once I have become familiar with the instruction set.

Details like exactly what inputs will be required for the various multiplexers, what constants are going to be required, and how each of the different blocks work will need to be worked out as I get deeper into the design. This design work is actually done by filling out the various worksheets to come.

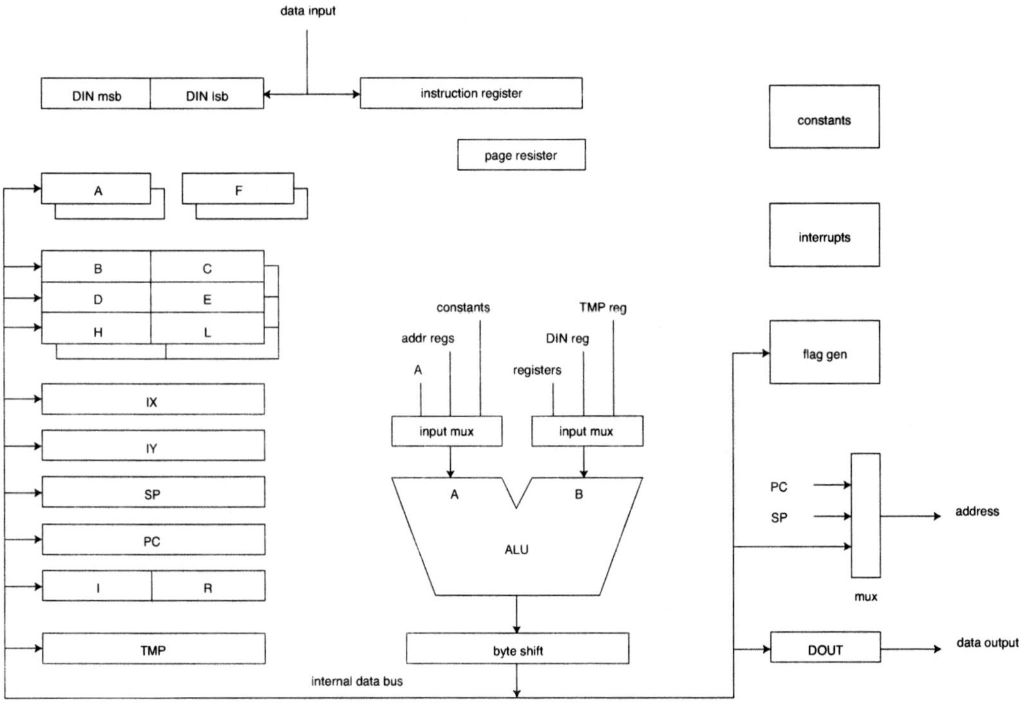

Figure 5-21. Block diagram of the datapath.v module

I have already mentioned that I plan to use a 16-bit ALU and internal data bus, and a 2-clock cycle machine cycle, and these choices should make the datapath.v module easier to design. The original Z80 employed 8-bit internal data buses and an 8-bit ALU, although the the ALU was extended to 16 bits for the increment operation required for the program counter update.

With two clock cycles per machine cycle the design should only require one ALU, as long the the ALU is capable of completing an operation in a single clock. In the worst case, which is a 1-byte instruction that executes in a single machine cycle, one clock cycle will use the ALU to increment the PC register, while the other clock cycle will use the ALU for the operation required by the instruction.

Interconnect was at a premium in the original Z80 design, so the registers were implemented as a small memory array. Given the size of the register file, such an implementation doesn't make sense in today's technologies, so I plan to use flip-flops for all of the registers. This allows the contents of all of the registers to be available in parallel, and I can use multiplexers on the inputs to the ALU to select the registers required by the instruction. This type of structure should lead to higher performance, by eliminating a pair of heavily-loaded buses coming out of the register file.

The 16-bit ALU will require some thought to take care of byte alignment issues. Aligning the data for the ALU inputs can be handled in the multiplexers on the ALU inputs, but I'll need a special block on the ALU output to shift the result from the lower byte to the upper byte. This shift is necessary, for example, when writing to the B, D, or H registers, because these registers need to reside on the upper byte of the data bus for word operations.

The 16-bit internal data path also means that data read from memory needs to be accumulated in a 16-bit data input register before it can be fed to the ALU. Only an 8-bit register is required for the output data, though, because I can only write one byte at a time externally.

Strictly speaking, the instruction register doesn't really need to be in the datapath.v module, but since it is loaded from the same data bus used by the data input register it's convenient to include it in this module. Having the instruction register in the datapath.v module also makes it simple to generate the bit mask required by the bit manipulation instructions as well as the restart vector.

Now that I know what the overall design will look like the next thing to do is to take a high-level view into the various machine cycles that are going to be required. I already know that the longest instruction will require seven machine cycles, but different types of machine cycles will be required for different instructions, so the total will be larger than this minimum.

Machine Cycle Details

At this point it's important to verify that the estimate for the machine cycles required for each instruction makes sense. This means going back through the *operation* column of the *Operation* worksheet, counting discrete operations. Then add the number of bytes that must be fetched for each instruction, which corresponds to the number of program counter increment operations.

The resulting number must be less than the number of available clock cycles, or the ALU will be oversubscribed. It turns out that most instructions have more than enough clock cycles available, and only the block instructions come close to requiring all of the available clock cycles.

To determine the different types of machine cycles required, I'll start with the obvious instruction fetches. Since there are up to three bytes of opcode in an instruction I'll need three distinct instruction fetch machine cycles, called *IF1*, *IF2* and *IF3*. The instruction register will be loaded at the end of each of these machine cycles. The first byte of the instruction will always use the *IF1* machine cycle, any second byte the *IF2* cycle, and any third byte the *IF3* cycle.

Many instructions contain immediate data, whether actual data, an address, or an address offset. I'll use dedicated machine cycles to fetch this data and load it into the data input register. Since there are never more than two bytes of immediate data I'll need two operand fetch machine cycles, called *OF1* and *OF2*. A single byte of immediate data or the first of two immediate bytes will use the *OF1* machine cycle, and any second byte will use the *OF2* cycle. Separating opcode fetches from operand fetches should simplify the control logic for the instruction register and the data input register, even though it means an extra type of machine cycle.

An address calculation will usually need a dedicated machine cycle, called *ADR*. Recall from the *Operation* worksheet that I assumed that for some instructions the address calculation would be done in parallel with an instruction fetch. I won't be able to verify this until much later in the design process, though. The *ADR* machine cycle is an idle cycle as far as the external bus is concerned.

Instructions that read memory or I/O can fetch one or two bytes, which leads to the *RD1* and *RD2* machine cycles. A word read will use an *RD1* cycle followed by an *RD2* cycle, but I'll always use only the *RD2* cycle to read a single byte. I do this to simplify the decision about the next state, because if the machine is in the *RD1* state the next state will always be the *RD2* state. This will probably complicate the loading of the data input register, so this may not be the best choice. Note that I don't use separate machine cycles for memory and I/O, because the only difference between the two cases is the status that is signalled externally.

Data writes are just like data reads, requiring *WR1* and *WR2* machine cycles. I'll apply the same rule about word and byte writes that I used for data reads, for the same reason.

Jump, Call and Return instructions need to load the program counter, and I anticipate that this will require a special machine cycle. In theory I could use the *ADR* machine cycle to do double duty, but since the operations required are fundamentally different I'm going to use a dedicated machine cycle for the program counter adjustment. I'll call this machine cycle *PCA*.

I won't go through the details here, but it turns out that the block compare instructions are going to require a dedicated machine cycle to perform some of the operations. These instructions only do a memory read during each iteration, and two clocks is not sufficient for all of the operations required. I'll call this machine cycle *BLK*, and it's already accounted for in the *Mach State* column in the *Operation* worksheet. The other block instructions do both a read and a write, so there should be sufficient clock cycles available in those cases.

All that remain are the three special cases. The *HLT* machine cycle will be used for the Halt state, the interrupt acknowledge machine cycle will be called *INTA*, and I'll reserve the *DMA* machine cycle for the bus release case. This is a total of fifteen distinct machine cycles, each two clock cycles long. Table 5-9 shows the different types of machine cycles.

Mnemonic	Function
IF1	Fetch first byte of opcode.
IF2	Fetch second byte of opcode.
IF3	Fetch third byte of opcode.
OF1	Fetch first byte of immediate data.
OF2	Fetch second byte of immediate data.
ADR	Calculate operand address.
RD1	Read first byte of a word operand.
RD2	Read second byte of a word operand or a byte operand.
WR1	Write first byte of a word operand.
WR2	Write second byte of a word operand or a byte operand.
BLK	Internal operation for block instruction.
PCA	Adjust program counter.
HLT	Halt cycle.
INTA	Interrupt acknowledge cycle.
DMA	Bus release cycle.

Table 5-9. Different types of machine cycles.

If you have been following closely you'll realize that there is a huge problem here that I haven't addressed, namely how to determine the next state after fetching an opcode byte. The problem is illustrated clearly in the timing shown in Figure 4-2, where the first byte of the opcode is not available until the end of the fetch machine cycle. This is too late to decide what type of machine cycle should be next. This type of complication is typical of a pipelined design, and solving it requires rethinking the definition of a machine cycle.

The problem is also apparent in the excerpt from the Machine State worksheet shown in Figure 5-22 for the Add instructions. Notice that for both the *IF1* and *IF2* states the next state in the sequence varies as a function of the opcode, but during these machine cycles the opcode isn't yet known. The sequence after the *OF1* state also varies, but since the opcode is already valid by this time the same problem does not occur here.

The way around this issue becomes obvious once I realize that no matter what the next state in the sequence is after the *IF1* or *IF2* state, the machine cycle can be identical as far as the external bus is concerned. True, the *ADR* machine cycle isn't really a memory access, but it doesn't hurt anything to start out the machine cycle that way.

Instruction	instruction code	IF1	IF2	OF1	OF2	IF3	ADR	RD1	RD2	WR1	WR2	BLK	PCA	Mach State
ADC A,(HL)	12'b000010001110	ADR					RD2		IF1					3
ADC A,(IX+d)	12'b010010001110	IF2	OF1	ADR			RD2		IF1					5
ADC A,(IY+d)	12'b010110001110	IF2	OF1	ADR			RD2		IF1					5
ADC A,n	12'b000011001110	OF1		IF1										2
ADC A,r	12'b000010001rrr	IF1												1
ADC HL,ss	12'b1xxx01xx1010	IF2	IF1											2
ADD A,(HL)	12'b000010000110	ADR					RD2		IF1					3
ADD A,(IX+d)	12'b010010000110	IF2	OF1	ADR			RD2		IF1					5
ADD A,(IY+d)	12'b010110000110	IF2	OF1	ADR			RD2		IF1					5
ADD A,n	12'b000011000110	OF1		IF1										2
ADD A,r	12'b000010000rrr	IF1												1
ADD HL,ss	12'b000000xx1001	IF1												1
ADD IX,xx	12'b010000xx1001	IF2	IF1											2
ADD IY,yy	12'b010100xx1001	IF2	IF1											2

Figure 5-22. *Machine State* worksheet for the Add instructions.

The bottom line here is that the first clock cyle after the *IF1* of *IF2* machine cycle should be fixed, with only the subsequent clock cycles specific to a particular machine cycle. I'll go ahead and give each clock cycle in the different machine cycles a mnemonic, according to Table 5-10. These individual clock cycles will then form the basis for the remainder of the worksheets.

Mnemonic	Function
if1a	First clock of *IF1* machine cycle. (Fetch first instruction byte.)
if1b	Second clock of *IF1* machine cycle.
dec1	Decode first byte of opcode. The first clock after an *IF1* machine cycle. May be the first clock of an *IF1, IF2, OF1, ADR* or *PCA* machine cycle.
if2b	Second clock of *IF2* machine cycle. (Fetch second byte of instruction.)
dec2	Decode second byte of opcode. The first clock after the *IF2* machine cycle. May be the first clock of an *IF1, OF1, ADR* or *PCA* machine cycle.
of1b	Second clock of *OF1* machine cycle. (Fetch first byte of immediate data.)
of2a	First clock of *OF2* machine cycle. (Fetch second byte of immediate data.)
of2b	Second clock of *OF2* machine cycle.
if3a	First clock of *IF3* machine cycle. (Fetch third instruction byte.)
if3b	Second clock of *IF3* machine cycle.
adr1	First clock of *ADR* machine cycle. (Calculate operand address.)
adr2	Second clock of *ADR* machine cycle.
rd1a	First clock of *RD1* machine cycle. (Read first byte of operand.)
rd1b	Second clock of *RD1* machine cycle.
rd2a	First clock of *RD2* machine cycle. (Read second byte of operand.)
rd2b	Second clock of *RD2* machine cycle.
wr1a	First clock of *WR1* machine cycle. (Write first byte of result.)
wr1b	Second clock of *WR1* machine cycle.
wr2a	First clock of *WR2* machine cycle. (Write second byte of result.)
wr2b	Second clock of *WR2* machine cycle.
blk1	First clock of *BLK* machine cycle. (Block instruction internal operation.)
blk2	Second clock of *BLK* machine cycle.
pca	First clock of *PCA* machine cycle. (Program counter adjust.)
pco	Second clock of *PCA* machine cycle.
hlta	First clock of *HLT* machine cycle. (Halt state.)
hltb	Second clock of *HLT* machine cycle.
inta	First clock of *INTA* machine cycle. (Interrupt acknowledge.)
intb	Second clock of *INTA* machine cycle.
dma1	First clock of *DMA* machine cycle. (Bus release.)
dma2	Second clock of *DMA* machine cycle.

Table 5-10. Clock cycle mnemonics versus machine cycles.

At this point I am done with the top level design, and can start the detailed design of the various functions. As I mentioned before, this design is really done by filling out individual worksheets in the design spreadsheet, specifying what data needs to be presented to the ALU, what ALU operation to perform, where to write the result, and so on. The requirements for the connections for data in the datapath.v module will become apparent as these worksheets are completed.

There is a logical sequence to completing these worksheets, as most worksheets draw on the information in previous worksheets. I'll go over the organization of the different worksheets shortly, but the most important one specifies the state sequence clock cycle by clock cycle. The *Machine State* worksheet is mostly for documentation, but I can still use it as the basis for the *Next State* worksheet, by adding columns to each machine cycle so that the individual columns correspond to clock cycles.

The *Next State* Worksheet

The *Next State* worksheet is the template for all of the remaining worksheets, so it is important to make sure that it is set up properly. Clearly we want to use one column for each clock cycle, but where do we start and stop the template for each instruction? Looking at the timing diagram in Figure 5-23 for a one-machine-cycle instruction, it becomes clear that the fetch of the first byte of an opcode should be treated as part of the previous instruction, and that the current instruction doesn't start until the instruction register has been loaded with the first byte of the opcode.

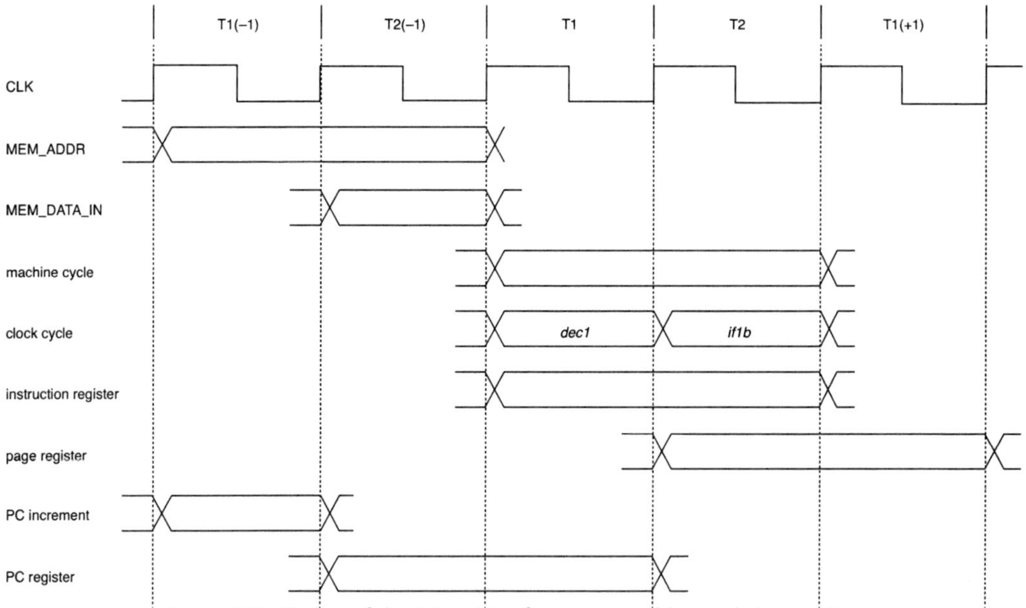

Figure 5-23. Timing of the PC register for a one-machine-cycle instruction.

This means that every instruction will start with the *dec1* state and finish up with the *if1b* state, with from zero to twelve states (six machine cycles) in between. Since a full row from the workbook won't fit on a page, I'll only show the relevant columns for each example here. Refer to the full spreadsheet for the compete set of state possibilities in order.

The *dec1* state is the first instruction decode state. This state is unique because the state of the page register is not yet valid for this instruction. We could always initialize the page register whenever the next state is going to be *dec1*. But we already know that this is the first byte of the opcode anyway, so that complication isn't really necessary. The end result of this is that any control signal decoding done in the *dec1* state should only use the instruction register and ignore the page register.

The *if1b* state is the second half of an instruction fetch machine cycle for the first byte of an instruction, at least as far as the external bus is concerned. To the internal logic it's the last clock cycle of any instruction.

Many instructions will use exactly the same sequence of states so I won't show every instruction in this section. I will go through each unique state sequence though, building up the required states just as I did when I started the design. Before I start with each unique sequence, take a look at the different cases for the Add instructions, in Figure 5-24.

	Instruction	internal code (fetch)	dec1	if2b	dec2	of1b	adr1	adr2	rd2a	rd2b	if1a	if1b	Mach State
7	ADD A,(HL)	`12'b000010000110`	adr2					rd2a	rd2b	if1a	if1b	dec1	3
8	ADD A,(IX+d)	`12'b010010000110`	if2b	dec2	of1b	adr1	adr2	rd2a	rd2b	if1a	if1b	dec1	5
9	ADD A,(IY+d)	`12'b010110000110`	if2b	dec2	of1b	adr1	adr2	rd2a	rd2b	if1a	if1b	dec1	5
10	ADD A,n	`12'b000011000110`	of1b			if1a					if1b	dec1	2
11	ADD A,r	`12'b000010000rrr`	if1b					rd2a	rd2b	if1a	if1b	dec1	1
12	ADD HL,ss	`12'b000000xx1001`	if1b									dec1	1
13	ADD IX,xx	`12'b010000xx1001`	if2b	dec2	if1b							dec1	2
14	ADD IY,yy	`12'b010100xx1001`	if2b	dec2	if1b							dec1	2

Figure 5-24. *Next State* worksheet for the Add instructions.

The state sequence always proceeds from left to right (except for some of the block instructions shown later) and unused states for a particular instruction are shaded to make it easy to see the sequence. Unused states will normally be empty, but the instruction in row *11* is a special case. Row *11* has an *rrr* bit field, which only uses seven out of eight possible encodings, and the other encoding is used by the instruction in row *7*. We can make the decoding for row *7* easier by taking advantage of some of the unused states in row *11*.

For example, when we sort the worksheet group based on the contents of the *adr2* column rows *7* and *11* will both be in the group with *rd2a* as the next state. This will allow the logic synthesis tool to combine these two rows and simplify the logic, without affecting the desired function.

All instructions that use just one machine cycle look just like row *12* in the above example, but there are several different cases for instructions that use two machine cycles, shown in Figure 5-25.

	Instruction	internal code (fetch)	dec1	if2b	dec2	of1b	pco	if1a	if1b	Mach State
4	ADC A,n	`12'b000011001110`	of1b			if1a		if1b	dec1	2
6	ADC HL,ss	`12'b1xxx01xx1010`	if2b	dec2	if1b				dec1	2
71	JP (HL)	`12'b000011101001`	pco				if1a	if1b	dec1	2

Figure 5-25. *Next State* worksheet for two-machine-cycle instructions.

All instructions that use a prefix byte go through the *if2b* state. As far as the external bus is concerned this state is the second half of the machine cycle that fetches the second byte of the opcode. Not much can happen internally during this state, because the instruction isn't known yet.

The *dec2* state is where the second byte of the opcode is decoded. Although not shown here, if the decoded byte is a second prefix byte, we will proceed directly to the fetch of the displacement for indexed addressing mode.

The *of1b* state is the second half of a machine cycle that is fetching an immediate operand. I use a separate state for this operation because the operand needs to be loaded into a different register from where the second byte of opcode will be loaded, and a unique state makes this easier to implement.

Instructions that change the normal program flow need time to start up the pipeline that places the PC on the address bus. This is what the *pco* state is used for.

The *if1a* state is required whenever the normal sequence of fetching an instruction has been interrupted. In the case of an immediate operand or program flow change we need a state to act as the first clock of an instruction fetch machine cycle that will finish up with the *if1b* state.

As the number of machine cycles required goes up, so does the number of different sequences that are possible. The different sequences used for three-machine-cycle instructions are shown in Figure 5-26.

	Instruction	internal code (fetch)	dec1	if2b	dec2	of1b	of2a	of2b	adr2	rd2a	rd2b	wr2a	wr2b	pca	pco	if1a	if1b	Mach State
1	ADC A,(HL)	12'b000010001110	adr2						rd2a	rd2b	if1a					if1b	dec1	3
46	DJNZ j	12'b000000010000	of1b			pca								pco	if1a	if1b	dec1	3
54	HALT	12'b000001110110	pco												hlta	if1b	dec1	3
72	JP (IX)	12'b010011101001	if2b	dec2	pco										if1a	if1b	dec1	3
78	LD (BC),A	12'b000000000010	adr2						wr2a			wr2b	if1a			if1b	dec1	3
80	LD (HL),n	12'b000000110110	of1b			wr2a						wr2b	if1a			if1b	dec1	3
97	LD dd,mn	12'b000000xx0001	of1b			of2a	of2b	if1a								if1b	dec1	3

Figure 5-26. *Next State* worksheet for three-machine-cycle instructions.

With three-machine-cycle instructions we have to add the states *of2a* and *of2b* to fetch the second immediate operand byte. The Z80 instruction set only supports 1-byte and 2-byte operands, so we won't need any more of these kinds of states.

The *adr2* state is used to multiplex the operand address for output. If we hadn't gone with a uniform two-clock machine cycle this state would usually not be required.

The *rd2a* and *rd2b* states read a byte operand from memory, while the *wr2a* and *wr2b* states write a byte operand to memory. I know that the instruction set supports 2-byte operands, so we will need another set of these states.

The *hlta* and *hltb* states are not shown in the *Next State* worksheet because they are only used with the Halt instruction. This instruction just loops in these two states waiting for an interrupt, so taking up space in the spreadsheet for them isn't really necessary. We still need to remember to implement these two states though.

The *pca* state is the optional predecessor to the *pco* state, required when the PC needs to be changed prior to output.

The first set of four-machine-cycle sequences is shown in Figure 5-27. The only new state we need to add here is *adr1*, which is required in this case because the I/O address just barely became available.

	Instruction	internal code (fetch)	dec1	if2b	dec2	of1b	of2a	of2b	adr1	adr2	rd2a	rd2b	wr2a	wr2b	if1a	if1b	Mach State
20	BIT b,(HL)	12'b001001xxx110	if2b	dec2	adr2					rd2a	rd2b	if1a			if1b	dec1	4
38	DEC (HL)	12'b000000110101	adr2							rd2a	rd2b	wr2a	wr2b	if1a	if1b	dec1	4
58	IN A,(n)	12'b000011011011	of1b			adr1			adr2	rd2a	rd2b	if1a			if1b	dec1	4
101	LD IX,mn	12'b010000100001	if2b	dec2	of1b	of2a	of2b	if1a							if1b	dec1	4
126	OUT (C),r	12'b1xxx01rrr001	if2b	dec2	adr2					wr2a			wr2b	if1a	if1b	dec1	4

Figure 5-27. *Next State* worksheet for most four-machine-cycle instructions.

The four-machine-cycle instruction shown in Figure 5-28 does not add any new states. This is another case where the uniform two-clock machine cycle costs us an extra clock (the *pca* state).

	Instruction	internal code (fetch)	dec1	of1b	of2a	of2b	pca	pco	if1a	if1b	Mach State
75	JP mn	`12'b000011000011`	of1b	of2a	of2b	pca	pco	if1a	if1b	dec1	4

Figure 5-28. *Next State* worksheet for four-machine-cycle Jump instructions.

The last pair of four-machine-cycle instructions, shown in Figure 5-29, do either a 2-byte operand read or a 2-byte operand write. This adds the *rd1a* and *rd1b* states for the read and the *wr1a* and *wr1b* states for the write. The read-read-write-write sequence should be easier to implement than read-write-read-write because it will use consecutive addresses twice during the sequence.

	Instruction	internal code (fetch)	dec1	adr2	rd1a	rd1b	rd2a	rd2b	wr1a	wr1b	wr2a	wr2b	if1a	if1b	Mach State
132	POP tt	`12'b000011xx0001`	adr2	rd1a	rd1b	rd2a	rd2b	if1a					if1b	dec1	4
135	PUSH tt	`12'b000011xx0101`	adr2	wr1a					wr1b	wr2a	wr2b	if1a	if1b	dec1	4

Figure 5-29. *Next State* worksheet for four-machine-cycle Push and Pop instructions.

When we get to the five-machine-cycle instructions the sequences get even more varied, because at this point we start to see the indexed addressing mode and 2-byte instruction prefixes. This is shown in Figure 5-30.

	Instruction	internal code (fetch)	dec1	if2b	dec2	of1b	if3a	if3b	adr1	adr2	rd2a	rd2b	wr2a	wr2b	if1a	if1b	Mach State
2	ADC A,(IX+d)	`12'b010010001110`	if2b	dec2	of1b	adr1			adr2	rd2a	rd2b	if1a			if1b	dec1	5
21	BIT b,(IX+d)	`12'b011001xxx110`	if2b	dec2	of1b	if3a	if3b	rd2a			rd2b	if1a			if1b	dec1	5
83	LD (IX+d),r	`12'b010001110rrr`	if2b	dec2	of1b	adr1			adr2	wr2a			wr2b	if1a	if1b	dec1	5
144	RL (HL)	`12'b001000010110`	if2b	dec2	adr2					rd2a	rd2b	wr2a	wr2b	if1a	if1b	dec1	5

Figure 5-30. *Next State* worksheet for most five-machine-cycle instructions.

Two new states are introduced here, *if3a* and *if3b*, for use with a 4-byte opcode. Notice that this is a special case, where I am assuming that the address calculation can be performed in parallel with the fetch of the last byte of the opcode. You'll also notice that the is no decode state for the last byte of the opcode. This is because every instruction on these pages will always go immediately to fetch an operand.

The five-machine-cycle sequence shown in Figure 5-31 is unique, because the instruction has both immediate data and an offset for indexed addressing mode. Although it doesn't require any new states, we will need to be careful with the routing of the immediate data to the appropriate register, because normally the *of2a* and *of2b* states would be reading the most-significant byte of a 2-byte operand.

	Instruction	internal code (fetch)	dec1	if2b	dec2	of1b	of2a	of2b	wr2a	wr2b	if1a	if1b	Mach State
82	LD (IX+d),n	12'b010000110110	if2b	dec2	of1b	of2a	of2b	wr2a	wr2b	if1a	if1b	dec1	5

Figure 5-31. *Next State* worksheet for five-machine-cycle Load instructions.

You might expect the Call instruction in Figure 5-32 to require the *pca* and *pco* states, but we should be able to use the wr2b state to output the new PC value, as is done with other instructions that do memory writes.

	Instruction	internal code (fetch)	dec1	of1b	of2a	of2b	wr1a	wr1b	wr2a	wr2b	if1a	if1b	Mach State
25	CALL mn	12'b000011001101	of1b	of2a	of2b	wr1a	wr1b	wr2a	wr2b	if1a	if1b	dec1	5

Figure 5-32. *Next State* worksheet for five-machine-cycle Call instructions.

The Return instruction in Figure 5-33 can't use this shortcut though, because the new PC value will not be available until the end of the *rd2b* state, which is too late. Here is another case where the uniform two-clock machine cycle hurts us.

	Instruction	internal code (fetch)	dec1	adr2	rd1a	rd1b	rd2a	rd2b	pca	pco	if1a	if1b	Mach State
140	RET	12'b000011001001	adr2	rd1a	rd1b	rd2a	rd2b	pca	pco	if1a	if1b	dec1	5

Figure 5-33. *Next State* worksheet for five-machine-cycle Return instructions.

The two five-machine-cycle instructions in Figure 5-34 use sequences identical to some already shown, except that these have 2-byte opcodes.

	Instruction	internal code (fetch)	dec1	if2b	dec2	adr2	rd1a	rd1b	rd2a	rd2b	wr1a	wr1b	wr2a	wr2b	if1a	if1b	Mach State
130	POP IX	12'b010011100001	if2b	dec2	adr2	rd1a	rd1b	rd2a	rd2b	if1a					if1b	dec1	5
133	PUSH IX	12'b010011100101	if2b	dec2	adr2	wr1a					wr1b	wr2a	wr2b	if1a	if1b	dec1	5

Figure 5-34. *Next State* worksheet for five-machine-cycle Push and Pop instructions.

The five-machine-cycle sequence shown in Figure 5-35 is unique, which is only fitting for the interrupt acknowledge. Actually, this is only part of the sequence, because I don't want to take up space in the spreadsheet with states that are only used for one case. So there really is a interrupt acknowledge machine cycle that is inserted after an *if1b* cycle in the case of an interrupt. At the end of these two states, called *inta* and *intb*, we start the sequence shown here to fetch the interrupt vector and write the PC to the stack.

	Instruction	internal code (fetch)	adr1	adr2	rd1a	rd1b	rd2a	rd2b	wr1a	wr1b	wr2a	wr2b	if1a	if1b	Mach State
200	ZINTACK	12'b0001xxxxxxxx	adr2	rd1a	rd1b	rd2a	rd2b	wr1a	wr1b	wr2a	wr2b	if1a	if1b	dec1	5

Figure 5-35. *Next State* worksheet for five-machine-cycle Interrupt Acknowledge sequence.

None of the six-machine-cycle instructions need any new states, but they are all different enough that they won't fit in a single figure. Two cases of read-modify-write instructions with indexed addressing shown in Figure 5-36 are nearly identical, except that one needs an additional opcode byte.

	Instruction	internal code (fetch)	dec1	if2b	dec2	of1b	adr1	adr2	rd2a	rd2b	wr2a	wr2b	if1a	if1b	Mach State
39	DEC (IX+d)	12'b010000110101	if2b	dec2	of1b	adr1	adr2	rd2a	rd2b	wr2a	wr2b	if1a	if1b	dec1	6

	Instruction	internal code (fetch)	dec1	if2b	dec2	of1b	if3a	if3b	rd2a	rd2b	wr2a	wr2b	if1a	if1b	Mach State
137	RES b,(IX+d)	12'b011010xxx110	if2b	dec2	of1b	if3a	if3b	rd2a	rd2b	wr2a	wr2b	if1a	if1b	dec1	6

Figure 5-36. *Next State* worksheet for six-machine-cycle read-modify-write instructions.

The instruction exchanging the top of the stack with the HL register is one of only three instructions that both read a 2-byte quantity from memory and write a 2-byte quantity to memory. The sequence is shown in Figure 5-37.

	Instruction	internal code (fetch)	dec1	adr2	rd1a	rd1b	rd2a	rd2b	wr1a	wr1b	wr2a	wr2b	if1a	if1b	Mach State
48	EX (SP),HL	12'b000011100011	adr2	rd1a	rd1b	rd2a	rd2b	wr1a	wr1b	wr2a	wr2b	if1a	if1b	dec1	6

Figure 5-37. *Next State* worksheet for six-machine-cycle Exchange instruction.

Moving a 2-byte operand to or from the HL register also requires six machine cycles, as shown in Figure 5-38. But here half of the machine cycles are used to fetch the address that is part of the instruction.

	Instruction	internal code (fetch)	dec1	of1b	of2a	of2b	adr1	adr2	wr1a	wr1b	wr2a	wr2b	if1a	if1b	Mach State
87	LD (mn),HL	12'b000000100010	of1b	of2a	of2b	adr1	adr2	wr1a	wr1b	wr2a	wr2b	if1a	if1b	dec1	6

	Instruction	internal code (fetch)	dec1	of1b	of2a	of2b	adr1	adr2	rd1a	rd1b	rd2a	rd2b	if1a	if1b	Mach State
98	LD HL,(mn)	12'b000000101010	of1b	of2a	of2b	adr1	adr2	rd1a	rd1b	rd2a	rd2b	if1a	if1b	dec1	6

Figure 5-38. *Next State* worksheet for six-machine-cycle word Load instructions.

The Return-From-Interrupt (RETI) instruction shown in Figure 5-39 is just like a normal return from a subroutine, except that it uses a 2-byte opcode. In the Z80 this instruction was seen by peripherals that monitored the data bus to control the operation of the interrupt daisy chain. This technique of monitoring the data bus is not appropriate for an FPGA or ASIC implementation, so I will just generate a dedicated signal that pulses whenever the RETI instruction is executed.

	Instruction	internal code (fetch)	dec1	if2b	dec2	adr2	rd1a	rd1b	rd2a	rd2b	pca	pco	if1a	if1b	Mach State
142	RETI	12'b1xxx01001101	if2b	dec2	adr2	rd1a	rd1b	rd2a	rd2b	pca	pco	if1a	if1b	dec1	6

Figure 5-39. *Next State* worksheet for six-machine-cycle Return-From-Interrupt instruction.

All of the seven-machine-cycle instructions shown in Figure 5-40 have corresponding six-machine-cycle instructions. The only difference is that these instructions use 2-byte opcodes, usually because they deal with the index registers. The ED-page instructions here were obviously added to allow 16-bit loads to registers other than the HL register.

	Instruction	internal code (fetch)	dec1	if2b	dec2	adr2	rd1a	rd1b	rd2a	rd2b	wr1a	wr1b	wr2a	wr2b	if1a	if1b	Mach State
49	EX (SP),IX	`12'b010011100011`	if2b	dec2	adr2	rd1a	rd1b	rd2a	rd2b	wr1a	wr1b	wr2a	wr2b	if1a	if1b	dec1	7

	Instruction	internal code (fetch)	dec1	if2b	dec2	of1b	of2a	of2b	adr1	adr2	wr1a	wr1b	wr2a	wr2b	if1a	if1b	Mach State
88	LD (mn),IX	`12'b010000100010`	if2b	dec2	of1b	of2a	of2b	adr1	adr2	wr1a	wr1b	wr2a	wr2b	if1a	if1b	dec1	7

	Instruction	internal code (fetch)	dec1	if2b	dec2	of1b	of2a	of2b	adr1	adr2	rd1a	rd1b	rd2a	rd2b	if1a	if1b	Mach State
96	LD dd,(mn)	`12'b1xxx01xx1011`	if2b	dec2	of1b	of2a	of2b	adr1	adr2	rd1a	rd1b	rd2a	rd2b	if1a	if1b	dec1	7

Figure 5-40. *Next State* worksheet for seven-machine-cycle instructions.

The block instructions are all special cases, so I'll treat them separately here. The block compare instructions shown in Figure 5-41 don't have enough clock cycles to do all of the operations required for each iteration, so we have to add two new states just for this case. The *blk1* and *blk2* states are idle cycles as far as the external bus is concerned.

	Instruction	internal code (fetch)	dec1	if2b	dec2	adr2	rd1a	rd1b	rd2a	rd2b	blk1	blk2	pca	pco	if1a	if1b	Mach State
32	CPD	`12'b1xxx10101001`	if2b	dec2	adr2	rd1a	rd1b	blk1	rd2b	blk1	blk2	if1a	pco	if1a	if1b	dec1	5
33	CPDR	`12'b1xxx10111001`	if2b	dec2	adr2	rd1a	rd1b	blk1	rd2b	blk1	blk2	pca rd2a	pco	if1a	if1b	dec1	4+2i

Figure 5-41. *Next State* worksheet for the block compare instructions.

All of the block instructions operate on bytes, so why are both *rd1a*, *rd1b*, *rd2a* and *rd2b* (as well as *wra1*, *wr1b*, *wr2a* and *wr2b* for the block moves) shown in Figure 5-42 used? I'll get to this later, but what I discovered is that the internal operations need to be slightly different for the first time through the loop of read and write. Trying to make the operation conditional was much more difficult than just using *rd1a*, *rd1b*, *wr1a* and *wr1b* for the first iteration and *rd2a*, *rd2b*, *wr2a* and *wr2b* for all subsequent iterations. Using one set of states would have required a separate status bit to distinguish the first iteration from subsequent iterations.

	Instruction	internal code (fetch)	dec1	if2b	dec2	adr2	rd1a	rd1b	rd2a	rd2b	wr1a	wr1b	wr2a	wr2b	pca	pco	if1a	if1b	Mach State
67	IND	`12'b1xxx10101010`	if2b	dec2	adr2	rd1a	rd1b	wr1a	rd2b	wr2a	wr1b	if1a	wr2b	pca rd2a	pco	if1a	if1b	dec1	5
68	INDR	`12'b1xxx10111010`	if2b	dec2	adr2	rd1a	rd1b	wr1a	rd2b	wr2a	wr1b	pca rd2a	wr2b	pca rd2a	pco	if1a	if1b	dec1	4+2i

Figure 5-42. *Next State* worksheet for the block instructions.

Prior to the block instructions every state sequence was linear, proceeding from left to right in order in the worksheet. But the block instructions need to jump backwards to repeat the operation until the loop count is zero. The Z80 implemented the repeat operation by decrementing the PC and then re-fetching the instruction, but it is much more efficient the way I do it here. But this technique requires that the next state be conditional, which is denoted by a pair of entries in a cell in the *Next State* worksheet.

When I sort the worksheet these special entries will be grouped by themselves, and I'll need to manually code the Verilog with the appropriate test. This case happens so rarely that the manual intervention isn't a problem.

I use the same technique to implement the various conditional branch instructions shown in Figure 5-43. In these cases, instead of looping back to a previous state, I conditionally skip over a number of states. With the instructions shown below skipping over the operand fetch is possible, but does not save any machine cycles because of the timing of the increment of the PC. If I were willing to bypass the pipeline for the PC increment it might be possible to remove one machine cycle. But the cost, in terms of both circuit complexity and possibly propagation delay, is probably not worth the effort.

	Instruction	internal code (fetch)	dec1	of1b	of2a	of2b	wr1a	wr1b	wr2a	wr2b	pca	pco	if1a	if1b	Mach State
24	CALL f,mn	`12'b000011fff100`	of1b	of2a	of2b	if1a wr1a	wr1b	wr2a	wr2b	if1a			if1b	dec1	5/3
74	JP f,mn	`12'b000011fff010`	of1b	of2a	of2b	if1a pca					pco	if1a	if1b	dec1	4/3
76	JR cc,e	`12'b0000001cc000`	of1b	if1a pca							pco	if1a	if1b	dec1	3/2

Figure 5-43. *Next State* worksheet for the conditional branch instructions.

The conditional Return instruction shown in Figure 5-44 is a different case completely, because it is a 1-byte opcode. I don't even need to do anything special to make this a one-machine-cycle instruction.

	Instruction	internal code (fetch)	dec1	adr2	rd1a	rd1b	rd2a	rd2b	pca	pco	if1a	if1b	Mach State
141	RET f	`12'b000011fff000`	if1b adr2	rd1a	rd1b	rd2a	rd2b	pca	pco	if1a	if1b	dec1	5/1

Figure 5-44. *Next State* worksheet for the conditional Return instructions.

That covers all of the different cases in the *Next State* worksheet, but I don't want to give you the impression that it is a simple exercise to come up with all of these sequences of machine cycles. When starting from scratch it requires an intimate knowledge of the operation of each instruction, and that's why I always start with an *Operation* worksheet.

Once you have the *Operation* worksheet done it's easy to determine at least how many operand fetches, memory reads and memory writes are going to be required, as a starting point for the state sequences. But then you need to think about some implementation realities, like how to put an address on the address bus if it is just being sampled as an input by the same clock edge. With a dedicated path for the data it can be done, but is it worth the cost? You will have to make trade-offs like this throughout the design.

It is also important to remember that you probably won't be able to think of every possible case as you are developing the *Next State* worksheet. You may find yourself needing to go back and modify the sequence for a particular instruction. The spreadsheet makes this fairly painless, because it is just a cut and paste operation between the different worksheets. I have had to go back and make changes after finding a problem in the simulation!

When to Add a Worksheet

Now that the *Next State* worksheet is complete it can be used as the template for the remainder of the worksheets, but first we need to determine what other worksheets will be required. Even with a starting template it takes a fair amount of work to populate a worksheet, so I only use a worksheet where the time investment will pay off. There are some obvious things that will need a worksheet, shown in Table 5-9.

Worksheet Name	Function
Address bus	Load control for the address register.
Pre-address	Source select for the address register. One clock early.
Load PC	Load control for the PC. Also controls the sampling of interrupts.
ALU Op	ALU operation. One clock early.
ALU A	First input to the ALU. One clock early.
ALU B	Second input to the ALU. One clock early.
Register Write	Register select and register write enable.

Table 5-9. The basic worksheets that will be required.

Some worksheets can perform double or even triple duty, if the number of different cases isn't too large. This is the case for the *Load PC* worksheet, where in many cases the load of the PC will coincide with the cycle where the interrupt request needs to be sampled. I started out trying to do this with the various flags but ended up separating them into the individual worksheets shown in Table 5-10 when the number of permutations became too large.

Worksheet Name	Function
S Flag	Source select and load enable for the Sign flag.
Z Flag	Source select and load enable for the Zero flag.
H Flag	Source select and load enable for the Half-Carry flag.
PV Flag	Source select and load enable for the Parity/Overflow flag.
N Flag	Source select and load enable for the Negate flag.
C Flag	Source select and load enable for the Carry flag.
T Flag	Source select and load enable for the Temporary flag.

Table 5-10. The flag worksheets that will be required.

Where did the Temporary flag come from? There are a couple of cases where an instruction uses the result of an operation but does not update any of the flags. The Temporary flag stores the result of the operation for use during the instruction execution. The DJNZ instruction is the best example of this, where the B register is decremented and tested for zero. The result of this test determines whether the jump is taken or not, but no flags are affected.

There are a few other cases where it might be possible to do without a worksheet, shown in Table 5-11, but I use one anyway because there are a few special cases that I don't want to forget.

Worksheet Name	Function
Tran Type	Controls the transaction type status for the next bus transaction.
DinDout	Source select and load control for the data in and data out registers.

Table 5-11. Two worksheets that might be optional.

An example of control signals that don't really need a worksheet, or could all share a common worksheet, are the controls for the interrupt enable bits and the interrupt mode bits, controls associated with the halt state and the controls associated with the register bank select. All of these cases apply to just one or two instructions, so I don't usually bother with a worksheet for them.

Several of these worksheet descriptions include a comment that says "one clock early." This is because the operation selected in a particular column will be registered in flip-flops before use. I register control signals so that they will be valid as early in the clock cycle as possible. The best example is the ALU controls. If these control signals were not registered, they would not be settled to their final value until well into the clock cycle. This would mean either less time for the ALU operation to complete or a longer clock cycle time.

Completing one of these pipelined worksheets can be a very error-prone proposition, because it's easy to forget that you are dealing with a pipelined signal. I usually do this type of worksheet in a two-step process. I first complete the worksheet as if the signals were not pipelined, and carefully verify that it is correct. Then I create a copy of the worksheet and manually move each of the entries back to the previous clock cycle in the instruction, row by row.

In the case of the ALU control I only have to do the manual move for the *ALU Op* worksheet, because then I can use that worksheet as the template for the *ALU A* and *ALU B* worksheets. After all, the ALU inputs only matter when an ALU operation is specified.

In all of the previous worksheet examples every cell that wasn't shaded contained an entry. For all of the remaining worksheets this is not the case. Where a shaded cell in a worksheet is always a "don't care" as far as the value is concerned, a blank cell that is not shaded can either mean "don't care" or "inactive."

The exact meaning depends on the worksheet. For example, the *DinDout* worksheet controls both the source select and the load enable for these registers. Clearly the load enable must be inactive for the clock cycles corresponding to blank worksheet cells. Keep this in mind when working with the remaining worksheets.

With that background complete, I can now discuss the individual worksheets. I won't go over them line by line, but will try to summarize them like I did for the *Next State* worksheet. I'll try to pick a representative instruction and go over it in full, and then add the special cases that also need to be covered.

The *Tran Type* Worksheet

The *Tran Type* worksheet is probably the easiest to complete, and that's why I like to start with it. This is the transaction type identifier for the external bus. It may appear that I have made it more complicated than necessary, but this is a case of thinking for the future. With separate memory and I/O address spaces, we need to distinguish these transaction types, and there are also the cases where the external bus is idle. Excerpts from the *Tran Type* worksheet are shown in Figures 5-41 and 5-42.

Some CPUs distinguish program memory, data memory and stack memory, and that is what I have done in this worksheet, just in case. Even though they are identified as separate memory spaces in the worksheet I don't have to make the encoding unique in the design.

	Instruction	internal code (fetch)	dec1	if2b	dec2	of1b	adr1	adr2	rd2a	rd2b	if1a	if1b	Mach State
7	ADD A,(HL)	12'b000010000110						mem		if		if	3
8	ADD A,(IX+d)	12'b010010000110		if		idl		mem		if		if	5
9	ADD A,(IY+d)	12'b010110000110		if		idl		mem		if		if	5
10	ADD A,n	12'b000011000110				if						if	2
11	ADD A,r	12'b000010000rrr										if	1
12	ADD HL,ss	12'b000000xx1001										if	1
13	ADD IX,xx	12'b010000xx1001		if								if	2
14	ADD IY,yy	12'b010100xx1001		if								if	2

Figure 5-45a. *Tran Type* worksheet for the Add instructions.

The transaction type information needs to be valid during the clock before the transaction starts on the external bus so that it can be latched along with the address. That's why it looks as though it's a pipelined signal.

	Instruction	internal code (fetch)	dec1	if2b	dec2	of1b	of2a	of2b	adr1	adr2	wr1a	wr1b	wr2a	wr2b	if1a	if1b
24	CALL f,mn	12'b000011fff100				if		if stk				stk		if		if
25	CALL mn	12'b000011001101				if		stk				stk		if		if
126	OUT (C),r	12'b1xxx01rrr001		if						io				if		if
127	OUT (n),A	12'b000011010011				idl				io				if		if

Figure 5-45b. *Tran Type* worksheet showing different identifiers.

These examples show all of the possibilities for the *Tran Type* worksheet. The meanings of the various identifiers should be obvious, but I'll list them here anyway.

The *iak* identifier does not appear anywhere in the *Tran Type* worksheet, but only because I haven't bothered to include that state in the spreadsheet as a whole to save space.

Identifier	Meaning
iak	Interrupt Acknowledge transaction.
idl	The bus is idle for this machine cycle.
if	Instruction fetch transaction, from the program memory address space.
io	I/O transaction.
mem	Memory read or write transaction, from the data memory address space.
stk	Stack read or write transaction, from the stack memory address space.

Table 5-12. *Tran Type* worksheet identifier definitions.

The *Address Bus* Worksheet

The *Address Bus* worksheet is another simple worksheet that is nearly identical to the *Tran Type* worksheet. An excerpt from this worksheet is shown in Figure 5-46. Instead of the transaction type information, it shows the source for the register that drives the address bus. I can't use the information in this worksheet to directly control the address multiplexer though, because of the settling time issue that I discussed earlier. Instead, any entry signifies the load control signal for the address register. I'll discuss the identifiers used here in the description of the next worksheet.

	Instruction	internal code (fetch)	dec1	if2b	dec2	of1b	adr1	adr2	rd2a	rd2b	if1a	if1b	Mach State
7	ADD A,(HL)	12'b000010000110						hl		pc		pc	3
8	ADD A,(IX+d)	12'b010010000110		pc		pc		alu		pc		pc	5
9	ADD A,(IY+d)	12'b010110000110		pc		pc		alu		pc		pc	5
10	ADD A,n	12'b000011000110				pc						pc	2
11	ADD A,r	12'b000010000rrr										pc	1
12	ADD HL,ss	12'b000000ss1001										pc	1
13	ADD IX,xx	12'b010000xx1001		pc								pc	2
14	ADD IY,yy	12'b010100yy1001		pc								pc	2

Figure 5-46. *Address Bus* worksheet for the Add instructions.

The *Pre-address* Worksheet

The *Pre-address* worksheet shown in Figure 5-47 is created from the *Address Bus* worksheet by moving the identifiers back in time to the previous clock cycle so that they can be registered.

	Instruction	internal code (fetch)	dec1	if2b	dec2	of1b	adr1	adr2	rd2a	rd2b	if1a	if1b	Mach State
7	ADD A,(HL)	12'b000010000110	hl						pc		pc		3
8	ADD A,(IX+d)	12'b010010000110	pc		pc		alu		pc		pc		5
9	ADD A,(IY+d)	12'b010110000110	pc		pc		alu		pc		pc		5
10	ADD A,n	12'b000011000110	pc								pc		2
11	ADD A,r	12'b000010000rrr	pc										1
12	ADD HL,ss	12'b000000xx1001	pc										1
13	ADD IX,xx	12'b010000xx1001	pc		pc								2
14	ADD IY,yy	12'b010100xx1001	pc		pc								2

Figure 5-47. *Pre-address* worksheet for the Add instructions.

There is one other identifier used in this (and the previous) worksheet, as shown in Figure 5-48.

	Instruction	internal code (fetch)	dec1	if2b	dec2	adr2	rd1a	rd1b	rd2a	rd2b	if1a	if1b	Mach State
130	POP IX	`12'b010011100001`	pc		sp		alu		pc		pc		5
131	POP IY	`12'b010111100001`	pc		sp		alu		pc		pc		5

Figure 5-48. *Pre-address* worksheet showing different identifiers.

The meaning of the identifiers should be obvious. After all, that's the whole point of using mnemonics like these, but I'll list them here in Table 5-13 for completeness.

Identifier	Meaning
alu	Output of the ALU. Used whenever none of the other identifiers apply.
hl	Contents of the HL register is the address.
pc	Contents of the PC register is the address.
sp	Contents of the SP register is the address.

Table 5-13. *Address Bus* and *Pre-address* worksheet identifier definitions.

In reality, I should be able to get by with just using the output of the ALU as the source for the address register, because I can pass anything through the ALU. I'm using a dedicated path for the PC register in the hope that it will save some power. My thinking is that with a direct path I won't have to worry about generating the ALU control signals and have more internal nodes changing state as often.

The HL and SP register paths are included for similar reasons. When we get to the ALU control worksheets we'll see that avoiding the use of the ALU to pass the HL register simplifies the decoding for opcodes that use the *rrr* register select field. Remember that this register select field is also used to select the indirect addressing using the HL register.

The *Load PC* Worksheet

At first glance, the *Load PC* worksheet seems like it should be another easy one, because I've already worked out the timing for the increment of the PC register. But the increment of the PC register is affected by the presence an interrupt request, so I'll also use this worksheet to control the sampling of interrupts. This makes the *Load PC* worksheet much more complex, but it reduces the chance of introducing an error between this pair of closely related functions.

This is also the time to think about the bus request/bus acknowledge function. The original Z80 could release the bus between any bus transaction. This made sense when the CPU clock frequency was 2.5MHz, but this design should easily run at ten times that speed. In addition, machine cycles for this design are only two clock cycles, versus four for the Z80. So I probably don't need to accept a bus request after every machine cycle.

Limiting the bus release to instruction boundaries means that it operates almost identically to an interrupt. In fact the only difference is that a bus release will not need to go through the interrupt acknowledge sequence, but can just sit in an idle state until the bus is restored to the CPU. So I will just treat the bus request like a special interrupt and use the same timing.

The timing diagram in Figure 5-49 shows what will be required to interrupt instruction execution. Since I want the interrupt acknowledge machine cycle to directly follow an *if1b* state the increment of the PC register during the state just prior to *if1b* must be inhibited. The inhibited increment of the PC register dictates that the interrupt request be sampled during the same clock cycle. Otherwise there is going to be a possibility that things will get out of sync.

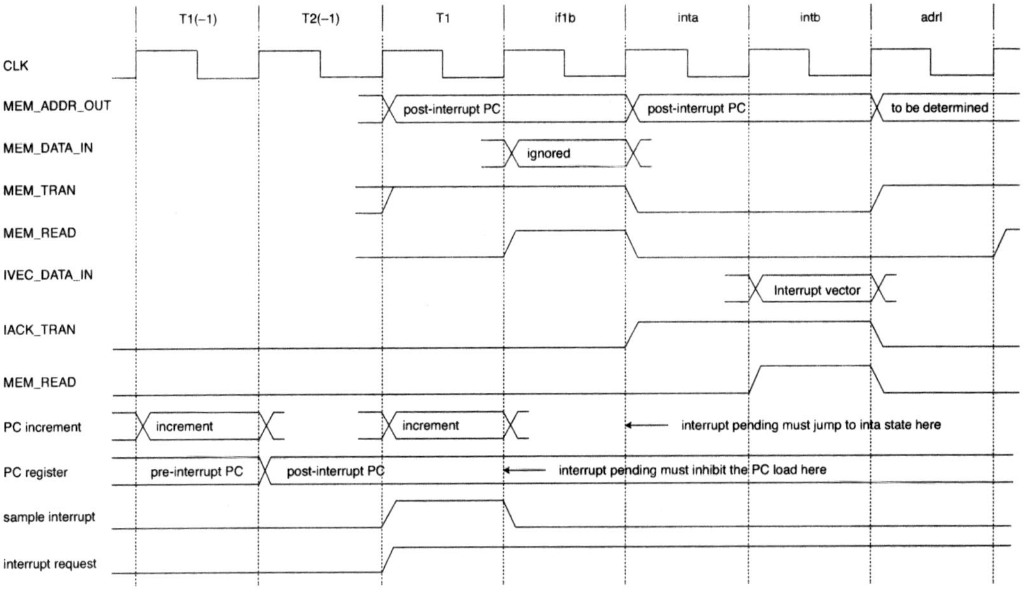

Figure 5-49. Interrupt Acknowledge timing.

Figure 5-50 is the *Load PC* worksheet for the Add instruction. Since this worksheet is describing a register load signal, blank cells that are not shaded really do matter. A blank cell means that no operation should take place. Depending on what I choose as the default case for a particular column, it is sometimes necessary to enter a "do nothing" identifier instead of leaving a cell blank. This type of identifier helps when sorting the column by identifier. I'll go over what each of the identifiers mean after the different examples.

As you can see, the case of instructions that execute sequentially is not complicated. The PC register is incremented once for each byte of opcode and interrupts are sampled at the end of each instruction.

	Instruction	internal code (fetch)	dec1	if2b	dec2	of1b	adr1	adr2	rd2a	rd2b	if1a	if1b	Mach State
7	ADD A,(HL)	`12'b000010000110`	hld								nild	jmp	3
8	ADD A,(IX+d)	`12'b010010000110`	ld		ld						nild	jmp	5
9	ADD A,(IY+d)	`12'b010110000110`	ld		ld						nild	jmp	5
10	ADD A,n	`12'b000011000110`	ld								nild	jmp	2
11	ADD A,r	`12'b000010000rrr`	nild									jmp	1
12	ADD HL,ss	`12'b000000xx1001`	nild									jmp	1
13	ADD IX,xx	`12'b010000xx1001`	ld		nild							jmp	2
14	ADD IY,yy	`12'b010100xx1001`	ld		nild							jmp	2

Figure 5-50. *Load PC* worksheet for the Add instructions.

The cases of branch instructions are much more complex, as shown in Figure 5-51. These instructions start off just like any other but then quickly become unique. Conditional branch instructions where the execution time is different for the taken/not taken case don't need anything special as far as the controls for the PC register. But when the execution time is the same either way I have to make the controls for the PC register conditional.

	Instruction	internal code (fetch)	dec1	of1b	of2a	of2b	wr1a	wr1b	wr2a	wr2b	pca	pco	if1a	if1b	Mach State
24	CALL f,mn	`12'b000011fff100`	ld		ld					ld			nild	jmp	5/3
25	CALL mn	`12'b000011001101`	ld		ld					ld			nild	jmp	5
46	DJNZ j	`12'b000000010000`	ld								cld	hld	nild	jmp	3
71	JP (HL)	`12'b000011101001`	ld									ld	nild	jmp	2
74	JP f,mn	`12'b000011fff010`	ld		ld						ld	hld	nild	jmp	4/3
75	JP mn	`12'b000011000011`	ld		ld						ld	hld	nild	jmp	4
76	JR cc,e	`12'b0000001cc000`	ld								ld	hld	nild	jmp	3/2
77	JR e	`12'b000000011000`	ld								ld	hld	nild	jmp	3

Figure 5-51. *Load PC* worksheet for the branch instructions.

The block instructions must sample interrupts once per iteration, which means that I can't just sample the interrupts at the end of the instruction. I use a dedicated identifier to control this interrupt sampling, as shown in Figure 5-52.

	Instruction	internal code (fetch)	dec1	if2b	dec2	adr2	rd1a	rd1b	rd2a	rd2b	blk1	blk2	pca	pco	if1a	if1b	Mach State
32	CPD	`12'b1xxx10101001`	ld		hld										nild	jmp	5
33	CPDR	`12'b1xxx10111001`	ld		hld			int		int				ld	nild2	jmp	4+2i
34	CPI	`12'b1xxx10100001`	ld		hld										nild	jmp	5
35	CPIR	`12'b1xxx10110001`	ld		hld			int		int				ld	nild2	jmp	4+2i

Figure 5-52. *Load PC* worksheet for the block instructions.

Normally the interrupts are sampled at the end of every instruction. One exception is the interrupt acknowledge sequence shown in Figure 5-53. The interrupt status will still be latched at this time, which means that the logic would attempt to do another interrupt acknowledge, looping forever.

	Instruction	internal code (fetch)	adr1	adr2	rd1a	rd1b	rd2a	rd2b	wr1a	wr1b	wr2a	wr2b	if1a	if1b	Mach State
200	ZINTACK	`12'b0001xxxxxxxx`	hld									ld	ld	hld	5

Figure 5-53. *Load PC* worksheet for the interrupt acknowledge sequence.

The definitions of the identifiers used in the *Load PC* worksheet are shown in Table 5-14. This worksheet controls the loading of the PC register and the sampling of interrupts and the bus request.

Identifier	Meaning
cld	Conditional load of the PC. Use the condition specified in the opcode.
dma	Sample the dma request only (no interrupts allowed).
hld	Do not load the PC.
int	Sample dma and interrupt requests only.
jmp	Divert to the inta or dma1 state if an interrupt or bus request is pending.
ld	Load the PC.
nild	Load the PC, but only if the interrupt request is inactive. Sample the interrupt request at the same time.
nild2	Load the PC, but only if the latched interrupt request is active.

Table 5-14. *Load PC* worksheet identifier definitions.

With the two-clock-cycle machine cycle I always have a clock cycle available for the increment of the PC register. This simplifies things, because it means that the source for the PC register will always be the output of the ALU. A single-clock machine cycle would mean a dedicated path, potentially with multiple sources, for the input to the PC register.

The *DinDout* Worksheet

The *DinDout* worksheet is supposed to be simple, but there are several subtle issues relating to byte order that I need to keep track of. There is also the issue of the width of these registers. Since the external data bus width is 8 bits, and I have already decided to use a 16-bit internal data bus, the question becomes where and how to do the byte lane swapping.

Clock cycles are at a premium during memory read machine cycles, so I expect that it will be easier to use a 16-bit data input register and assemble the data directly from the data input bus. Using a byte-wide data input register and then assembling the data using the normal internal data paths might get in the way of other operations required during these machine cycles.

With a byte-wide source and a 2-byte destination register there are a couple of ways to handle the byte-lane control. Besides the obvious individual byte enables, I'm going to allow both enables to be active at the same time, replicating the input data. This will allow me to load the register with bytes presented on the data bus in either order, just in case.

The data output register is a different matter. During data write machine cycles there should be spare clock cycles available to do any required byte-lane swapping. In addition, there are not that many cases where two bytes a written by an instruction. So for the data output register I will use a multiplexer on the register input and load the register from either the high byte or the low byte of the internal data bus.

The I/O data output bus could be identical to the memory data output bus, but in an effort to save power, I'll use a separate I/O data output register that will only be loaded by I/O instructions.

I expect that the data input and data output controls will be fairly uniform, with only a few special cases. This means that generating the control signals should not be too complicated and I can probably get by without registering these control signals. This is just a guess based on experience at this point, and only the timing analysis after the design is complete will say for sure. If you are at all concerned about meeting timing it's better to be conservative up front.

Figure 5-54 is the excerpt from the *DinDout* worksheet for the Add instruction. I am loading both halves of the data input register with the address offset or immediate data, even though it really only needs to be loaded in the lower byte, just to make sure that the register contains known data. The operand fetches are loaded only to the lower byte because that is the alignment that will be needed for the operation.

	Instruction	internal code (fetch)	dec1	if2b	dec2	of1b	tran	adr1	rd2a	rd2b	if1a	if1b	Mach State
7	ADD A,(HL)	12'b000010000110								din0			3
8	ADD A,(IX+d)	12'b010010000110				din10				din0			5
9	ADD A,(IY+d)	12'b010110000110				din10				din0			5
10	ADD A,n	12'b000011000110				din10							2
11	ADD A,r	12'b000010000rrr											1
12	ADD HL,ss	12'b000000xx1001											1
13	ADD IX,xx	12'b010000xx1001											2
14	ADD IY,yy	12'b010100xx1001											2

Figure 5-54. *DinDout* worksheet for the Add instructions.

The *DinDout* worksheet excerpt in Figure 5-55 shows a few of the load instructions. It turns out that the *of1b* state should always load both halves of the data input register, independent of the instruction. This makes the coding and logic simpler. The *of2b* state is different, solely because of instructions in rows *82* and *84*.

The output register controls here are the usual case. Byte writes load the data output register from the lower byte of the data bus. Word writes start with the lower byte, followed by the upper byte.

	Instruction	internal code (fetch)	dec1	if2b	dec2	of1b	of2a	of2b	tran	adr1	wr1a	wr1b	wr2a	wr2b	if1a	if1b	Mach State
80	LD (HL),n	12'b000000110110				din10							dout				3
81	LD (HL),r	12'b000001110rrr											dout				3
82	LD (IX+d),n	12'b010000110110				din10		din0					dout				5
83	LD (IX+d),r	12'b010001110rrr				din10							dout				5
84	LD (IY+d),n	12'b010100110110				din10		din0					dout				5
85	LD (IY+d),r	12'b010101110rrr				din10							dout				5
86	LD (mn),A	12'b000000110010				din10		din1					dout				5
87	LD (mn),HL	12'b000000100010				din10		din1			dout		douth				6
88	LD (mn),IX	12'b010000100010				din10		din1			dout		douth				7
89	LD (mn),IY	12'b010100100010				din10		din1			dout		douth				7
90	LD (mn),ss	12'b1xxx01xx0011				din10		din1			dout		douth				7

Figure 5-55. *DinDout* worksheet for several Load instructions.

But stack writes are just the opposite, because the stack grows downward in memory. This leads to the arrangement shown in Figure 5-56, where the pushing data on to the stack is unique.

	Instruction	internal code (fetch)	dec1	if2b	dec2	adr1	adr2	rd1b	rd2a	rd2b	wr1a	wr1b	wr2a	wr2b	if1a	if1b	Mach State
48	EX (SP),HL	12'b000011100011						din0		din1	dout		douth				6
49	EX (SP),IX	12'b010011100011						din0		din1	dout		douth				7
130	POP IX	12'b010011100001						din0		din1							5
132	POP tt	12'b000011xx0001						din0		din1							4
133	PUSH IX	12'b010011100101									douth		dout				5
135	PUSH tt	12'b000011xx0101									douth		dout				4

Figure 5-56. *DinDout* worksheet for instructions that access the stack.

There are no 16-bit I/O instructions, so I only need one identifier for the I/O data output register, as shown in Figure 5-57. In theory, I could just use the transaction type information to control the routing of these load enable signals. But I expect to locate these registers in the same module as the ALU, where the transaction type information will not normally be available. Hence the separate identifier.

	Instruction	internal code (fetch)	dec1	if2b	dec2	of1b	tran	adr1	adr2	rd1b	wr1a	wr1b	wr2a	wr2b	if1a	if1b
126	OUT (C),r	12'b1xxx01rrr001											douti			
127	OUT (n),A	12'b000011010011				din10							douti			
128	OUTD	12'b1xxx10101011								din0	douti		douti			
129	OUTI	12'b1xxx10100011								din0	douti		douti			

Figure 5-57. *DinDout* worksheet for Output instructions.

I'm not going to use separate identifiers for the I/O and interrupt vector cases of the input data bus. I prefer to do the source selection on the input side of the registers, which will be in the external interface module. The transaction type information will certainly be available in that module so separate identifiers are not required. Even at this early stage of the design you need to be thinking about how the different functions will be arranged in the Verilog code.

The definitions of the identifiers used to control the data input registers in the *DinDout* worksheet are shown in Table 5-15. Remember that the data input register is loaded from either the memory data input bus, the I/O input data bus or the interrupt vector bus, depending on the transaction type.

Identifier	Meaning
din0	Load the least-significant byte of the data input register.
din1	Load the most-significant byte of the data input register.
din10	Load both bytes of the data input register in parallel.

Table 5-15. *DinDout* worksheet data input identifier definitions.

The definitions of the identifiers used to control the data output registers in the *DinDout* worksheet are shown in Table 5-16. The data output register and the I/O data output register is loaded from the lower byte of the internal data bus.

Identifier	Meaning
dout	Load the data output register from the least-significant byte of the internal data bus.
douth	Load the data output register from the most-significant byte of the internal data bus.
douti	Load the I/O data output register from the least-significant byte of the internal data bus.

Table 5-16. *DinDout* worksheet data output identifier definitions.

That takes care of all of the easy worksheets. I have the machine state sequence, the controls for the PC register and the controls for the transaction type, address and data on the external bus worked out. Now things start to get complex, with the operation of the ALU.

Even though it will be somewhat cumbersome, I will go through the three worksheets related to the ALU together. I always work on all three worksheets at the same time, switching back and forth between the worksheets as I fill them out row by row. I don't find it necessary to try to fill out the flag worksheets at the same time. After all, it is easy to use the *ALU Op* worksheet as the starting template for a flag worksheet.

The *ALU Op*, *ALU A* and *ALU B* Worksheets

The *ALU Op*, *ALU A* and *ALU B* worksheets are the heart of the design, and are probably the most complex part of the overall design spreadsheet. The ALU control signals will need to be registered to allow the entire clock cycle for the ALU output to resolve. If you aren't yet comfortable working with registered cell entries directly, feel free to create unregistered versions first like I did with the *Address Bus* worksheet.

The order that you use to fill in the ALU worksheets is a personal choice. In general I find it useful to group rows by execution time to start with, filling in operations that are common between different instructions with the same timing. Once I have the common operations complete I usually switch to grouping the rows by instruction type. This helps me visualize the different types of operations and inputs required for each group of instructions. This is how I'll present the ALU worksheets.

The *ALU Op* worksheet excerpt in Figure 5-58 shows the various Add instructions. If you recall the timing for the different machine cycles, the increment of the PC register occurs during the *dec1*, *dec2* and *if1a* states, among others. With the registering of the ALU controls this means that the operation during the *if1b* and *if2b* states will always be an increment. The same is true for whichever state occurs before the *if1a* state.

There are five different types of add operation required here: add and add-with-carry, both byte and word, and the special add with sign-extend for the indexed addressing mode. I prefer to explicitly keep track of the width of the operation this way, and then use the ALU identifier to modify the flag operation as appropriate.

	Instruction	internal code	dec1	if2b	dec2	of1b	adr1	adr2	rd2a	rd2b	if1a	if1b	Mach State
1	ADC A,(HL)	12'b000010001110	badc							add	badc	add	3
2	ADC A,(IX+d)	12'b010010001110		add		add	ads			add	badc	add	5
3	ADC A,(IY+d)	12'b010110001110		add		add	ads			add	badc	add	5
4	ADC A,n	12'b000011001110				add					badc	add	2
5	ADC A,r	12'b000010001rrr	badc							add	badc	add	1
6	ADC HL,ss	12'b1xxx01xx1010		add	adc							add	2
7	ADD A,(HL)	12'b000010000110	badd							add	badd	add	3
8	ADD A,(IX+d)	12'b010010000110		add		add	ads			add	badd	add	5
9	ADD A,(IY+d)	12'b010110000110		add		add	ads			add	badd	add	5
10	ADD A,n	12'b000011000110				add					badd	add	2
11	ADD A,r	12'b000010000rrr	badd							add	badd	add	1
12	ADD HL,ss	12'b000000xx1001	add									add	1
13	ADD IX,xx	12'b010000xx1001		add	add							add	2
14	ADD IY,yy	12'b010100xx1001		add	add							add	2

Figure 5-58. *ALU Op* worksheet for the Add instructions.

Notice that I always try to fill in the spreadsheet to take advantage of the "don't-care" cases of bit fields. This is why there are identifiers in shaded cells as well as identifiers in the *dec1* states of instructions using indirect addressing. Without the direct path for the HL register for the address these identifiers in the *dec1* states would not be possible, because the ALU would need to pass the HL register during this state.

The corresponding *ALU A* worksheet excerpt is shown in Figure 5-59. I will use this ALU input for the accumulator and the registers that are both source and destination for the instruction. All of the *one* identifiers are for the increment of the PC register. Theoretically I could use a dedicated increment operation and not worry about driving this ALU input bus. But in reality the bus has to be driven with some value every clock cycle anyway, and this as a good a choice as any other.

	Instruction	internal code	dec1	if2b	dec2	of1b	adr1	adr2	rd2a	rd2b	if1a	if1b	Mach State
1	ADC A,(HL)	12'b000010001110	a							one	a	one	3
2	ADC A,(IX+d)	12'b010010001110		one		one	ix			one	a	one	5
3	ADC A,(IY+d)	12'b010110001110		one		one	iy			one	a	one	5
4	ADC A,n	12'b000011001110				one					a	one	2
5	ADC A,r	12'b000010001rrr	a							one	a	one	1
6	ADC HL,ss	12'b1xxx01xx1010		one	hl							one	2
7	ADD A,(HL)	12'b000010000110	a							one	a	one	3
8	ADD A,(IX+d)	12'b010010000110		one		one	ix			one	a	one	5
9	ADD A,(IY+d)	12'b010110000110		one		one	iy			one	a	one	5
10	ADD A,n	12'b000011000110				one					a	one	2
11	ADD A,r	12'b000010000rrr	a							one	a	one	1
12	ADD HL,ss	12'b000000xx1001	hl									one	1
13	ADD IX,xx	12'b010000xx1001		one	ix							one	2
14	ADD IY,yy	12'b010100xx1001		one	iy							one	2

Figure 5-59. *ALU A* worksheet for the Add instructions.

The *ALU B* worksheet excerpt is shown in Figure 5-60. This is one place where the value of the bit fields matter, so I have to use identifiers that indicate this fact. When I group these identifiers to transfer them to the Verilog I'll have to expand them into the corresponding individual cases. This is one of only a few worksheets where the value of a bit field is important, but the extra work is worth the simplified worksheet.

	Instruction	internal code	dec1	if2b	dec2	of1b	adr1	adr2	rd2a	rd2b	if1a	if1b	Mach State
1	ADC A,(HL)	12'b000010001110	r210							pc	din	pc	3
2	ADC A,(IX+d)	12'b010010001110		pc		pc	din			pc	din	pc	5
3	ADC A,(IY+d)	12'b010110001110		pc		pc	din			pc	din	pc	5
4	ADC A,n	12'b000011001110				pc					din	pc	2
5	ADC A,r	12'b000010001rrr	r210							pc	din	pc	1
6	ADC HL,ss	12'b1xxx01xx1010		pc	s54							pc	2
7	ADD A,(HL)	12'b000010000110	r210							pc	din	pc	3
8	ADD A,(IX+d)	12'b010010000110		pc		pc	din			pc	din	pc	5
9	ADD A,(IY+d)	12'b010110000110		pc		pc	din			pc	din	pc	5
10	ADD A,n	12'b000011000110				pc					din	pc	2
11	ADD A,r	12'b000010000rrr	r210							pc	din	pc	1
12	ADD HL,ss	12'b000000xx1001	s54									pc	1
13	ADD IX,xx	12'b010000xx1001		pc	x54							pc	2
14	ADD IY,yy	12'b010100xx1001		pc	y54							pc	2

Figure 5-60. *ALU B* worksheet for the Add instructions.

Figure 5-61 shows the *ALU Op* worksheet excerpt for the Compare and Subtract instructions. It is basically identical to the add instruction excerpt with different ALU operations in the columns that aren't incrementing the PC register. The *ALU A* and *ALU B* worksheets for these instructions do not add anything new, so I won't show them here.

	Instruction	internal code	dec1	if2b	dec2	of1b	adr1	adr2	rd2a	rd2b	if1a	if1b	Mach State
27	CP (HL)	`12'b000010111110`	bsub							add	bsub	add	3
28	CP (IX+d)	`12'b010010111110`		add		add	ads			add	bsub	add	5
29	CP (IY+d)	`12'b010110111110`		add		add	ads			add	bsub	add	5
30	CP n	`12'b000011111110`				add					bsub	add	2
31	CP r	`12'b000010111rrr`	bsub							add	bsub	add	1
167	SBC (IX+d)	`12'b010010011110`		add		add	ads			add	bsbc	add	5
168	SBC (IY+d)	`12'b010110011110`		add		add	ads			add	bsbc	add	5
169	SBC A,(HL)	`12'b000010011110`	bsbc							add	bsbc	add	3
170	SBC A,n	`12'b000011011110`				add					bsbc	add	2
171	SBC A,r	`12'b000010011rrr`	bsbc							add	bsbc	add	1
172	SBC HL,ss	`12'b1xxx01xx0010`		add	sbc							add	2
190	SUB (HL)	`12'b000010010110`	bsub							add	bsub	add	3
191	SUB (IX+d)	`12'b010010010110`		add		add	ads			add	bsub	add	5
192	SUB (IY+d)	`12'b010110010110`		add		add	ads			add	bsub	add	5
193	SUB n	`12'b000011010110`				add					bsub	add	2
194	SUB r	`12'b000010010rrr`	bsub							add	bsub	add	1

Figure 5-61. *ALU Op* worksheet for the Subtract and Compare instructions.

Figure 5-62 is the *ALU Op* worksheet excerpt for the Increment and Decrement instructions. Why does the Decrement instruction use the *add* identifier but not the *badd* identifier? With an addition operation the order of the operands on the ALU inputs doesn't matter, but it does matter with a subtract operation. I am trying to keep all constant values on the ALU A input, which dictates an addition operation. Since the byte decrement instructions affect the Carry flag and Half-Carry flag doing it this way requires that these signals be inverted out of the ALU to create the borrow that a subtract would generate. The *bdec* operation flags this special inversion operation.

	Instruction	internal code	dec1	if2b	dec2	of1b	adr1	adr2	rd2a	rd2b	wr2a	wr2b	if1a	if1b	Mach State
38	DEC (HL)	12'b000000110101	bdec							bdec		add		add	4
39	DEC (IX+d)	12'b010000110101		add		add	ads		pass	bdec		add		add	6
40	DEC (IY+d)	12'b010100110101		add		add	ads		pass	bdec		add		add	6
41	DEC IX	12'b010000101011		add	add									add	2
42	DEC IY	12'b010100101011		add	add									add	2
43	DEC r	12'b000000rrr101	bdec							bdec				add	1
44	DEC ss	12'b000000xx1011	add											add	1
60	INC (HL)	12'b000000110100	badd							badd		add		add	4
61	INC (IX+d)	12'b010000110100		add		add	ads		pass	badd		add		add	6
62	INC (IY+d)	12'b010100110100		add		add	ads		pass	badd		add		add	6
63	INC IX	12'b010000100011		add	add									add	2
64	INC IY	12'b010100100011		add	add									add	2
65	INC r	12'b000000rrr100	badd							badd		add		add	1
66	INC ss	12'b000000xx0011	add											add	1

Figure 5-62. *ALU Op* worksheet for the Decrement and Increment instructions.

The corresponding *ALU A* and *ALU B* worksheet excerpts are shown in Figure 5-63 and Figure 5-64. To save a little power I will use a temporary register to hold the calculated address. Otherwise I would need to do the calculation twice, first for the read and then again for the write.

	Instruction	internal code	dec1	if2b	dec2	of1b	adr1	adr2	rd2a	rd2b	wr2a	wr2b	if1a	if1b	Mach State
38	DEC (HL)	12'b000000110101	neg1							neg1		one		one	4
39	DEC (IX+d)	12'b010000110101		one		one	ix			neg1		one		one	6
40	DEC (IY+d)	12'b010100110101		one		one	iy			neg1		one		one	6
41	DEC IX	12'b010000101011		one	neg1									one	2
42	DEC IY	12'b010100101011		one	neg1									one	2
43	DEC r	12'b000000rrr101	neg1							neg1				one	1
44	DEC ss	12'b000000xx1011	neg1											one	1
60	INC (HL)	12'b000000110100	one							one		one		one	4
61	INC (IX+d)	12'b010000110100		one		one	ix			one		one		one	6
62	INC (IY+d)	12'b010100110100		one		one	iy			one		one		one	6
63	INC IX	12'b010000100011		one	one									one	2
64	INC IY	12'b010100100011		one	one									one	2
65	INC r	12'b000000rrr100	one											one	1
66	INC ss	12'b000000xx0011	one											one	1

Figure 5-63. *ALU A* worksheet for the Decrement and Increment instructions.

Using a temporary register like this is a classic example of adding more hardware to save power. It may seem counter-intuitive, but it makes sense because CMOS technology uses very little static power. If the technology being used required static power the choice might go the opposite way.

	Instruction	internal code	dec1	if2b	dec2	of1b	adr1	adr2	rd2a	rd2b	wr2a	wr2b	if1a	if1b	Mach State
38	DEC (HL)	12'b000000110101	r543							din		pc		pc	4
39	DEC (IX+d)	12'b010000110101		pc		pc	din		tmp	din		pc		pc	6
40	DEC (IY+d)	12'b010100110101		pc		pc	din		tmp	din		pc		pc	6
41	DEC IX	12'b010000101011		pc	ix									pc	2
42	DEC IY	12'b010100101011		pc	iy									pc	2
43	DEC r	12'b000000rrr101	r543							din		pc		pc	1
44	DEC ss	12'b000000xx1011	s54											pc	1
60	INC (HL)	12'b000000110100	r543							din		pc		pc	4
61	INC (IX+d)	12'b010000110100		pc		pc	din		tmp	din		pc		pc	6
62	INC (IY+d)	12'b010100110100		pc		pc	din		tmp	din		pc		pc	6
63	INC IX	12'b010000100011		pc	ix									pc	2
64	INC IY	12'b010100100011		pc	iy									pc	2
65	INC r	12'b000000rrr100	r543							din		pc		pc	1
66	INC ss	12'b000000xx0011	s54											pc	1

Figure 5-64. *ALU B* worksheet for the Decrement and Increment instructions.

The next *ALU Op* worksheet excerpt, in Figure 5-65, shows the logical operations. I only show a few cases because the order of operations is identical to the add and subtract operations. I don't show the *ALU A* or *ALU B* worksheet excerpts here for the same reason.

There are no word-wide logical operations, but I still like to mark the identifiers as byte for consistency. If I happen to add word-wide logical operations in the future, this will come in handy.

	Instruction	internal code	dec1	if2b	dec2	of1b	adr1	adr2	rd2a	rd2b	if1a	if1b	Mach State
16	AND (IX+d)	12'b010010100110		add		add	ads			add	band	add	5
120	OR (IX+d)	12'b010010110110		add		add	ads			add	bor	add	5
196	XOR (IX+d)	12'b010010101110		add		add	ads			add	bxor	add	5

Figure 5-65. *ALU Op* worksheet for the logical instructions.

The special arithmetic instructions shown in Figure 5-66 are really simple. But why have special ALU operations for setting and complementing the Carry flag? I think it will be easier to implement this way, because it will gather all of the different possibilities for the Carry flag into one section of the Verilog code.

	Instruction	internal code	dec1	if2b	dec2	if1b	Mach State
26	CCF	12'b000000111111	ccf			add	1
36	CPL	12'b000000101111	bxor			add	1
37	DAA	12'b000000100111	daa			add	1
117	NEG	12'b1xxx01000100		add	bsub	add	2
173	SCF	12'b000000110111	scf			add	1

Figure 5-66. *ALU Op* worksheet for the special arithmetic instructions.

Obviously decimal adjust gets its own operation, but it's too early to tell exactly how it will work. Since the operation is really just an addition with variable data, I expect that this will be the easiest way to implement this instruction. Figure 5-67 is the *ALU A* worksheet for these cases.

	Instruction	internal code	dec1	if2b	dec2	if1b	Mach State
26	CCF	12'b000000111111				one	1
36	CPL	12'b000000101111	neg1			one	1
37	DAA	12'b000000100111	daa			one	1
117	NEG	12'b1xxx01000100		one	zer	one	2
173	SCF	12'b000000110111				one	1

Figure 5-67. *ALU A* worksheet for the special arithmetic instructions.

Figure 5-68 shows that the *ALU B* worksheet for these cases is simple. Now you see why I assigned all of the constant values to the ALU A input.

	Instruction	internal code	dec1	if2b	dec2	if1b	Mach State
26	CCF	12'b000000111111				pc	1
36	CPL	12'b000000101111	a			pc	1
37	DAA	12'b000000100111	a			pc	1
117	NEG	12'b1xxx01000100		pc	a	pc	2
173	SCF	12'b000000110111				pc	1

Figure 5-68. *ALU B* worksheet for the special arithmetic instructions.

Next come the *ALU Op*, *ALU A* and *ALU B* worksheet excerpts for the bit instructions, shown in Figure 5-69, Figure 5-70 and Figure 5-71 respectively. These instructions can use the existing logical operations with the proper choice of a masking bit pattern. The Bit Test and Bit Set cases will need a one-hot mask, while the Bit Reset will need the complement of this. I expect to create this mask outside of the ALU itself and then supply it to the ALU A input. The mask can be continuously generated from the bits in the opcode with this type of implementation, although enabling the mask only when required will save a little bit of power.

	Instruction	internal code	dec1	if2b	dec2	of1b	if3a	if3b	adr2	rd2a	rd2b	wr2a	wr2b	if1a	if1b	Mach State
20	BIT b,(HL)	12'b001001xxx110		add	band						add			band	add	4
21	BIT b,(IX+d)	12'b011001xxx110		add		add	ads			pass	add			band	add	5
22	BIT b,(IY+d)	12'b011101xxx110		add		add	ads			pass	add			band	add	5
23	BIT b,r	12'b001001xxxrrr		add	band						add			band	add	2
136	RES b,(HL)	12'b001010xxx110		add	band						band		add		add	5
137	RES b,(IX+d)	12'b011010xxx110		add		add	ads			pass	band		add		add	6
138	RES b,(IY+d)	12'b011110xxx110		add		add	ads			pass	band		add		add	6
139	RES b,r	12'b001010xxxrrr		add	band						band		add		add	2
174	SET b,(HL)	12'b001011xxx110		add	bor						bor		add		add	5

Figure 5-69. *ALU Op* worksheet for the bit instructions.

I have chosen not to make the two different bit masks separate options for the ALU A input. This will make the ALU A input multiplexer a little less complicated, which will hopefully mean a little more speed. The bit mask, which can be generated from the instruction register starting with the *dec2* state, will be valid at least one clock before being selected by the multiplexer.

	Instruction	internal code	dec1	if2b	dec2	of1b	if3a	if3b	adr2	rd2a	rd2b	wr2a	wr2b	if1a	if1b	Mach State
20	BIT b,(HL)	12'b001001xxx110		one	bit						one			bit	one	4
21	BIT b,(IX+d)	12'b011001xxx110		one		one	ix				one			bit	one	5
22	BIT b,(IY+d)	12'b011101xxx110		one		one	iy				one			bit	one	5
23	BIT b,r	12'b001001xxxrrr		one	bit						one			bit	one	2
136	RES b,(HL)	12'b001010xxx110		one	bit						bit		one		one	5
137	RES b,(IX+d)	12'b011010xxx110		one		one	ix				bit		one		one	6
138	RES b,(IY+d)	12'b011110xxx110		one		one	iy				bit		one		one	6
139	RES b,r	12'b001010xxxrrr		one	bit						bit				one	2
174	SET b,(HL)	12'b001011xxx110		one	bit						bit		one		one	5

Figure 5-70. *ALU A* worksheet for the bit instructions.

I am able to do the address calculation during the *if3a* and *if3b* states, so no separate address calculation machine cycle is required with the indexed address mode.

	Instruction	internal code	dec1	if2b	dec2	of1b	if3a	if3b	adr2	rd2a	rd2b	wr2a	wr2b	if1a	if1b	Mach State
20	BIT b,(HL)	12'b001001xxx110		pc	r210						pc			din	pc	4
21	BIT b,(IX+d)	12'b011001xxx110		pc		pc	din			tmp	pc			din	pc	5
22	BIT b,(IY+d)	12'b011101xxx110		pc		pc	din			tmp	pc			din	pc	5
23	BIT b,r	12'b001001xxxrrr		pc	r210						pc			din	pc	2
136	RES b,(HL)	12'b001010xxx110		pc	r210					hl	din		pc		pc	5
137	RES b,(IX+d)	12'b011010xxx110		pc		pc	din			tmp	din		pc		pc	6
138	RES b,(IY+d)	12'b011110xxx110		pc		pc	din			tmp	din		pc		pc	6
139	RES b,r	12'b001010xxxrrr		pc	r210					hl	din		pc		pc	2
174	SET b,(HL)	12'b001011xxx110		pc	r210						din		pc		pc	5

Figure 5-71. *ALU B* worksheet for the bit instructions.

Some of the shift and rotate cases are shown in Figure 5-72. Each case is nearly identical to the bit operations, except for the unique ALU operation for each different shift or rotate.

	Instruction	internal code	dec1	if2b	dec2	of1b	if3a	if3b	adr2	rd2a	rd2b	wr2a	wr2b	if1a	if1b	Mach State
144	RL (HL)	12'b001000010110		add	rl						rl		add		add	5
145	RL (IX+d)	12'b011000010110		add		add	ads			pass	rl		add		add	6
146	RL (IY+d)	12'b011100010110		add		add	ads			pass	rl		add		add	6
147	RL r	12'b001000010rrr		add	rl						rl		add		add	2
149	RLC (HL)	12'b001000000110		add	rlc						rlc		add		add	5
155	RR (HL)	12'b001000011110		add	rr						rr		add		add	5
160	RRC (HL)	12'b001000001110		add	rrc						rrc		add		add	5
178	SLA (HL)	12'b001000100110		add	sla						sla		add		add	5
182	SRA (HL)	12'b001000101110		add	sra						sra		add		add	5
186	SRL (HL)	12'b001000111110		add	srl						srl		add		add	5

Figure 5-72. *ALU Op* worksheet for some of the shift and rotate instructions.

Shift and rotate operations only have one operand, so the *ALU A* worksheet excerpt is almost empty for these instructions, as shown in Figure 5-73.

	Instruction	internal code	dec1	if2b	dec2	of1b	if3a	if3b	adr2	rd2a	rd2b	wr2a	wr2b	if1a	if1b	Mach State
144	RL (HL)	12'b001000010110		one									one		one	5
145	RL (IX+d)	12'b011000010110		one		one	ix						one		one	6
146	RL (IY+d)	12'b011100010110		one		one	iy						one		one	6
147	RL r	12'b001000010rrr		one									one		one	2
149	RLC (HL)	12'b001000000110		one									one		one	5
155	RR (HL)	12'b001000011110		one									one		one	5
160	RRC (HL)	12'b001000001110		one									one		one	5
178	SLA (HL)	12'b001000100110		one									one		one	5
182	SRA (HL)	12'b001000101110		one									one		one	5
186	SRL (HL)	12'b001000111110		one									one		one	5

Figure 5-73. *ALU A* worksheet for some of the shift and rotate instructions.

The ALU B worksheet excerpt shown in Figure 5-74 is pretty simple for these cases also. Like the Bit Test/Set/Reset instructions, I am able to do the address calculation during the *if3a* and *if3b* states.

	Instruction	internal code	dec1	if2b	dec2	of1b	if3a	if3b	adr2	rd2a	rd2b	wr2a	wr2b	if1a	if1b	Mach State
144	RL (HL)	12'b001000010110		pc	r210						din		pc		pc	5
145	RL (IX+d)	12'b011000010110		pc		pc	din			tmp	din		pc		pc	6
146	RL (IY+d)	12'b011100010110		pc		pc	din			tmp	din		pc		pc	6
147	RL r	12'b001000010rrr		pc	r210						din		pc		pc	2
149	RLC (HL)	12'b001000000110		pc	r210						din		pc		pc	5
155	RR (HL)	12'b001000011110		pc	r210						din		pc		pc	5
160	RRC (HL)	12'b001000001110		pc	r210						din		pc		pc	5
178	SLA (HL)	12'b001000100110		pc	r210						din		pc		pc	5
182	SRA (HL)	12'b001000101110		pc	r210						din		pc		pc	5
186	SRL (HL)	12'b001000111110		pc	r210						din		pc		pc	5

Figure 5-74. *ALU B* worksheet for some of the shift and rotate instructions.

The next *ALU Op*, *ALU A* and *ALU B* worksheet excerpts show the special rotate instructions, in Figure 5-75, Figure 5-76 and Figure 5-77 respectively. At this point I'm not sure that the dedicated *rla*, *rlca*, *rra* and *rrca* operations are really going to be required. I can always change this later during the implementation. The rotate digit instructions are expensive, with two dedicated ALU operations for each of the two instructions.

The *rld1* operation sends the lower nibble of the Data Input register concatenated with the lower nibble of the A register to the output of the ALU. This will be written back to memory. Then the *rld2* operation sends the upper nibble of the A register concatenated with the upper nibble of the Data Input register to the output of the ALU. This is written back to the A register. The net effect is the rotate left of a digit from memory into the lower nibble of the accumulator.

In the same way, the *rrd1* operation sends the lower nibble of the A register concatenated with the upper nibble of the Data Input register to the output of the ALU. This will be written back to memory. Then the *rrd2* operation sends the upper nibble of the A register concatenated with the lower nibble of the Data Input register to the output of the ALU. This is written back to the A register. The net effect is the rotate right of a digit from memory into the lower nibble of the accumulator.

	Instruction	internal code	dec1	if2b	dec2	adr2	rd2a	rd2b	wr2a	wr2b	if1a	if1b	Mach State
148	RLA	12'b000000010111	rla									add	1
153	RLCA	12'b000000000111	rlca									add	1
154	RLD	12'b1xxx01101111		add				rld1		add	rld2	add	5
159	RRA	12'b000000011111	rra									add	1
164	RRCA	12'b000000001111	rrca									add	1
165	RRD	12'b1xxx01100111		add				rrd1		add	rrd2	add	5

Figure 5-75. *ALU Op* worksheet for the special rotate instructions.

	Instruction	internal code	dec1	if2b	dec2	adr2	rd2a	rd2b	wr2a	wr2b	if1a	if1b	Mach State
148	RLA	12'b000000010111										one	1
153	RLCA	12'b000000000111										one	1
154	RLD	12'b1xxx01101111		one				a		one	a	one	5
159	RRA	12'b000000011111										one	1
164	RRCA	12'b000000001111										one	1
165	RRD	12'b1xxx01100111		one				a		one	a	one	5

Figure 5-76. *ALU A* worksheet for the special rotate instructions.

	Instruction	internal code	dec1	if2b	dec2	adr2	rd2a	rd2b	wr2a	wr2b	if1a	if1b	Mach State
148	RLA	`12'b000000010111`	a									pc	1
153	RLCA	`12'b000000000111`	a									pc	1
154	RLD	`12'b1xxx01101111`		pc				din		pc	din	pc	5
159	RRA	`12'b000000011111`	a									pc	1
164	RRCA	`12'b000000001111`	a									pc	1
165	RRD	`12'b1xxx01100111`		pc				din		pc	din	pc	5

Figure 5-77. *ALU B* worksheet for the special rotate instructions.

At first glance the 8-bit load *ALU Op* worksheet excerpt in Figure 5-78 is nothing special, because data just passes through the ALU. However, there are a number of byte-lane swapping issues to think about. The easiest assumption to make is that byte operations will always use the lower byte. This probably means byte-lane swapping on one of the ALU inputs and the ALU output, but this should reduce the possibility of error because of an oversight.

For example, the B, D and H registers want to normally reside on the high byte of the ALU input and the internal data bus for the cases where they are used to hold an address. The same is true of the A register when it is paired with the F register for a Push or Pop instruction. The I register also should be on the high byte so that it can be concatenated with the interrupt vector.

This byte swapping is not really amenable to control in the spreadsheet because I use register-select fields. This is something that I'll need to remember during the implementation, but it's easy because the rule is simple. The A, B, D, H, I and R registers always get swapped to the low byte.

In this worksheet I am assuming that the *pass* ALU operation passes the ALU B input directly to the ALU output, and this is the most common case. But because of the input loading issue I will also need to be able to pass the ALU A input directly to the output. This is the special *apas* identifier used I rows *94* and *95*.

	Instruction	internal code	dec1	if2b	dec2	of1b	of2a	of2b	adr1	adr2	rd2a	rd2b	wr2a	wr2b	if1a	if1b	Mach State
78	LD (BC),A	12'b000000000010	pass							pass				add		add	3
79	LD (DE),A	12'b000000010010	pass							pass				add		add	3
80	LD (HL),n	12'b000000110110				pass								add		add	3
81	LD (HL),r	12'b000001110rrr	pass							pass				add		add	3
82	LD (IX+d),n	12'b010000110110		add		add	ads	pass						add		add	5
83	LD (IX+d),r	12'b010001110rrr		add		add			ads	pass				add		add	5
84	LD (IY+d),n	12'b010100110110		add		add	ads	pass						add		add	5
85	LD (IY+d),r	12'b010101110rrr		add		add			ads	pass				add		add	5
86	LD (mn),A	12'b000000110010				add			pass	pass				add		add	5
91	LD A,(BC)	12'b000000001010	pass									add			pass	add	3
92	LD A,(DE)	12'b000000011010	pass									add			pass	add	3
93	LD A,(mn)	12'b000000111010				add			pass			add			pass	add	5
94	LD A,I	12'b1xxx01010111		add	apas											add	2
95	LD A,R	12'b1xxx01011111		add	apas											add	2
99	LD I,A	12'b1xxx01000111		add	pass											add	2
104	LD r,(HL)	12'b000001rrr110	pass									add		add	pass	add	3
105	LD r,(IX+d)	12'b010001rrr110		add		add			ads			add			pass	add	5
106	LD r,(IY+d)	12'b010101rrr110		add		add			ads			add			pass	add	5
107	LD R,A	12'b1xxx01001111		add	pass											add	2
108	LD r,n	12'b000000rrr110				add									pass	add	2
109	LD rd,rs	12'b000001rdrrsr	pass									add		add	pass	add	1

Figure 5-78. *ALU Op* worksheet for the byte load instructions.

There are only a couple of special cases for the *ALU A* worksheet for the 8-bit loads, having to do with the special *apas* operation. These cases are shown in Figure 5-79.

	Instruction	internal code	dec1	if2b	dec2	of1b	of2a	of2b	adr1	adr2	rd2a	rd2b	wr2a	wr2b	if1a	if1b	Mach State
94	LD A,I	12'b1xxx01010111		one	ii											one	2
95	LD A,R	12'b1xxx01011111		one	rr											one	2

Figure 5-79. *ALU A* worksheet for the special byte load instructions.

The only special cases in the *ALU B* worksheet for the 8-bit loads are for the instructions that use indirect addressing with the BC or DE registers. These cases are shown in Figure 5-80. Notice how the timing for the write cases works out nicely, with the address register accessed during one clock cycle and the data to be written accessed during the next clock cycle.

	Instruction	internal code	dec1	if2b	dec2	of1b	of2a	of2b	adr1	adr2	rd2a	rd2b	wr2a	wr2b	if1a	if1b	Mach State
78	LD (BC),A	12'b000000000010	bc							a				pc		pc	3
79	LD (DE),A	12'b000000010010	de							a				pc		pc	3
91	LD A,(BC)	12'b000000001010	bc									pc			din	pc	3
92	LD A,(DE)	12'b000000011010	de									pc			din	pc	3

Figure 5-80. *ALU B* worksheet for other special byte load instructions.

The *ALU Op* worksheet excerpt for 16-bit memory writes is shown in Figure 5-81. The only thing new here is the increment of the address between the first and second writes. This is the *add* identifier in the *wr1a* column.

The indexed addressing case is a bit of a problem here. I need the regular indexed address calculation for the first byte, but this same address incremented by one for the second byte. There are two ways to do this. I could do the calculation a second time and use the Carry-in to the ALU for the increment. Alternatively, I can store the original address in the temporary register and then increment it for the second byte. I will use the temporary register option to save power. For consistency in the group I'll do the same thing for the other cases even though it isn't necessary.

	Instruction	internal code	dec1	if2b	dec2	of1b	of2a	of2b	adr1	adr2	wr1a	wr1b	wr2a	wr2b	if1a	if1b	Mach State
87	LD (mn),HL	12'b000000100010				add			pass	pass	add	pass		add		add	6
88	LD (mn),IX	12'b010000100010		add		add			pass	pass	add	pass		add		add	7
89	LD (mn),IY	12'b010100100010		add		add			pass	pass	add	pass		add		add	7
90	LD (mn),ss	12'b1xxx01xx0011		add		add			pass	pass	add	pass		add		add	7

Figure 5-81. *ALU Op* worksheet for word memory write instructions.

There is nothing interesting about the *ALU A* worksheet for this case so I won't show it here. The *ALU B* worksheet excerpt is a different matter, though, and is shown in Figure 5-82. This shows the case where I do need to control the byte lane swapping explicitly, because the registers selected do not use the normal register-select bit field.

	Instruction	internal code	dec1	if2b	dec2	of1b	of2a	of2b	adr1	adr2	wr1a	wr1b	wr2a	wr2b	if1a	if1b	Mach State
87	LD (mn),HL	12'b000000100010				pc		pc	din	hl	tmp	h		pc		pc	6
88	LD (mn),IX	12'b010000100010		pc		pc		pc	din	ix	tmp	ixh		pc		pc	7
89	LD (mn),IY	12'b010100100010		pc		pc		pc	din	iy	tmp	iyh		pc		pc	7
90	LD (mn),ss	12'b1xxx01xx0011		pc		pc		pc	din	s54	tmp	s54h		pc		pc	7

Figure 5-82. *ALU B* worksheet for word memory write instructions.

The *ALU Op* worksheet excerpt in Figure 5-83, for 16-bit memory reads and 16-bit internal transfers, is basically the same as the previous example.

	Instruction	internal code	dec1	if2b	dec2	of1b	of2a	of2b	adr1	adr2	rd1a	rd1b	rd2a	rd2b	if1a	if1b	Mach State
96	LD dd,(mn)	12'b1xxx01xx1011		add		add			pass		add			add	pass	add	7
97	LD dd,mn	12'b000000xx0001				add		add							pass	add	3
98	LD HL,(mn)	12'b000000101010				add			pass		add			add	pass	add	6
100	LD IX,(mn)	12'b010000101010		add		add			pass		add			add	pass	add	7
101	LD IX,mn	12'b010000100001		add		add		add							pass	add	4
102	LD IY,(mn)	12'b010100101010		add		add			pass		add			add	pass	add	7
103	LD IY,mn	12'b010100100001		add		add		add							pass	add	4
110	LD SP,HL	12'b000011111001	pass													add	1
111	LD SP,IX	12'b010011111001		add	pass											add	2
112	LD SP,IY	12'b010111111001		add	pass											add	2

Figure 5-83. *ALU Op* worksheet for other word transfer instructions.

Again, it is easier to use the temporary register to hold the address for these instructions, as shown in Figure 5-84.

	Instruction	internal code	dec1	if2b	dec2	of1b	of2a	of2b	adr1	adr2	rd1a	rd1b	rd2a	rd2b	if1a	if1b	Mach State
96	LD dd,(mn)	12'b1xxx01xx1011		pc		pc		pc	din		tmp			pc	din	pc	7
97	LD dd,mn	12'b000000xx0001				pc		pc							din	pc	3
98	LD HL,(mn)	12'b000000101010				pc		pc	din		tmp			pc	din	pc	6
100	LD IX,(mn)	12'b010000101010		pc		pc		pc	din		tmp			pc	din	pc	7
101	LD IX,mn	12'b010000100001		pc		pc		pc							din	pc	4
102	LD IY,(mn)	12'b010100101010		pc		pc		pc	din		tmp			pc	din	pc	7

Figure 5-84. *ALU B* worksheet for other word transfer instructions.

The exchange instructions aren't much more complicated. I read the top of the stack into the data input register, write the CPU register to the top of the stack, and then update the CPU register.

The bank exchange instructions will use dedicated signals, so nothing special is needed in the spreadsheet. The 16-bit register exchange uses a separate direct connect for the DE register input, while the HL register input uses the normal path through the ALU. I chose the direct path for the DE register because the HL register is much more heavily used, and I didn't want to add any complexity to the HL register input. The Exchange instructions are shown in Figure 5-85.

	Instruction	internal code	dec1	if2b	dec2	adr2	rd1a	rd1b	rd2a	rd2b	wr1a	wr1b	wr2a	wr2b	if1a	if1b	Mach State
48	EX (SP),HL	12'b000011100011	add				add		pass	pass	add	pass		add	pass	add	6
49	EX (SP),IX	12'b010011100011		add			add		pass	pass	add	pass		add	pass	add	7
50	EX (SP),IY	12'b010111100011		add			add		pass	pass	add	pass		add	pass	add	7
51	EX AF,AF'	12'b000000001000														add	1
52	EX DE,HL	12'b000011101011	pass													add	1
53	EXX	12'b000011011001														add	1

Figure 5-85. *ALU Op* worksheet for the Exchange instructions.

Figure 5-86 shows that there is no need for the temporary register here. I can use the SP register directly to create the address for all four transactions.

	Instruction	internal code	dec1	if2b	dec2	adr2	rd1a	rd1b	rd2a	rd2b	wr1a	wr1b	wr2a	wr2b	if1a	if1b	Mach State
48	EX (SP),HL	12'b000011100011					sp		sp	hl	sp	h		pc	din	pc	6
49	EX (SP),IX	12'b010011100011		pc			sp		sp	ix	sp	ixh		pc	din	pc	7
50	EX (SP),IY	12'b010111100011		pc			sp		sp	iy	sp	iyh		pc	din	pc	7
51	EX AF,AF'	12'b000000001000														pc	1
52	EX DE,HL	12'b000011101011	de													pc	1
53	EXX	12'b000011011001														pc	1

Figure 5-86. *ALU B* worksheet for the Exchange instructions.

The *ALU Op* and *ALU A* worksheet excerpts for the Push and Pop instructions are shown in Figure 5-87 and Figure 5-88 respectively. The only difference between these instructions and the normal 16-bit read and write instructions is the update of the SP register.

	Instruction	internal code	dec1	if2b	dec2	adr2	rd1a	rd1b	rd2a	rd2b	wr1a	wr1b	wr2a	wr2b	if1a	if1b	Mach State
130	POP IX	12'b010011100001		add			add		add	add					pass	add	5
131	POP IY	12'b010111100001		add			add		add	add					pass	add	5
132	POP tt	12'b000011xx0001					add		add	add					pass	add	4
133	PUSH IX	12'b010011100101		add	add	pass					add	pass		add		add	5
134	PUSH IY	12'b010111100101		add	add	pass					add	pass		add		add	5
135	PUSH tt	12'b000011xx0101	add			pass					add	pass		add		add	4

Figure 5-87. *ALU Op* worksheet for the Push and Pop instructions.

	Instruction	internal code	dec1	if2b	dec2	adr2	rd1a	rd1b	rd2a	rd2b	wr1a	wr1b	wr2a	wr2b	if1a	if1b	Mach State
130	POP IX	12'b010011100001		one			one		one	one						one	5
131	POP IY	12'b010111100001		one			one		one	one						one	5
132	POP tt	12'b000011xx0001					one		one	one						one	4
133	PUSH IX	12'b010011100101		one	neg1						neg1			one		one	5
134	PUSH IY	12'b010111100101		one	neg1						neg1			one		one	5
135	PUSH tt	12'b000011xx0101	neg1								neg1			one		one	4

Figure 5-88. *ALU A* worksheet for the Push and Pop instructions.

As I have mentioned previously, the push instructions are unique because they write to the higher address first. To avoid this complication I could decrement the SP register by two for the first write, increment the address normally, and then perform another decrement of the SP register. It isn't clear which method is better, so I'll stick with the more intuitive sequence, shown in Figure 5-89.

	Instruction	internal code	dec1	if2b	dec2	adr2	rd1a	rd1b	rd2a	rd2b	wr1a	wr1b	wr2a	wr2b	if1a	if1b	Mach State
130	POP IX	12'b010011100001		pc			sp		sp	pc					din	pc	5
131	POP IY	12'b010111100001		pc			sp		sp	pc					din	pc	5
132	POP tt	12'b000011xx0001					sp		sp	pc					din	pc	4
133	PUSH IX	12'b010011100101		pc	sp	ixh					sp	ix		pc		pc	5
134	PUSH IY	12'b010111100101		pc	sp	iyh					sp	iy		pc		pc	5
135	PUSH tt	12'b000011xx0101	sp			z54h					sp	z54		pc		pc	4

Figure 5-89. *ALU B* worksheet for the Push and Pop instructions.

The Jump, Call and Restart instructions are shown in Figure 5-90. Whenever the operation is conditional it is critical that you always use the same order for the two cases on different worksheets. Here I am using the "not taken" case on the top and the "taken" case on the bottom, which is identical to how I specified the cases in the *Next State* worksheet.

	Instruction	internal code	dec1	if2b	dec2	of1b	of2a	of2b	adr2	wr1a	wr1b	wr2a	wr2b	pca	pco	if1a	if1b	Mach State
24	CALL f,mn	12'b000011fff100				add	add	add pass		add	pass	pass	add				add	5/3
25	CALL mn	12'b000011001101				add	add	pass		add	pass	pass	add				add	5
46	DJNZ j	12'b000000010000	badd			ads									add		add	3
71	JP (HL)	12'b000011101001	pass												add		add	2
72	JP (IX)	12'b010011101001		add	pass										add		add	3
73	JP (IY)	12'b010111101001		add	pass										add		add	3
74	JP f,mn	12'b000011fff010				add		add pass							add		add	4/3
75	JP mn	12'b000011000011				add		pass							add		add	4
76	JR cc,e	12'b0000001cc000				add ads									add		add	3/2
77	JR e	12'b000000011000				ads									add		add	3
166	RST v	12'b000011vvv111	add						pass	add	pass	apas	add				add	4

Figure 5-90. *ALU Op* worksheet for the Jump, Call and Restart instructions.

There are two special cases for the Jump, Call and Restart instructions, shown in Figure 5-91. Even though the conditional jump relative executes in the same number of machine cycles whether the branch is taken or not taken, the contents of the ALU A bus needs to be different. The second special case is the *apas* operation in row *166*. This is where the restart vector is output to the address register and loaded into the PC register. I place the restart vector on the ALU A input to help equalize the loading on the two ALU input buses.

	Instruction	internal code	dec1	if2b	dec2	of1b	of2a	of2b	adr2	wr1a	wr1b	wr2a	wr2b	pca	pco	if1a	if1b	Mach State
76	JR cc,e	12'b0000001cc000				one pc									one		one	3/2
166	RST v	12'b000011vvv111	neg1							neg1		rst	one				one	4

Figure 5-91. *ALU A* worksheet for the Jump, Call and Restart instructions.

The *ALU B* worksheet excerpt in Figure 5-92 shows similar conditional sources for the conditional call and jump instructions. I still have to do the byte alignment for the PC when it is pushed to the stack.

	Instruction	internal code	dec1	if2b	dec2	of1b	of2a	of2b	adr2	wr1a	wr1b	wr2a	wr2b	pca	pco	if1a	if1b	Mach State
24	CALL f,mn	`12'b000011fff100`				pc	sp	pc pch		sp	pc	din	pc				pc	5/3
25	CALL mn	`12'b000011001101`				pc	sp	pch		sp	pc	din	pc				pc	5
46	DJNZ j	`12'b000000010000`	b			din									pc		pc	3
71	JP (HL)	`12'b000011101001`	hl												pc		pc	2
72	JP (IX)	`12'b010011101001`		pc	ix										pc		pc	3
73	JP (IY)	`12'b010111101001`		pc	iy										pc		pc	3
74	JP f,mn	`12'b000011fff010`				pc		pc din							pc		pc	4/3
75	JP mn	`12'b000011000011`				pc		din							pc		pc	4
76	JR cc,e	`12'b0000001cc000`				pc din									pc		pc	3/2
77	JR e	`12'b000000011000`				din									pc		pc	3
166	RST v	`12'b000011vvv111`	sp						pch	sp	pc		pc				pc	4

Figure 5-92. *ALU B* worksheet for the Jump, Call and Restart instructions.

By this time the Return instructions in Figure 5-93 are unremarkable, except when you notice that only about half of the clock cycles use the ALU. This is one argument in favor of a one-clock machine cycle.

	Instruction	internal code	dec1	adr2	rd1a	rd1b	rd2a	rd2b	pca	pco	if1a	if1b	Mach State
140	RET	`12'b000011001001`			add		add	pass		add		add	5
141	RET f	`12'b000011fff000`			add		add	pass		add		add	5/1

Figure 5-93. *ALU Op* worksheet for the Return instructions.

The conditional Return instruction in Figure 5-94 doesn't require anything special in the ALU controls, because the not-taken cases skips all of the states used for the stack operations.

	Instruction	internal code	dec1	adr2	rd1a	rd1b	rd2a	rd2b	pca	pco	if1a	if1b	Mach State
140	RET	`12'b000011001001`			sp		sp	din		pc		pc	5
141	RET f	`12'b000011fff000`			sp		sp	din		pc		pc	5/1

Figure 5-94. *ALU B* worksheet for the Return instructions.

The ALU Op worksheet excerpt for the input and output instructions is shown in Figure 5-95. Note the *band* operation in one of the input instructions. This is required because this instruction sets the flags based on the input data. There isn't anything special about the *ALU A* worksheet for these instructions, so I won't show it here.

	Instruction	internal code	dec1	if2b	dec2	of1b	adr1	adr2	rd2a	rd2b	wr2a	wr2b	if1a	if1b	Mach State
58	IN A,(n)	12'b000011011011				add	pass			add				add	4
59	IN r,(C)	12'b1xxx01rrr000		add	pass					add			band	add	4
126	OUT (C),r	12'b1xxx01rrr001		add	pass			pass				add		add	4
127	OUT (n),A	12'b000011010011				add	pass	pass				add		add	4

Figure 5-95. *ALU Op* worksheet for the input and output instructions.

The ALU B worksheet excerpt for the input and output instructions in Figure 5-96 has two things worth noting. The input and output instructions using direct addressing place the contents of the A register on the high byte of the address bus and the immediate port address on the low byte of the address bus, and this requires a special case for the ALU B input.

In addition, the input and output instructions using indirect addressing use a different set of bits in the instruction to select the register, requiring a separate identifier.

	Instruction	internal code	dec1	if2b	dec2	of1b	adr1	adr2	rd2a	rd2b	wr2a	wr2b	if1a	if1b	Mach State
58	IN A,(n)	12'b000011011011				pc	io			pc				pc	4
59	IN r,(C)	12'b1xxx01rrr000		pc	bc					pc			din	pc	4
126	OUT (C),r	12'b1xxx01rrr001		pc	bc			r543				pc		pc	4
127	OUT (n),A	12'b000011010011				pc	io	a				pc		pc	4

Figure 5-96. *ALU B* worksheet for the input and output instructions.

The *ALU Op, ALU A* and *ALU B* worksheet excerpts in Figure 5-97, Figure 5-98 and Figure 5-99 show the block compare instructions.

In contrast with most of the previous cases, the majority of clock cycles here are used, because I need to update an address, update a byte count, and compare two bytes during each iteration.

	Instruction	internal code	dec1	if2b	dec2	adr2	rd1a	rd1b	rd2a	rd2b	blk1	blk2	pca	pco	if1a	if1b	Mach State
32	CPD	12'b1xxx10101001		add	pass	add		bsub		bsub	add	add	add	add		add	5
33	CPDR	12'b1xxx10111001		add	pass	add		bsub		bsub	add	add	add	add		add	4+2i
34	CPI	12'b1xxx10100001		add	pass	add		bsub		bsub	add	add	add	add		add	5
35	CPIR	12'b1xxx10110001		add	pass	add		bsub		bsub	add	add	add	add		add	4+2i

Figure 5-97. *ALU Op* worksheet for the block compare instructions.

The *pca* and *pco* states are used to finish up these instructions. The *pca* state just passes the PC register in the case of a normal completion. If one of these instructions is terminated early because of an interrupt, the PC register must be decremented by two so that the instruction will be fetched again and execution will continue after the interrupt is serviced.

	Instruction	internal code	dec1	if2b	dec2	adr2	rd1a	rd1b	rd2a	rd2b	blk1	blk2	pca	pco	if1a	if1b	Mach State
32	CPD	12'b1xxx10101001		one		neg1		a		a	neg1	one	neg2 zer	one		one	5
33	CPDR	12'b1xxx10111001		one		neg1		a		a	neg1	neg1	neg2 zer	one		one	4+2i
34	CPI	12'b1xxx10100001		one		neg1		a		a	one	one	neg2 zer	one		one	5
35	CPIR	12'b1xxx10110001		one		neg1		a		a	one	neg1	neg2 zer	one		one	4+2i

Figure 5-98. *ALU A* worksheet for the block compare instructions.

In the *ALU B* worksheet excerpt I select the HL register during the *rd1a* and *rd2a* states only to share the selection with the remainder of the block instructions.

	Instruction	internal code	dec1	if2b	dec2	adr2	rd1a	rd1b	rd2a	rd2b	blk1	blk2	pca	pco	if1a	if1b	Mach State
32	CPD	12'b1xxx10101001		pc	hl	bc	hl	din	hl	din	hl	pc	pc	pc		pc	5
33	CPDR	12'b1xxx10111001		pc	hl	bc	hl	din	hl	din	hl	bc	pc	pc		pc	4+2i
34	CPI	12'b1xxx10100001		pc	hl	bc	hl	din	hl	din	hl	pc	pc	pc		pc	5
35	CPIR	12'b1xxx10110001		pc	hl	bc	hl	din	hl	din	hl	bc	pc	pc		pc	4+2i

Figure 5-99. *ALU B* worksheet for the block compare instructions.

The *ALU Op* worksheet excerpt in Figure 5-100 shows that the remainder of the block instructions need nearly every single clock cycle available, because they need to do more operations for each iteration.

This efficiency is the reason that CISC machines tended to become more and more complex over time. This complexity required more time for design and verification though, which led to the development of RISC machines. In a RISC machine simple instructions could be combined by the compiler to build equivalents of these types of complex operations.

	Instruction	internal code	dec1	if2b	dec2	adr2	rd1a	rd1b	rd2a	rd2b	wr1a	wr1b	wr2a	wr2b	pca	pco	if1a	if1b	Mach State
69	INI	12'b1xxx10100010		add	pass	badd	pass	band	add	band	pass	add	pass	badd	add	add	add	add	5
70	INIR	12'b1xxx10110010		add	pass	badd	pass	band	add	band	pass	badd	pass	badd	add	add	add	add	4+2i
113	LDD	12'b1xxx10101000		add	pass	add	pass	pass	add	pass	add	add	add	add	add	add	add	add	5
114	LDDR	12'b1xxx10111000		add	pass	add	pass	pass	add	pass	add	add	add	add	add	add	add	add	4+2i
115	LDI	12'b1xxx10100000		add	pass	add	pass	pass	add	pass	add	add	add	add	add	add	add	add	5
116	LDIR	12'b1xxx10110000		add	pass	add	pass	pass	add	pass	add	add	add	add	add	add	add	add	4+2i
124	OTDR	12'b1xxx10111011		add	pass	band	pass	band	pass	band	add	badd	add	badd	add	add	badd	add	4+2i
128	OUTD	12'b1xxx10101011		add	pass	band	pass	band	pass	band	add	add	add	badd	add	add	badd	add	5

Figure 5-100. *ALU Op* worksheet for the block instructions.

Because these block instructions do both a read and a write, they don't need the special *blk1* and *blk2* states used by the block compare instructions. The *ALU A* worksheet for these cases is shown in Figure 5-101.

	Instruction	internal code	dec1	if2b	dec2	adr2	rd1a	rd1b	rd2a	rd2b	wr1a	wr1b	wr2a	wr2b	pca	pco	if1a	if1b	Mach State
69	INI	12'b1xxx10100010		one		neg1		neg1	one	neg1		one		neg1	neg2 zer	one	one	one	5
70	INIR	12'b1xxx10110010		one		neg1		neg1	one	neg1		neg1		neg1	neg2 zer	one	one	one	4+2i
113	LDD	12'b1xxx10101000		one		neg1			neg1		neg1	one	neg1	neg1	neg2 zer	one	neg1	one	5
114	LDDR	12'b1xxx10111000		one		neg1			neg1		neg1	neg1	neg1	neg1	neg2 zer	one	neg1	one	4+2i
115	LDI	12'b1xxx10100000		one		neg1			one		one	one	one	neg1	neg2 zer	one	one	one	5
116	LDIR	12'b1xxx10110000		one		neg1			one		one	neg1	one	neg1	neg2 zer	one	one	one	4+2i
124	OTDR	12'b1xxx10111011		one		neg1		neg1		neg1	neg1	neg1	neg1	neg1	neg2 zer	one	neg1	one	4+2i
128	OUTD	12'b1xxx10101011		one		neg1		neg1		neg1	neg1	one	neg1	neg1	neg2 zer	one	neg1	one	5

Figure 5-101. *ALU A* worksheet for the block instructions.

But here the *ALU B* input cases shown in Figure 5-102 are more complex, because the I/O block instructions use different register for the I/O address and a byte register for the loop counter.

	Instruction	internal code	dec1	if2b	dec2	adr2	rd1a	rd1b	rd2a	rd2b	wr1a	wr1b	wr2a	wr2b	pca	pco	if1a	if1b	Mach State
69	INI	12'b1xxx10100010		pc	bc	b	hl	din	hl	din	bc	pc	bc	b	pc	pc	hl	pc	5
70	INIR	12'b1xxx10110010		pc	bc	b	hl	din	hl	din	bc	b	bc	b	pc	pc	hl	pc	4+2i
113	LDD	12'b1xxx10101000		pc	hl	bc	de	din	de	din	hl	pc	hl	bc	pc	pc	de	pc	5
114	LDDR	12'b1xxx10111000		pc	hl	bc	de	din	de	din	hl	bc	hl	bc	pc	pc	de	pc	4+2i
115	LDI	12'b1xxx10100000		pc	hl	bc	de	din	de	din	hl	pc	hl	bc	pc	pc	de	pc	5
116	LDIR	12'b1xxx10110000		pc	hl	bc	de	din	de	din	hl	bc	hl	bc	pc	pc	de	pc	4+2i
124	OTDR	12'b1xxx10111011		pc	hl	b	bc	din	bc	din	hl	b	hl	b	pc	pc	b	pc	4+2i
128	OUTD	12'b1xxx10101011		pc	hl	b	bc	din	bc	din	hl	pc	hl	b	pc	pc	b	pc	5

Figure 5-102. *ALU B* worksheet for the block instructions.

Up to now the choice and sequence of ALU operations should have been fairly obvious, but you're probably wondering how I came up with the sequence of operations for the block instructions. It turns out that the sequence is completely determined by the order of the machine cycles. I know that the sequence has to be a read followed immediately by a write, in a loop, and that constrains where the address and data will need to be available. I'll go though the sequence to show what I mean.

In the *dec2* state I need to *pass* the address for the first read and in the *rd1a* state I need to *pass* the address for the first write. Remember that the ALU controls are registered, so this means that these addresses are on the internal bus during the *adr2* and *rd1b* states, ready to be sampled at the end of these states. Continuing with the address requirements, during the *wr1a* state I need to *add* (increment or decrement) or *pass* the address for the second read. Then during the *rd2a* state I need to *add* (increment or decrement) or *pass* the address for the second write. Since the loop continues with the sequence *rd2a*, *rd2b*, *wr2a* and *wr2b*, you can see how both addresses are updated and output to the external address bus.

The read data is loaded into the data input register at the end of the *rd1b* and *rd2b* states, so the pass operation is required during these states to have the data available during the *wr1a* and *wr2a* states to be driven on the external data bus at the end of those states. That leaves just the *wr1b* and *wr2b* states for the decrement of the loop counter.

For the single-transfer versions of the instructions I can use the *wr1b* state to *pass* the PC register in preparation for the next instruction fetch. Although it isn't shown here (refer back to the *Next State* worksheet) the repeating versions test for an interrupt pending during the *wr1b* and *wr2b* states will exit the loop and proceed to the *pca* and *pco* states if an interrupt is pending. This will also happen if the loop count decrements to zero.

If you think about the timing, you'll realize that the loop count decrement appears to happen too late to be tested during the *wr1b* and *wr2b* states. In reality the loop count decrement that is occurring at during these states is for the next transfer that will happen. This is why there is a loop count decrement during the *adr2* state. The loop count decrement actually happens before the corresponding transfer occurs.

This illustrates why it is so important to start with the *Operation* and *Next State* worksheets. Once you have a good guess at the state sequence and the operations required, it becomes fairly easy to work backwards to determine the sequence of internal operations.

Only one of the interrupt-related instructions in the *ALU Op* worksheet excerpt in Figure 5-103 requires anything out of the ordinary, so I'll only show the *ALU A* and *ALU B* excerpts for that case. I have to remember that the *hlta* and *hltb* states are not shown in the worksheets, but the *hlta* state does need to sample interrupts. The *pass* identifier in the *dec1* state of line *54* is not necessary for that instruction, and is only there to simplify the decoding for similar opcodes.

	Instruction	internal code	dec1	if2b	dec2	adr2	rd1a	rd1b	rd2a	rd2b	pca	pco	if1a	if1b	Mach State
45	DI	12'b000011110011												add	1
47	EI	12'b000011111011												add	1
54	HALT	12'b000001110110	pass									add		add	3
55	IM 0	12'b1xxx01000110		add										add	2
56	IM 1	12'b1xxx01010110		add										add	2
57	IM 2	12'b1xxx01011110		add										add	2
142	RETI	12'b1xxx01001101		add	pass		add		add	pass		add		add	6
143	RETN	12'b1xxx01000101		add	pass		add		add	pass		add		add	6

Figure 5-103. *ALU Op* worksheet for the interrupt-related instructions.

The Halt instruction in row *54* is basically just a "wait-for-interrupt" instruction, but since I am implementing the bus request like an interrupt, I need some special handling in the case of a bus request. Normally the Halt instruction will resume execution with the next instruction after an interrupt. But a bus request during the Halt instruction should do nothing as far as the machine state is concerned. I'll need to remember this special case when I implement the logic for the interrupts and bus request.

As I mentioned back in the *Next State* worksheet, the interrupt acknowledge cycle uses the special *inta* and *intb* states, which are not shown in the spreadsheet. The *intb* state needs to load the contents of the I register concatenated with interrupt vector data bus contents into the temporary register. This is required so that the resulting address will be available for the *rd1a* state.

If vectored interrupts are enabled, the entire sequence shown in Figure 5-104 is executed, but if no vector is used the *intb* state goes directly to the *wr1a* state to push the contents of the PC register to the stack. I use the ALU A input and an *apas* identifier to load the PC register after the stack has been written. All of this requires manual work, but I prefer not to have single-use columns in the spreadsheet.

	Instruction	internal code	adr1	adr2	rd1a	rd1b	rd2a	rd2b	wr1a	wr1b	wr2a	wr2b	if1a	if1b	Mach State
200	ZINTACK	`12'b0001xxxxxxxx`	pass		add		add	pass	add	pass	apas	add		add	5

	Instruction	internal code	adr1	adr2	rd1a	rd1b	rd2a	rd2b	wr1a	wr1b	wr2a	wr2b	if1a	if1b	Mach State
200	ZINTACK	`12'b0001xxxxxxxx`			one		neg1		neg1		int	one		one	5

	Instruction	internal code	adr1	adr2	rd1a	rd1b	rd2a	rd2b	wr1a	wr1b	wr2a	wr2b	if1a	if1b	Mach State
200	ZINTACK	`12'b0001xxxxxxxx`	tmp		tmp		sp	pch	sp	pc		pc		pc	5

Figure 5-104. *ALU Op, ALU A* and *ALU B* worksheets for the interrupt acknowledge sequence.

That takes care of all of the *ALU Op, ALU A* and *ALU B* worksheets except for the NOP instruction. I won't bother showing excerpts for this instruction here, because it is pretty boring.

Table 5-17 shows the definitions of the identifiers used in the *ALU Op* worksheet. The Word or Byte designation controls the source for the Flag results.

Identifier	Meaning
add	Word: Add
badd	Byte: Add
bdec	Byte: Add (but invert the Carry and Half-Carry)
ads	Word: Add (ALU B[7:0] sign-extended to sixteen bits)
adc	Word: Add With Carry
badc	Byte: Add With Carry
sub	Word: Subtract (ALU A - ALU B)
bsub	Byte: Subtract (ALU A - ALU B)
sbc	Word: Subtract With Carry (ALU A - ALU B - Carry Flag)
bsbc	Byte: Subtract With Carry (ALU A - ALU B - Carry Flag)
daa	Byte: Decimal Adjust Accumulator (actually a Byte Add)
pass	Word: Pass B Input
band	Byte: Logical AND
bor	Byte: Logical OR
bxor	Byte: Logical XOR
ccf	Complement Carry Flag.
scf	Set Carry Flag
rld1	Rotate Left Digit, for memory write
rld2	Rotate Left Digit, for Accumulator write
rrd1	Rotate Right Digit, for memory write
rrd2	Rotate Right Digit, for Accumulator write
apas	Word: Pass A Input
rl	Byte: Rotate Left
rla	Byte: Rotate Left Accumulator
rlc	Byte: Rotate Left Circular
rlca	Byte: Rotate Left Circular Accumulator
rr	Byte: Rotate Right
rra	Byte: Rotate Right Accumulator
rrc	Byte: Rotate Right Circular
rrca	Byte: Rotate Right Circular Accumulator
sla	Byte: Shift Left Arithmetic
srl	Byte: Shift Right Logical
sra	Byte: Shift Right Arithmetic

Table 5-17. *ALU Op worksheet identifier definitions.*

Table 5-18 shows the definitions of the identifiers used in the *ALU A* worksheet. For byte values the most-significant byte is all zeros. The advantage of an accumulator-based machine is that only a few registers need to be available on one of the ALU inputs.

Identifier	Meaning
zer	Zero, 0x0000
one	One, 0x0001
neg1	Negative One, 0xFFFF
neg2	Negative Two, 0xFFFE
hl	HL Register
ix	IX Register
iy	IY Register
pc	PC Register
a	Accumulator (byte, on the lsb)
bit	Bit Mask (byte, on the lsb)
daa	Decimal Adjust Accumulator Constant (byte, on the lsb)
i	I Register (byte, on the lsb)
r	R Register (byte, on the lsb)
int	Interrupt Vector: I Register concatenated with byte vector
rst	Restart Vector

Table 5-18. *ALU A* worksheet identifier definitions.

Table 5-19 shows the definitions of the identifiers used to in the *ALU B* worksheet. For byte values the most-significant byte is all zeros. Several of the identifiers need to be manually expanded into individual identifiers. Even though it looks like there are a large number of cases, in reality there are only twenty-five unique cases. This compares well with the sixteen unique cases for the *ALU A* worksheet.

Identifier	Meaning
a	A Register (byte, on the lsb)
bc	BC Register
b	B Register (byte, on the lsb)
de	DE Register
hl	HL Register
h	H register (byte, on the lsb)
ix	IX Register
ixh	IX Register msb (byte, on the lsb)
iy	IY Register
iyh	IY Register msb (byte, on the lsb)
sp	SP Register
pc	PC Register
pch	PC Register msb (byte, on the lsb)
din	Data Input Register
tmp	Temporary Register
r210	3-bit field with the following definition: (all byte, on the lsb) 000: B Register 001: C Register 010: D Register 011: E Register 100: H Register 101: L Register 111: A Register
r543	3-bit field with the following definition: (all byte, on the lsb) 000: B Register 001: C Register 010: D Register 011: E Register 100: H Register 101: L Register 111: A Register
s54	2-bit field with the following definition: 00: BC Register 01: DE Register 10: HL Register 11: SP Register
s54h	2-bit field with the following definition: (all byte, on the lsb) 00: B Register 01: D Register 10: H Register 11: SP Register msb

x54	2-bit field with the following definition: 00: BC Register 01: DE Register 10: IX Register 11: SP Register
x54h	2-bit field with the following definition: (all byte, on the lsb) 00: B Register 01: D Register 10: IX Register msb 11: SP Register msb
y54	2-bit field with the following definition: 00: BC Register 01: DE Register 10: IY Register 11: SP Register
y54h	2-bit field with the following definition: (all byte, on the lsb) 00: B Register 01: D Register 10: IY Register msb 11: SP Register msb
z54	2-bit field with the following definition: 00: BC Register 01: DE Register 10: HL Register 11: AF Register
z54h	2-bit field with the following definition: (all byte, on the lsb) 00: B Register 01: D Register 10: H Register 11: A Register

Table 5-19. *ALU B* worksheet identifier definitions.

The *ALU Op*, *ALU A* and *ALU B* worksheets contain most of the information necessary to design the data path for the CPU, but there are still a number of details that I'll have to work out when I start coding. For example, generating the *daa* adjust value, the *rst* vector and the *bit* mask value. I also need to make sure that the byte lane shuffling on the ALU input and output is done correctly. From the point of view of the spreadsheet these are all implementation details.

At this point it all that remains are the worksheets for the Flags and the register writes. I usually do the *Register Wr* worksheet next, because it's slightly more complicated than the flag worksheets. I usually use the *ALU Op* worksheet as the starting point for all of the remaining worksheets, because it clearly shows where I need to be writing a register or a flag.

The *Register Wr* Worksheet

The *Register Wr* worksheet is a nice change after the three ALU worksheets. After all, most instructions only write once to a register, and some don't write at all. In addition, those instructions that do write to a register usually do so in the last clock cycle of the instruction. The register write controls do not need to be registered, because there is a full clock cycle for them to settle.

Just like an accumulator-based machine simplified the ALU inputs, such a machine also simplifies the required options when writing to a register. I'll show the case of a complete instruction, and then only go through the interesting or special cases.

The *Register Wr* worksheet excerpt for the Add instructions is shown in Figure 5-105. Register writes occur only during the last clock of the instruction, and only to a limited set of registers.

	Instruction	internal code	dec1	if2b	dec2	of1b	adr1	adr2	rd2a	rd2b	if1a	if1b	Mach State
7	ADD A,(HL)	12'b000010000110										a	3
8	ADD A,(IX+d)	12'b010010000110										a	5
9	ADD A,(IY+d)	12'b010110000110										a	5
10	ADD A,n	12'b000011000110										a	2
11	ADD A,r	12'b000010000rrr										a	1
12	ADD HL,ss	12'b000000xx1001										hl	1
13	ADD IX,xx	12'b010000xx1001										ix	2
14	ADD IY,yy	12'b010100xx1001										iy	2

Figure 5-105. *Register Wr* worksheet for the Add instructions.

The Compare and Subtract instructions are essentially the same as the Add instruction case, but the Decrement and Increment instructions add something new, as shown in Figure 5-106. This is one case where any register can be affected by the instruction, and I use a single identifier just as I did in the *ALU B* worksheet. In addition, I write the computed address to the temporary register rather than doing the computation again.

You might be tempted to just inhibit the write to the address register. After all, this is a read-modify-write operation to the same address. I actually did this once in a design, but it ended up being more trouble than it was worth. The problem is that you need some kind of signal that marks the start of a bus transaction to generate Wait states, and the address register load signal works perfectly for this function. That is, unless there isn't always an address register load signal present before the start of a bus transaction. So now I just use a temporary register.

	Instruction	internal code	dec1	if2b	dec2	of1b	adr1	adr2	rd2a	rd2b	wr2a	wr2b	if1a	if1b	Mach State
38	DEC (HL)	12'b000000110101													4
39	DEC (IX+d)	12'b010000110101						tmp							6
40	DEC (IY+d)	12'b010100110101						tmp							6
41	DEC IX	12'b010000101011												ix	2
42	DEC IY	12'b010100101011												iy	2
43	DEC r	12'b000000rrr101												r543	1
44	DEC ss	12'b000000xx1011												s54	1

Figure 5-106. *Register Wr worksheet for the Decrement instructions.*

The next new cases are for the Bit Set and Bit Reset instructions shown in the *Register Wr* worksheet excerpt in Figure 5-107. The temporary register is again loaded with the calculated address and a new 3-bit field selects the destination register.

	Instruction	internal code	dec1	if2b	dec2	of1b	if3a	if3b	adr2	rd2a	rd2b	wr2a	wr2b	if1a	if1b	Mach State
136	RES b,(HL)	12'b001010xxx110														5
137	RES b,(IX+d)	12'b011010xxx110						tmp								6
138	RES b,(IY+d)	12'b011110xxx110						tmp								6
139	RES b,r	12'b001010xxxrrr													r210	2
174	SET b,(HL)	12'b001011xxx110														5
175	SET b,(IX+d)	12'b011011xxx110						tmp								6
176	SET b,(IY+d)	12'b011111xxx110						tmp								6
177	SET b,r	12'b001011xxxrrr													r210	2

Figure 5-107. *Register Wr* worksheet for the Bit Set and Bit Reset instructions.

Only the writes to the I register and the R register are new in the worksheet excerpt shown in Figure 5-108.

	Instruction	internal code	dec1	if2b	dec2	of1b	of2a	of2b	adr1	adr2	rd2a	rd2b	if1a	if1b	Mach State
91	LD A,(BC)	12'b000000001010												a	3
92	LD A,(DE)	12'b000000011010												a	3
93	LD A,(mn)	12'b000000111010												a	5
94	LD A,I	12'b1xxx01010111												a	2
95	LD A,R	12'b1xxx01011111												a	2
99	LD I,A	12'b1xxx01000111												i	2
104	LD r,(HL)	12'b000001rrr110												r543	3
105	LD r,(IX+d)	12'b010001rrr110												r543	5
106	LD r,(IY+d)	12'b010101rrr110												r543	5
107	LD R,A	12'b1xxx01001111												r	2
108	LD r,n	12'b000000rrr110												r543	2
109	LD rd,rs	12'b000001rdrrsr												r543	1

Figure 5-108. *Register Wr* worksheet for several byte Load instructions.

Up to this point I've only had to write to 8-bit registers, but the worksheet excerpt in Figure 5-109 shows some of the 16-bit writes that will be required. In the original Z80 16-bit writes took two clock cycles, because the internal data path was only eight bits wide, but I am avoiding that bottleneck.

	Instruction	internal code	dec1	if2b	dec2	of1b	of2a	of2b	adr1	adr2	rd1a	rd1b	rd2a	rd2b	if1a	if1b	Mach State
96	LD dd,(mn)	12'b1xxx01xx1011								tmp						d54	7
97	LD dd,mn	12'b000000xx0001														d54	3
98	LD HL,(mn)	12'b000000101010								tmp						hl	6
100	LD IX,(mn)	12'b010000101010								tmp						ix	7
101	LD IX,mn	12'b010000100001														ix	4
102	LD IY,(mn)	12'b010100101010								tmp						iy	7
103	LD IY,mn	12'b010100100001														iy	4
110	LD SP,HL	12'b000011111001														sp	1
111	LD SP,IX	12'b010011111001														sp	2
112	LD SP,IY	12'b010111111001														sp	2

Figure 5-109. *Register Wr* worksheet for several word Load instructions.

The *Register Wr* worksheet excerpt in Figure 5-110 shows the Exchange instructions. The *dehl* case is going to require some care to implement. It is the one special instance where I need to write to two registers in the same clock cycle. Remember that the register bank exchanges only toggle an enable bit and don't actually move any data. That's why there are no register writes for these instructions.

	Instruction	internal code	dec1	if2b	dec2	adr2	rd1a	rd1b	rd2a	rd2b	wr1a	wr1b	wr2a	wr2b	if1a	if1b	Mach State
48	EX (SP),HL	12'b000011100011														hl	6
49	EX (SP),IX	12'b010011100011														ix	7
50	EX (SP),IY	12'b010111100011														iy	7
51	EX AF,AF'	12'b000000001000															1
52	EX DE,HL	12'b000011101011														dehl	1
53	EXX	12'b000011011001															1

Figure 5-110. *Register Wr* worksheet for the Exchange instructions.

The Push and Pop instructions are the first instructions that write to something other than the temporary register in the middle of execution. The timing of the writes to the SP register in Figure 5-111 clearly show the pre-decrement operation for the Push instruction and the post-increment operation for the Pop instruction.

	Instruction	internal code	dec1	if2b	dec2	adr2	rd1a	rd1b	rd2a	rd2b	wr1a	wr1b	wr2a	wr2b	if1a	if1b	Mach State
130	POP IX	12'b010011100001						sp		sp						ix	5
131	POP IY	12'b010111100001						sp		sp						iy	5
132	POP tt	12'b000011xx0001						sp		sp						z54	4
133	PUSH IX	12'b010011100101				sp						sp					5
134	PUSH IY	12'b010111100101				sp						sp					5
135	PUSH tt	12'b000011xx0101				sp						sp					4

Figure 5-111. *Register Wr* worksheet for the Push and Pop instructions.

The conditional Call instruction is the only case where the write of a register is conditional, and that's only because of where I have chosen to make the taken/not taken decision. The DJNZ instruction timing dictates that the B register be decremented very early so that the taken/not taken decision can be made in the *pca* state. These cases are shown in Figure 5-112.

	Instruction	internal code	dec1	of1b	of2a	of2b	wr1a	wr1b	wr2a	wr2b	pca	pco	if1a	if1b	Mach State
24	CALL f,mn	12'b000011fff100				null sp		sp							5/3
25	CALL mn	12'b000011001101				sp		sp							5
46	DJNZ j	12'b000000010000		b											3

Figure 5-112. *Register Wr* worksheet for some branch instructions.

As usual, the block move instructions are the most complex, as shown in the *Register Wr* worksheet excerpt in Figure 5-113. The register writes during the *if1b* state are required to compensate for the location of the corresponding writes during the loop operation. Otherwise the contents of those registers will be off by one when these instructions resume or finish.

	Instruction	internal code	dec1	if2b	dec2	adr2	rd1a	rd1b	rd2a	rd2b	wr1a	wr1b	wr2a	wr2b	pca	pco	if1a	if1b	Mach State
67	IND	12'b1xxx10101010					b		b	hl								hl	5
68	INDR	12'b1xxx10111010					b		b	hl								hl	4+2i
69	INI	12'b1xxx10100010					b		b	hl								hl	5
70	INIR	12'b1xxx10110010					b		b	hl								hl	4+2i
113	LDD	12'b1xxx10101000					bc		bc	de		hl		hl				de	5
114	LDDR	12'b1xxx10111000					bc		bc	de		hl		hl				de	4+2i
115	LDI	12'b1xxx10100000					bc		bc	de		hl		hl				de	5
116	LDIR	12'b1xxx10110000					bc		bc	de		hl		hl				de	4+2i
124	OTDR	12'b1xxx10111011					b		b			hl		hl				b	4+2i
125	OTIR	12'b1xxx10110011					b		b			hl		hl				b	4+2i
128	OUTD	12'b1xxx10101011					b		b			hl		hl				b	5
129	OUTI	12'b1xxx10100011					b		b			hl		hl				b	5

Figure 5-113. *Register Wr* worksheet for the block move instructions.

The *Register Wr* worksheet contents are used for both the write enable and the register select, so blank un-shaded cells are important. That is why there are blank cells in the worksheet excerpt for the block move instructions.

The definitions of the identifiers used to in the *Register Wr* worksheet are shown in Table 5-20. A few of the identifiers need to be manually expanded into individual identifiers.

Identifier	Meaning
a	A Register
bc	BC Register
b	B Register
de	DE Register
hl	HL Register
ix	IX Register
iy	IY Register
sp	SP Register
pc	PC Register
tmp	Temporary Register
i	I Register
r	R Register
dehl	DE Register and HL Register
r210	3-bit field with the following definition: 000: B Register 001: C Register 010: D Register 011: E Register 100: H Register 101: L Register 111: A Register
r543	3-bit field with the following definition: 000: B Register 001: C Register 010: D Register 011: E Register 100: H Register 101: L Register 111: A Register
d54	3-bit field with the following definition: 00: BC Register 01: DE Register 10: HL Register 11: SP Register
s54	2-bit field with the following definition: 00: BC Register 01: DE Register 10: HL Register 11: SP Register
z54	2-bit field with the following definition: 00: BC Register 01: DE Register 10: HL Register 11: AF Register

Table 5-20. *Register Wr* worksheet identifier definitions.

The *S flag* Worksheet

The *S flag* worksheet is very simple, because the Sign flag is only used to hold the most-significant bit of an arithmetic result. Since I plan to control the byte/word operation via the *ALU Op* identifiers this worksheet only controls the enable for the load of the Sign flag. The *S flag* worksheet excerpt in Figure 5-114 shows the Add instruction cases.

	Instruction	internal code	dec1	if2b	dec2	of1b	adr1	adr2	rd2a	rd2b	if1a	if1b	Mach State
7	ADD A,(HL)	12'b000010000110										s	3
8	ADD A,(IX+d)	12'b010010000110										s	5
9	ADD A,(IY+d)	12'b010110000110										s	5
10	ADD A,n	12'b000011000110										s	2
11	ADD A,r	12'b000010000rrr										s	1
12	ADD HL,ss	12'b000000xx1001											1
13	ADD IX,xx	12'b010000xx1001											2
14	ADD IY,yy	12'b010100xx1001											2

Figure 5-114. *S flag* worksheet for the Add instructions.

I won't show any other cases from the worksheet because none of them are in any way special. The definition of the identifier used to in the *S flag* worksheet in Table 5-21 is also straightforward.

Identifier	Meaning
s	Load the Sign flag with the most-significant bit of the arithmetic result.

Table 5-21. *S Flag* worksheet identifier definitions.

The *Z flag* Worksheet

The *Z flag* worksheet is also very simple, because the Zero flag is only used to hold the result for a test for all zeros. As in the case of the Sign flag, this worksheet only controls the enable for the load of the Zero flag. The *Z flag* worksheet excerpt in Figure 5-115 shows the Add instruction cases.

	Instruction	internal code	dec1	if2b	dec2	of1b	adr1	adr2	rd2a	rd2b	if1a	if1b	Mach State
7	ADD A,(HL)	12'b000010000110										z	3
8	ADD A,(IX+d)	12'b010010000110										z	5
9	ADD A,(IY+d)	12'b010110000110										z	5
10	ADD A,n	12'b000011000110										z	2
11	ADD A,r	12'b000010000rrr										z	1
12	ADD HL,ss	12'b000000xx1001											1
13	ADD IX,xx	12'b010000xx1001											2
14	ADD IY,yy	12'b010100xx1001											2

Figure 5-115. *Z flag* worksheet for the Add instructions.

I won't show any other cases from the worksheet because none of them are in any way special. The *Z flag* worksheet is not quite identical to the *S flag* worksheet, because there are a few cases where only the Zero flag is loaded. The definition of the identifier used to in the *Z flag* worksheet in Table 5-22 is also straightforward.

Identifier	Meaning
z	Load the Z Flag with the result of a test for all zeros.

Table 5-22. *Z Flag* worksheet identifier definitions.

The *H flag* Worksheet

The *H flag* worksheet is a little more complex that the previous two worksheets, because the Half-Carry flag has several uses. So this worksheet controls both the enable for the load of the Half-Carry flag as well as the source for this flag. The *H flag* worksheet excerpt in Figure 5-116 shows the Add instruction cases.

	Instruction	internal code	dec1	if2b	dec2	of1b	adr1	adr2	rd2a	rd2b	if1a	if1b	Mach State
7	ADD A,(HL)	12'b000010000110										h	3
8	ADD A,(IX+d)	12'b010010000110										h	5
9	ADD A,(IY+d)	12'b010110000110										h	5
10	ADD A,n	12'b000011000110										h	2
11	ADD A,r	12'b000010000rrr										h	1
12	ADD HL,ss	12'b000000xx1001										h	1
13	ADD IX,xx	12'b010000xx1001										h	2
14	ADD IY,yy	12'b010100xx1001										h	2

Figure 5-116. *H flag* worksheet for the Add instructions.

These are the normal functions for the Half-Carry flag, which is also the case for the subtract, byte decrement and byte increment instructions. But the logical functions are different, as shown in the *H flag* worksheet excerpt in Figure 5-117.

	Instruction	internal code	dec1	if2b	dec2	of1b	adr1	adr2	rd2a	rd2b	if1a	if1b	Mach State
15	AND (HL)	12'b000010100110										1	3
16	AND (IX+d)	12'b010010100110										1	5
17	AND (IY+d)	12'b010110100110										1	5
18	AND n	12'b000011100110										1	2
19	AND r	12'b000010100rrr										1	1
119	OR (HL)	12'b000010110110										0	3
120	OR (IX+d)	12'b010010110110										0	5
121	OR (IY+d)	12'b010110110110										0	5
122	OR n	12'b000011110110										0	2
123	OR r	12'b000010110rrr										0	1
195	XOR (HL)	12'b000010101110										0	3
196	XOR (IX+d)	12'b010010101110										0	5
197	XOR (IY+d)	12'b010110101110										0	5
198	XOR n	12'b000011101110										0	2
199	XOR r	12'b000010101rrr										0	1

Figure 5-117. *H flag* worksheet for the logical instructions.

In reality, this behavior probably fell out of the logic design in the original Z80, rather than serving any useful purpose, but I want to remain compatible so I need to match the behavior.

The special arithmetic instructions really are special when it comes to the Half-Carry flag, as shown in the *H flag* worksheet excerpt in Figure 5-118. The Complement Carry Flag (CCF) instruction copies the current state of the Carry flag into the Half-Carry flag. I'll use a separate identifier here to remind myself of this fact, but I expect to generate it automatically in the ALU. The specification for the Decimal Adjust Accumulator (DAA) instruction appears messy at first glance, but when I analyze it carefully I find that it is just the normal Half-Carry functionality.

	Instruction	internal code	dec1	if2b	dec2	if1b	Mach State
26	CCF	12'b000000111111				c	1
36	CPL	12'b000000101111				1	1
37	DAA	12'b000000100111				h	1
117	NEG	12'b1xxx01000100				h	2
173	SCF	12'b000000110111				0	1

Figure 5-118. *H flag* worksheet for the special arithmetic instructions.

For some reason the Bit Test instructions affect the Half-Carry flag, while the Bit Set and Bit Reset instructions do not. The Bit Test cases are shown in Figure 5-119.

	Instruction	internal code	dec1	if2b	dec2	of1b	if3a	if3b	adr2	rd2a	rd2b	if1a	if1b	Mach State
20	BIT b,(HL)	12'b001001xxx110											1	4
21	BIT b,(IX+d)	12'b011001xxx110											1	5
22	BIT b,(IY+d)	12'b011101xxx110											1	5
23	BIT b,r	12'b001001xxxrrr											1	2

Figure 5-119. *H flag* worksheet for the Bit Test instructions.

All of the rotate and shift instructions, including the special ones, clear the Half-Carry flag. I show a small excerpt of the *H flag* worksheet in Figure 5-120 to illustrate where during the execution of the instruction I have chosen to clear the flag. I am expecting that loading the Half-Carry flag at the same time that I do the ALU operation will save a bit of logic.

	Instruction	internal code	dec1	if2b	dec2	of1b	if3a	if3b	adr2	rd2a	rd2b	wr2a	wr2b	if1a	if1b	Mach State
144	RL (HL)	12'b001000010110										0				5
145	RL (IX+d)	12'b011000010110										0				6
146	RL (IY+d)	12'b011100010110										0				6
147	RL r	12'b001000010rrr										0			0	2

Figure 5-120. *H flag* worksheet for some rotate instructions.

For some reason two of the special 8-bit loads clear the Half-Carry flag. This is shown in Figure 5-121, and is probably another case of the functionality falling out of the logic design of the original Z80.

	Instruction	internal code	dec1	if2b	dec2	if1b	Mach State
94	LD A,I	12'b1xxx01010111				0	2
95	LD A,R	12'b1xxx01011111				0	2

Figure 5-121. *H flag* worksheet for some special load instructions.

There are a few more cases where instructions affect the Half-Carry flag, but there is nothing unique about them so I won't bother to show them here. The definitions of the identifiers used in the *H flag* worksheet are shown below.

Identifier	Meaning
h	Load the H flag with the carry out of bit 4 (byte operation) or bit 12 (word operation).
0	Clear the H flag.
1	Set the H flag.
c	Load the H flag with the contents of the C flag. This operation will fall out automatically when the H flag is generated in the ALU.

Table 5-23. *H Flag* worksheet identifier definitions.

The *PV flag* Worksheet

The *PV flag* worksheet is about the same as the *H flag* worksheet in terms of complexity, but instead of set-to-one and set-to-zero cases there are three separate generating functions for the Parity/ Overflow flag. I sometimes wonder if it wouldn't have been better to use the two unused bits in the F register rather than combining the different functions in the PV flag. But that would have meant more cases for the conditional branch instructions, so I understand the trade-off. The *PV flag* worksheet excerpt in Figure 5-122 shows the Add instruction cases.

	Instruction	internal code	dec1	if2b	dec2	of1b	adr1	adr2	rd2a	rd2b	if1a	if1b	Mach State
7	ADD A,(HL)	12'b000010000110										v	3
8	ADD A,(IX+d)	12'b010010000110										v	5
9	ADD A,(IY+d)	12'b010110000110										v	5
10	ADD A,n	12'b000011000110										v	2
11	ADD A,r	12'b000010000rrr										v	1
12	ADD HL,ss	12'b000000xx1001											1
13	ADD IX,xx	12'b010000xx1001											2
14	ADD IY,yy	12'b010100xx1001											2

Figure 5-122. *PV flag* worksheet for the Add instructions.

This is the normal overflow function for the Parity/Overflow flag, which is also true for the subtract, byte decrement and byte increment instructions. But the logical functions are different, as shown in the *PV flag* worksheet excerpt in Figure 5-123. The Parity/Overflow flag reports the parity for all of the logical operations.

	Instruction	internal code	dec1	if2b	dec2	of1b	adr1	adr2	rd2a	rd2b	if1a	if1b	Mach State
15	AND (HL)	12'b000010100110										p	3
16	AND (IX+d)	12'b010010100110										p	5
17	AND (IY+d)	12'b010110100110										p	5
18	AND n	12'b000011100110										p	2
19	AND r	12'b000010100rrr										p	1

Figure 5-123. *PV flag* worksheet for some logical instructions.

The special arithmetic instructions are a mixed bag, as shown in the PV flag worksheet excerpt in Figure 5-124. The Decimal Adjust Accumulator instruction reporting the parity of the result is inexplicable.

	Instruction	internal code	dec1	if2b	dec2	if1b	Mach State
26	CCF	12'b000000111111					1
36	CPL	12'b000000101111					1
37	DAA	12'b000000100111				p	1
117	NEG	12'b1xxx01000100				v	2
173	SCF	12'b000000110111					1

Figure 5-124. *PV flag* worksheet for the special arithmetic instructions.

None of the Bit Test, Bit Set or Bit Reset instructions affect the Parity/Overflow flag, but all of the normal shift and rotate instructions report the parity of the result. An example is shown in Figure 5-125.

	Instruction	internal code	dec1	if2b	dec2	of1b	if3a	if3b	adr2	rd2a	rd2b	wr2a	wr2b	if1a	if1b	Mach State
144	RL (HL)	12'b001000010110										p				5
145	RL (IX+d)	12'b011000010110										p				6
146	RL (IY+d)	12'b011100010110										p				6
147	RL r	12'b001000010rrr										p			p	2

Figure 5-125. *PV flag* worksheet for some rotate cases.

As far as the special rotate instructions, the instructions that were originally from the 8080 do not affect the Parity/Overflow flag, probably because the 8080 didn't include the parity functionality. But the rotate instructions that were included for working with BCD digits report the parity on the result, again for no obvious reason. This is shown in Figure 5-126.

	Instruction	internal code	dec1	if2b	dec2	adr2	rd2a	rd2b	wr2a	wr2b	if1a	if1b	Mach State
148	RLA	12'b000000010111											1
153	RLCA	12'b000000000111											1
154	RLD	12'b1xxx01101111										p	5
159	RRA	12'b000000011111											1
164	RRCA	12'b000000001111											1
165	RRD	12'b1xxx01100111										p	5

Figure 5-126. *PV flag* worksheet for the special rotate instructions.

Two of the special 8-bit loads return the status of the interrupt enable in the Parity/Overflow flag. This is actually a very useful feature for a programmer, and is shown in Figure 5-127.

	Instruction	internal code	dec1	if2b	dec2	if1b	Mach State
94	LD A,I	12'b1xxx01010111				f	2
95	LD A,R	12'b1xxx01011111				f	2

Figure 5-127. *PV flag* worksheet for some special load instructions.

The *PV flag* worksheet excerpt in Figure 5-128 shows the Block Compare instructions. For these instructions the Parity/Overflow flag is used to report the status of the decrement of the loop counter. Normally this kind of status would be reported in the Zero flag, but there are two reasons that this can't be done. First, the Zero flag is used to report the status of the compare, and second, the zero-detect is the result of a word decrement, but these are really byte instructions.

	Instruction	internal code	dec1	if2b	dec2	adr2	rd1a	rd1b	rd2a	rd2b	blk1	blk2	pca	pco	if1a	if1b	Mach State
32	CPD	12'b1xxx10101001					b		b								5
33	CPDR	12'b1xxx10111001					b		b								4+2i
34	CPI	12'b1xxx10100001					b		b								5
35	CPIR	12'b1xxx10110001					b		b								4+2i

Figure 5-128. *PV flag* worksheet for the Block Compare instructions.

Even though they don't use the Zero flag, some of the block move instructions use the Parity/Overflow flag in the same manner as do the Block Compare instructions, as shown in Figure 5-129.

	Instruction	internal code	dec1	if2b	dec2	adr2	rd1a	rd1b	rd2a	rd2b	wr1a	wr1b	wr2a	wr2b	pca	pco	if1a	if1b	Mach State
67	IND	12'b1xxx10101010																	5
68	INDR	12'b1xxx10111010																	4+2i
69	INI	12'b1xxx10100010																	5
70	INIR	12'b1xxx10110010																	4+2i
113	LDD	12'b1xxx10101000					b		b										5
114	LDDR	12'b1xxx10111000					b		b										4+2i
115	LDI	12'b1xxx10100000					b		b										5
116	LDIR	12'b1xxx10110000					b		b										4+2i
124	OTDR	12'b1xxx10111011																	4+2i
125	OTIR	12'b1xxx10110011																	4+2i
128	OUTD	12'b1xxx10101011																	5
129	OUTI	12'b1xxx10100011																	5

Figure 5-129. *PV flag* worksheet for the block load instructions.

There are a few more cases where instructions affect the Parity/Overflow flag, but there is nothing unique about them so I won't bother to show them here. The definitions of the identifiers used in the *PV flag* worksheet are shown in Table 5-24.

Identifier	Meaning
v	Load the PV flag with the overflow result from an arithmetic operation.
p	Load the PV flag with the parity of the result.
f	Load the PV flag with the state of the Interrupt Enable bit.
b	Load the PV flag with the result of the test for all zeros after the decrement of the loop counter.

Table 5-24. *PV Flag* worksheet identifier definitions.

As in the case of the Carry flag and the Half-Carry flag, signaling the overflow condition depends on whether the instruction operates on a byte or a word. Just as in those two cases I expect to generate the overflow status in the ALU itself, based on the ALU operation. This is why there is only one identifier for the overflow case.

The *N flag* Worksheet

The *N flag* worksheet is very simple because there are only three cases to implement. Except for the one special case I am going to always update the flags during the last clock of the instruction. In this case I don't believe that it will save any logic to have the Negate flag update coincident with the update of the other flags. The *N flag* worksheet excerpt in Figure 5-130 shows the Add instruction cases.

	Instruction	internal code	dec1	if2b	dec2	of1b	adr1	adr2	rd2a	rd2b	if1a	if1b	Mach State
7	ADD A,(HL)	12'b000010000110										0	3
8	ADD A,(IX+d)	12'b010010000110										0	5
9	ADD A,(IY+d)	12'b010110000110										0	5
10	ADD A,n	12'b000011000110										0	2
11	ADD A,r	12'b000010000rrr										0	1
12	ADD HL,ss	12'b000000xx1001										0	1
13	ADD IX,xx	12'b010000xx1001										0	2
14	ADD IY,yy	12'b010100xx1001										0	2

Figure 5-130. *N flag* worksheet for the Add instructions.

The Compare and Subtract cases are essentially identical except for the value of the Negate flag. The *N flag* worksheet excerpt in Figure 5-131 shows some of the subtract cases.

	Instruction	internal code	dec1	if2b	dec2	of1b	adr1	adr2	rd2a	rd2b	if1a	if1b	Mach State
190	SUB (HL)	12'b000010010110										1	3
191	SUB (IX+d)	12'b010010010110										1	5
192	SUB (IY+d)	12'b010110010110										1	5
193	SUB n	12'b000011010110										1	2
194	SUB r	12'b000010010rrr										1	1

Figure 5-131. *N flag worksheet* for the Compare and Subtract instructions.

There are some anomalies in the operation of the Negate flag, probably because it was only intended for use with the Decimal Adjust instruction. Since Decimal Adjust is inherently a byte operation, it's only really necessary to update the Negate flag for byte Add and Subtract instructions. That rule is followed for the Increment and Decrement instructions, as shown in Figure 5-132. But the same rule was not followed for the Add instructions in Figure 5-130.

	Instruction	internal code	dec1	if2b	dec2	of1b	adr1	adr2	rd2a	rd2b	wr2a	wr2b	if1a	if1b	Mach State
38	DEC (HL)	12'b000000110101												1	4
39	DEC (IX+d)	12'b010000110101												1	6
40	DEC (IY+d)	12'b010100110101												1	6
41	DEC IX	12'b010000101011													2
42	DEC IY	12'b010100101011													2
43	DEC r	12'b000000rrr101												1	1
44	DEC ss	12'b000000xx1011													1
60	INC (HL)	12'b000000110100												0	4
61	INC (IX+d)	12'b010000110100												0	6
62	INC (IY+d)	12'b010100110100												0	6
63	INC IX	12'b010000100011													2
64	INC IY	12'b010100100011													2
65	INC r	12'b000000rrr100												0	1
66	INC ss	12'b000000xx0011													1

Figure 5-132. *N flag* worksheet for the Decrement and Increment instructions.

I won't bother to show the relevant *N flag* worksheet excerpts here, but the logical instructions, the Bit Test instructions and all of the normal and special shift and rotate instructions also clear the Negate flag. The special arithmetic instructions follow their own rules, as shown in Figure 5-133.

	Instruction	internal code	dec1	if2b	dec2	if1b	Mach State
26	CCF	12'b000000111111				0	1
36	CPL	12'b000000101111				1	1
37	DAA	12'b000000100111					1
117	NEG	12'b1xxx01000100				1	2
173	SCF	12'b000000110111				0	1

Figure 5-133. *N flag* worksheet for the special arithmetic instructions.

The *N flag* worksheet excerpt in Figure 5-134 shows the Block Compare instructions. Even though these instructions only affect registers used for addressing and the loop counter, they still set the Negate flag.

	Instruction	internal code	dec1	if2b	dec2	adr2	rd1a	rd1b	rd2a	rd2b	blk1	blk2	pca	pco	if1a	if1b	Mach State
32	CPD	12'b1xxx10101001														1	5
33	CPDR	12'b1xxx10111001														1	4+2i
34	CPI	12'b1xxx10100001														1	5
35	CPIR	12'b1xxx10110001														1	4+2i

Figure 5-134. *N flag* worksheet for the special arithmetic instructions.

The block move instructions are even more strange, as shown in Figure 5-135. The Block Input and Block Output instructions set the Negate flag with the sign of the data byte being transferred. I should note that this operation does not agree with the official Zilog documentation for the Z80. But this is how the Z180, and all of the unofficial Z80 documentation says it works.

	Instruction	internal code	dec1	if2b	dec2	adr2	rd1a	rd1b	rd2a	rd2b	wr1a	wr1b	wr2a	wr2b	pca	pco	if1a	if1b	Mach State
67	IND	12'b1xxx10101010									s		s						5
68	INDR	12'b1xxx10111010									s		s						4+2i
69	INI	12'b1xxx10100010									s		s						5
70	INIR	12'b1xxx10110010									s		s						4+2i
113	LDD	12'b1xxx10101000																0	5
114	LDDR	12'b1xxx10111000																0	4+2i
115	LDI	12'b1xxx10100000																0	5
116	LDIR	12'b1xxx10110000																0	4+2i
124	OTDR	12'b1xxx10111011									s		s						4+2i
125	OTIR	12'b1xxx10110011									s		s						4+2i
128	OUTD	12'b1xxx10101011									s		s						5
129	OUTI	12'b1xxx10100011									s		s						5

Figure 5-135. *N flag* worksheet for the block move instructions.

The definitions of the identifiers used in the *N flag* worksheet are shown below.

Identifier	Meaning
0	Clear the N flag.
1	Set the N flag.
s	Load the N flag with bit 7 of the output of the ALU.

Table 5-25. *N Flag* worksheet identifier definitions.

The *C flag* Worksheet

The *C flag* worksheet really only controls the enable for the load signal for the Carry flag, because of the way that I have chosen to implement the carry functionality. I will use a three different identifiers in the worksheet just as a reminder to myself about how the Carry flag is supposed to operate. The *C flag* worksheet excerpt in Figure 5-136 shows the Add instruction cases.

	Instruction	internal code	dec1	if2b	dec2	of1b	adr1	adr2	rd2a	rd2b	if1a	if1b
7	ADD A,(HL)	12'b000010000110										c
8	ADD A,(IX+d)	12'b010010000110										c
9	ADD A,(IY+d)	12'b010110000110										c
10	ADD A,n	12'b000011000110										c
11	ADD A,r	12'b000010000rrr										c
12	ADD HL,ss	12'b000000xx1001										c
13	ADD IX,xx	12'b010000xx1001										c
14	ADD IY,yy	12'b010100xx1001										c

Figure 5-136. *C flag* worksheet for the Add instructions.

The Carry flag is updated for every Add and Subtract instruction, but not for any Decrement or Increment instruction. I still don't understand the rationale for excluding the Decrement and Increment instructions, because it makes multi-precision increments and decrement more difficult. All of the logical instructions clear the Carry flag.

The special arithmetic instructions shown in Figure 5-137 might appear to be unique, but are actually operating exactly as you would expect.

	Instruction	internal code	dec1	if2b	dec2	if1b	Mach State
26	CCF	12'b000000111111				c	1
36	CPL	12'b000000101111					1
37	DAA	12'b000000100111				c	1
117	NEG	12'b1xxx01000100				c	2
173	SCF	12'b000000110111				1	1

Figure 5-137. *C flag* worksheet for the special arithmetic instructions.

All of the normal shift and rotate instructions affect the Carry flag, each in their own way. This is the main reason for keeping the carry operation inside the ALU. Otherwise I would need several different identifiers that carry the same information that is inherent in the *ALU Op* worksheet. Only the special BCD rotates do not affect the Carry flag.

The definitions of the identifiers used in the *C flag* worksheet are shown below. All of the identifiers just enable the load of the Carry flag.

Identifier	Meaning
c	Load the C flag with the carry result appropriate for the operation.
0	Clear the C flag.
1	Set the C flag.

Table 5-26. *C Flag* worksheet identifier definitions.

The *T flag* Worksheet

The *T flag* worksheet controls the operation of the internal Temporary flag, which is not visible to the user. The Temporary flag is required by a few instructions that cannot use one of the regular flags.

For example, the Decrement-Jump-Non-Zero instruction decrements a loop counter and branches if the loop count is not zero. But none of the regular flags are affected by this instruction. The *T flag* worksheet excerpt for the jump instructions are shown in Figure 5-138, with the DJNZ instruction loading Temporary flag with the result of the decrement of the loop counter. The result of this decrement operation is used in the *pca* state.

	Instruction	internal code	dec1	if2b	dec2	of1b	of2a	of2b	pca	pco	if1a	if1b	Mach State
46	DJNZ j	12'b000000010000				z							3
71	JP (HL)	12'b000011101001											2
72	JP (IX)	12'b010011101001											3
73	JP (IY)	12'b010111101001											3
74	JP f,mn	12'b000011fff010											4/3
75	JP mn	12'b000011000011											4
76	JR cc,e	12'b0000001cc000											3/2
77	JR e	12'b000000011000											3

Figure 5-138. *T flag* worksheet for several branch instructions.

The block instructions also use the Temporary flag, but not always because they use a loop counter. The block compare instructions load the result of the decrement of the loop counter into both the Temporary flag and the normal Parity/Overflow flag during the *rd1a* and *rd2a* states.

But in this case the load of the Temporary flag is only there to share the decoding for those states and the real use of the Temporary flag occurs during the *blk1* state. In the *blk1* state the Temporary flag is loaded with the logical-OR of the result of the compare and the state of the Parity/Overflow flag. This complication is required because the loop must terminate on either a character match or the end of the loop count. This operation is shown in Figure 5-139.

	Instruction	internal code	dec1	if2b	dec2	adr2	rd1a	rd1b	rd2a	rd2b	blk1	blk2	pca	pco	if1a	if1b	Mach State
32	CPD	12'b1xxx10101001					z		z		b						5
33	CPDR	12'b1xxx10111001					z		z		b						4+2i
34	CPI	12'b1xxx10100001					z		z		b						5
35	CPIR	12'b1xxx10110001					z		z		b						4+2i

Figure 5-139. *T flag* worksheet for the Block Compare instructions.

The block move instructions are shown in Figure 5-140. All of these instructions use the Temporary flag to store the result of the decrement of the loop counter. So why is the block output instruction different? If you remember back to the *ALU Op*, *ALU A* and *ALU B* worksheets, in this case the loop counter is decremented near the end of the corresponding transfer. So the test during the *rd1a* and *rd2a* states for this instruction should be for a count of one rather than a count of zero to terminate the loop.

	Instruction	internal code	dec1	if2b	dec2	adr2	rd1a	rd1b	rd2a	rd2b	wr1a	wr1b	wr2a	wr2b	pca	pco	if1a	if1b	Mach State
67	IND	12'b1xxx10101010					z		z										5
68	INDR	12'b1xxx10111010					z		z										4+2i
69	INI	12'b1xxx10100010					z		z										5
70	INIR	12'b1xxx10110010					z		z										4+2i
113	LDD	12'b1xxx10101000					z		z										5
114	LDDR	12'b1xxx10111000					z		z										4+2i
115	LDI	12'b1xxx10100000					z		z										5
116	LDIR	12'b1xxx10110000					z		z										4+2i
124	OTDR	12'b1xxx10111011					1		1										4+2i
125	OTIR	12'b1xxx10110011					1		1										4+2i
128	OUTD	12'b1xxx10101011					1		1										5
129	OUTI	12'b1xxx10100011					1		1										5

Figure 5-140. *T flag* worksheet for the block move instructions.

The definitions of the identifiers used in the *T flag* worksheet are shown in Table 5-27. The identifiers select the source for the Temporary flag as well as enabling the loading of the flag.

Identifier	Meaning
z	Load the T flag with the zero-detect output of the ALU.
b	Load the T flag with the logical-OR of the zero-detect output of the ALU and the state of the P/V flag..
1	Load the T flag with the result of a byte test for a value of one.

Table 5-27. *T Flag* worksheet identifier definitions.

That's almost it for the spreadsheet. The final worksheet gathers some miscellaneous cases.

The *Special Case* Worksheet

The *Special Case* worksheet controls all of the special machine cycles that are not covered in the remainder of the spreadsheet. These include the interrupt acknowledge machine cycle, the halt machine cycle and the bus release machine cycle. This worksheet also shows the states that are necessary to exit the reset state and start up the registered control signals properly.

I could have put all of this information in the regular worksheets, by adding eight extra columns to each worksheet. Since these are all special cases that are unaffected by the instruction, I think that it makes more sense to do them separately. This also gives me the opportunity to present a different format for the worksheets.

So far the spreadsheet that I have presented here leads to Verilog code that is sorted by function and then arranged by clock cycle, with individual instruction codes selecting the exact function. I find that this format makes the most sense for me, but I have also seen designs described in Verilog sorted first by instruction, and then arranged by clock cycle, with all of the functions listed in each clock cycle. In this alternate format the design is presented more like software, with sequential step-by-step operation for each instruction. Designers with more of a software background may find this style makes more sense to them.

In the *Special* worksheet, the columns are still the individual clock cycles, while the rows correspond to the information in the individual worksheets. If this format were extended to the entire machine, each worksheet would correspond to a machine cycle, each column would be used for an instruction, and the rows would be used for the individual functions. The entire *Special* worksheet is shown in Figure 5-141.

Function	inta	intb		hlta	hltb		dma1	dma2		rst	rste
Next State	intb	wr1a adr1		hltb	hlta if1a		dma2	dma1 if1a		rste	if1a
Tran Type		stk idl			idl if			idl if			if
Address Bus		alu pc			pc			pc			pc
Pre-Address	alu pc			pc			pc			pc	
Load PC				int			dma				
DinDout		din0									
ALU Op	add	pass									
ALU A	neg1										
ALU B	sp	pch									
Register Wr		sp tmp									

Figure 5-141. *Special* worksheet in its entirety.

The *inta* and *intb* states are the first machine cycle in the interrupt acknowledge sequence, where the interrupt vector is read from the `ivec_data_in` bus. In the case of Interrupt Mode 1 this vector is not used, and the sequence jumps directly to the *wr1a* state for the stack write of the PC register. In this case the ALU output, which now contains the decremented SP register, must be output to the address register. The SP register is also updated during the *intb* state in this case.

In the case of Interrupt Mode 2 the interrupt vector will be used, and the sequence continues with the *adr1* state. Here the address register does not need to be loaded with the updated SP register, so the PC register is used instead. In this case the SP register is not updated during the *intb* state, because it will be done later during the *rd2b* state of the interrupt sequence. Instead, the Temporary register is written directly from the `ivec_data_in` bus in the low byte and the contents of the I register in the high byte. I could have done this concatenation in the ALU during the *adr1* state, but that would have required a special ALU operation just for this case, which I would rather avoid.

The *hlta* and *hltb* states are the machine cycle where the CPU sits waiting for an interrupt while the Halt instruction is executed. This machine cycle is inserted between the *pco* and *if1a* states for that instruction. Interrupts and bus requests are sampled during the *hlta* state and if none are pending then the machine cycle repeats. A pending interrupt request (but not a bus request) causes a transition to the *if1a* state where instruction execution resumes.

The *dma1* and *dma2* states are the machine cycle where the CPU sits in response to a bus request. This machine cycle is inserted after the *if1b* state just like an interrupt acknowledge machine cycle. Only bus requests are sampled during the *dma1* state because the bus request is higher priority than interrupts and as long as the bus is being requested this machine cycle repeats. When the bus is no longer being requested the next machine cycle will be a normal instruction fetch.

The *rst* state is forced as long as the master rest signal is active. On the release of the reset signal the machine transitions to the *rste* state. This state is required to allow all of the registered control signals to resume normal operation.

At this point we have all of the information necessary to start the Verilog coding. But this is a good time to review all of the worksheets looking for things that you might have missed. Remember, once you start coding it becomes more painful to go back and modify the spreadsheet.

6. Writing the Verilog

Introduction

The first step in writing the Verilog is to work out the definitions for all of the identifiers used in the spreadsheet. This requires much more care than just picking the necessary bit field width and assigning a binary value to each identifier. Choosing the encoding has a significant impact on both the performance of the design and the size of the design.

A related topic is assigning states in a state machine. All logic synthesis tools that I am aware of have the option where the tool can assign the encoding for a state machine. Presumably this results in the most compact logic and highest performance, but the are two problems with this approach. First, you have no way of knowing how the states were assigned, so simulating a post-synthesis netlist is going to be more work than necessary if you need to follow the state sequence. Second, and more important, is that the synthesis tool may make a completely different choice from one run to the next. This makes it almost impossible to do minor fixes without major changes to the resulting netlist. You are of course free to make your own choice, but I have never allowed a logic synthesis tool choose the state machine encoding for me.

The process of choosing the encoding for state machines and control signals is more than I want to attempt to cover in this chapter. The choices for encoding range from fully-encoded to one-hot, or something in between these two extremes. I will review some of the considerations that I use here and then discuss the individual trade-offs for each case.

The first consideration is the choice of an idle state. For state machines the obvious choice is all zeros, and this is usually my preferred choice. But there are also places where this may not be the best choice. For example, a synchronizer on an active-low input probably wants to be initialized to all ones if that is consistent with the default value for the input. In some cases a counter might best be initialized to the roll-over value so that the roll-over signal is always generated immediately after reset.

For control fields it makes sense to choose the default value identical to the value that is most commonly used, to minimize the logic required. This will often be the all-zeros case.

In this chapter I will go through nearly the entire design, explaining the rationale behind the Verilog code in each of the modules. I won't bother with the header or definition sections of the modules because that doesn't really contribute to understanding the design. I will only go through a few sections of the Verilog that is generated from the design spreadsheet, because all of the relevant information has already been covered.

In deference to readers who may be new to Verilog, I will include some basic connection diagrams here. But as you become more comfortable with using Verilog to represent a design you will find that such diagrams are usually not worth the time it takes to create them. The Verilog input/output listing contains all of the information you need to visualize how blocks are connected.

The defines.v file

The defines.v file contains all of the `` `define `` directives for the design, where the identifiers in the design spreadsheet are converted into real values. This is not a Verilog file, but is used by the Verilog compiler during the compilation process.

I used the first section of the defines.v file, shown in Listing 6-1, as an example in the Verilog chapter, so there isn't much more to say about it here. In reality I had to finalize this encoding before completing the *Internal Code* worksheet, and that is why these definitions should not be modified.

```
/*******************************************************************************************/
/*                                                                                         */
/* page register control - DO NOT MODIFY                                                   */
/*                                                                                         */
/*******************************************************************************************/
`define MAIN_PG      4'b0000           //no instruction prefix byte(s)
`define INTR_PG      4'b0001           //interrupt acknowledge
`define CB_PAGE      4'b0010           //CB instruction prefix
`define DMA_PG       4'b0011           //dma acknowledge
`define DD_PAGE      4'b0100           //DD instruction prefix
`define FD_PAGE      4'b0101           //FD instruction prefix
`define DDCB_PG      4'b0110           //DD-CB instruction prefix
`define FDCB_PG      4'b0111           //FD-CB instruction prefix
`define ED_PAGE      4'b1000           //ED instruction prefix
`define DEC_MAIN     4'b0x0x           //main page or DD page or FD page
`define DEC_ED       4'b1xxx           //ED page
```

Listing 6-1. defines.v section for page register control.

The next section of this file, in Listing 6-2, defines the encoding for the identifiers used in the *Load PC* worksheet. The six identifiers need at least three bits, and in this case there doesn't seem to be any advantage to using a wider bit field. I have chosen the encoding so that bit 0 marks all of the cases where the PC register might potentially be loaded, which should simplify the logic. The "no operation" case is assigned to all zeros, and the more rare the case the more bits that are set in the bit field.

```
/*****************************************************************************/
/*                                                                           */
/* program counter register control: pc_sel                                  */
/*                                                                           */
/*****************************************************************************/
`define PCCTL_IDX   2
`define PC_NUL      3'b000          //No operation on PC
`define PC_LD       3'b001          //PC loaded unconditionally
`define PC_NILD     3'b011          //PC loaded if no interrupt, sample interrupt
`define PC_INT      3'b100          //Sample interrupt/dma only
`define PC_DMA      3'b110          //Sample dma only
`define PC_NILD2    3'b111          //PC loaded if no latched interrupt
```

Listing 6-2. defines.v section for program counter control.

There are only four identifiers used in the *Address Bus* worksheet, so I could get by with a 2-bit field. I am going to go with a one-hot encoding for speed reasons. One-hot encoding saves at least two levels of logic where the signals are generated, and another two levels of logic at the destination end. In addition, using one-hot coding to control a multiplexer usually allows the multiplexer to be implemented using just two levels of logic. The definitions are shown in Listing 6-3.

```
/*****************************************************************************/
/*                                                                           */
/* address bus select: add_sel                                               */
/*                                                                           */
/*****************************************************************************/
`define ADCTL_IDX   3
`define ADD_RSTVAL  4'b0000         //Pipeline register reset value
`define ADD_PC      4'b0001         //Select address register from PC
`define ADD_HL      4'b0010         //Select address register from HL
`define ADD_SP      4'b0100         //Select address register from SP
`define ADD_ALU     4'b1000         //Select address register from ALU
```

```
`define AD_PC       0               //Address from PC
`define AD_HL       1               //Address from HL
`define AD_SP       2               //Address from SP
`define AD_ALU      3               //Address from ALU
```

Listing 6-3. defines.v section for address bus select control.

The identifiers used in the *Tran Type* worksheet naturally want to be one-hot encoded. After all, the individual cases will usually directly create the status signals that are output by the design. The only exception might be the *mem* and *stk* cases, if I choose not to separate the cases. There are two ways to handle this option. In either case I need to do a logical-OR of the two identifiers. But I could just define the two identifiers to have the same encoding, which would potentially save some logic. I'll keep them separate here for more flexibility, as shown in Listing 6-4.

```
/*******************************************************************************************/
/*                                                                                         */
/* transaction type select: tran_sel                                                       */
/*                                                                                         */
/*******************************************************************************************/
`define TTYPE_IDX   5
`define TRAN_RSTVAL 6'b000000       //Transaction type reset value
`define TRAN_IAK    6'b000001       //Intack transaction
`define TRAN_IDL    6'b000010       //Idle transaction
`define TRAN_IF     6'b000100       //Instruction fetch transaction
`define TRAN_IO     6'b001000       //I/O transaction
`define TRAN_MEM    6'b010000       //Memory (data) transaction
`define TRAN_STK    6'b100000       //Memory (stack) transaction

`define TT_IAK      0               //Interrupt acknowledge transaction
`define TT_IDL      1               //Idle transaction
`define TT_IF       2               //Instruction fetch transaction
`define TT_IO       3               //I/O transaction
`define TT_MEM      4               //Memory (data) transaction
`define TT_STK      5               //Memory (stack) transaction
```

Listing 6-4. defines.v section for transaction type select control.

The identifiers used for the data output registers in the *DinDout* worksheet are shown in Listing 6-5. Here I am going to use a modified one-hot encoding. Bit 2 of the control field will enable the load of the memory data output register, while bit 1 will enable the load of the I/O data output register. Then I'll use bit 0 to control the source for the memory data output register.

Clearly I don't expect to use this control field symbolically with this type of encoding, and that is why I do not want the encoding modified.

```
/*****************************************************************************************/
/*                                                                                       */
/* data output control: do_ctl - DO NOT MODIFY                                           */
/*                                                                                       */
/*****************************************************************************************/
`define DO_IDX        2
`define DO_NUL        3'b000              //No load
`define DO_IO         3'b010              //Load i/o data from lsb
`define DO_LSB        3'b100              //Load mem data from lsb
`define DO_MSB        3'b101              //Load mem data from msb
```

Listing 6-5. defines.v section for data output control.

The identifiers used for the data input register in the *DinDout* worksheet are shown in Listing 6-6. The encoding might look like straight binary, but is in fact one-hot. Bit 1 of the control field enables the load of the high byte of the data input register, while bit 0 enables the load of the low byte of the register. I don't expect to use this control field symbolically.

```
/*****************************************************************************************/
/*                                                                                       */
/* data input control: di_ctl - DO NOT MODIFY                                            */
/*                                                                                       */
/*****************************************************************************************/
`define DI_IDX        1
`define DI_NUL        2'b00               //No load
`define DI_DI0        2'b01               //Load din0
`define DI_DI1        2'b10               //Load din1
`define DI_DI10       2'b11               //Load both din0 and din1
```

Listing 6-6. defines.v section for data input control.

The next set of identifiers, in Listing 6-7, are not used directly in the design spreadsheet, but they correspond to several cases that are not treated explicitly in any of the worksheets. By now you should recognize how I like to encode bit fields for loading registers.

```
/*****************************************************************************************/
/*                                                                                       */
/* interrupt enable control: ief_ctl - DO NOT MODIFY                                     */
/*                                                                                       */
/*****************************************************************************************/
`define IEF_IDX     2
`define IEF_NUL     3'b000          //No load
`define IEF_0       3'b010          //Load zero
`define IEF_1       3'b011          //Load one
`define IEF_NMI     3'b100          //ief2 <= ief1, ief1 <= 0
`define IEF_RTN     3'b101          //ief1 <= ief2
```

Listing 6-7. defines.v section for interrupt enable control.

The interrupt identifiers in Listing 6-8 come from the instructions that set the interrupt mode. I am not sure how I will use them yet. Remember that I do not intend to implement the normal Interrupt Mode 0, so I'll have to decide what I want to do for that case when I get to that part of the design.

```
/*****************************************************************************************/
/*                                                                                       */
/* int mode control: imd_ctl - DO NOT MODIFY                                             */
/*                                                                                       */
/*****************************************************************************************/
`define IMD_IDX     1
`define IMD_NUL     2'b00           //No load
`define IMD_0       2'b01           //Set interrupt mode 0
`define IMD_1       2'b10           //Set interrupt mode 1
`define IMD_2       2'b11           //Set interrupt mode 2
```

Listing 6-8. defines.v section for interrupt mode control.

The identifiers from the *H Flag* worksheet are shown in Listing 6-9. I use the usual encoding for loading a register.

```
/*****************************************************************************************/
/*                                                                                       */
/* half-carry flag control: hflg_ctl - DO NOT MODIFY                                    */
/*                                                                                       */
/*****************************************************************************************/
`define HFLG_IDX    1
`define HFLG_NUL    2'b00           //No load
`define HFLG_H      2'b01           //Load half-carry result
`define HFLG_0      2'b10           //Load zero
`define HFLG_1      2'b11           //Load one
```

Listing 6-9. defines.v section for Half-Carry flag control.

The identifiers for the *PV Flag* worksheet are shown in Listing 6-10. The control for this flag is messy enough that I will just use binary encoding. I will choose codes with a single bit set for the most common cases of parity and overflow.

```
/*****************************************************************************************/
/*                                                                                       */
/* parity/overflow flag control: pflg_ctl                                               */
/*                                                                                       */
/*****************************************************************************************/
`define PFLG_IDX    2
`define PFLG_NUL    3'b000          //No load
`define PFLG_V      3'b001          //Load overflow result
`define PFLG_0      3'b010          //Load zero
`define PFLG_1      3'b011          //Load one
`define PFLG_P      3'b100          //Load parity result
`define PFLG_B      3'b101          //Load block count zero result
`define PFLG_F      3'b111          //Load ief
```

Listing 6-10. defines.v section for Parity/Overflow flag control.

The identifiers from the *N Flag* worksheet are shown in Listing 6-11. I use the usual encoding for loading a register.

```
/*****************************************************************************************/
/*                                                                                       */
/* negate flag control: nflg_ctl - DO NOT MODIFY                                         */
/*                                                                                       */
/*****************************************************************************************/
`define NFLG_IDX     1
`define NFLG_NUL     2'b00              //No load
`define NFLG_S       2'b01              //Load sign result
`define NFLG_0       2'b10              //Load zero
`define NFLG_1       2'b11              //Load one
```

Listing 6-11. defines.v section for Negate flag control.

The three identifiers from the *T Flag* worksheet are rare enough that the encoding doesn't really matter. This is shown in Listing 6-12.

```
/*****************************************************************************************/
/*                                                                                       */
/* temporary flag control: tflg_ctl                                                      */
/*                                                                                       */
/*****************************************************************************************/
`define TFLG_IDX     1
`define TFLG_NUL     2'b00              //No load
`define TFLG_Z       2'b01              //Load zero result
`define TFLG_1       2'b10              //Load one result (blk out)
`define TFLG_B       2'b11              //Load blk cp result
```

Listing 6-12. defines.v section for Temporary flag control.

The *Register Wr* worksheet uses a number of identifiers that represent bit fields, and one way to use those identifiers would be to pass the corresponding bit field from the instruction register directly to the control signals that select the register to write. But there are so many special cases in the instruction set that this approach is very cumbersome. It also requires extra signals to identify some of the special cases. Instead, I will use a modified one-hot encoding, as shown in Listing 6-13. Each bit selects one register, and selecting multiple registers is allowed. A separate write-enable bit is used to generate the load control signal.

This choice of encoding requires that I manually expand the identifiers that select a bit field in the instruction, but this is really just some extra cut-and-paste operations. The advantage of this type of encoding is obvious when looking at the `define statements for the various cases. The encoding completely eliminates any decoding in the logic for the register write, and should also simplify the logic that generates this control bus.

```
/*****************************************************************************************/
/*                                                                                       */
/* write register control: wr_sel - unencoded                                           */
/*                                                                                       */
/*****************************************************************************************/
`define WREG_IDX 14
`define WREG_BB    15'b110000000000000        //Select B to write
`define WREG_BC    15'b111000000000000        //Select BC to write
`define WREG_CC    15'b101000000000000        //Select C to write
`define WREG_DD    15'b100100000000000        //Select D to write
`define WREG_DE    15'b100110000000000        //Select DE to write
`define WREG_EE    15'b100010000000000        //Select E to write
`define WREG_HH    15'b100001000000000        //Select H to write
`define WREG_HL    15'b100001100000000        //Select HL to write
`define WREG_LL    15'b100000100000000        //Select L to write
`define WREG_DEHL  15'b100111100000000        //Select DEHL to write (ex case)
`define WREG_AA    15'b100000010000000        //Select A to write
`define WREG_AF    15'b100000011000000        //Select A and F to write
`define WREG_FF    15'b100000001000000        //Select F to write
`define WREG_SP    15'b100000000100000        //Select SP to write
`define WREG_TMP   15'b100000000010000        //Select TMP register to write
`define WREG_IX    15'b100000000001000        //Select IX to write
`define WREG_IY    15'b100000000000100        //Select IY to write
`define WREG_II    15'b100000000000010        //Select I register to write
`define WREG_RR    15'b100000000000001        //Select R register to write
`define WREG_NUL   15'b000000000000000        //No register write

`define WR_REG     14            //register write
`define WR_BB      13            //BB register index
`define WR_CC      12            //CC register index
`define WR_DD      11            //DD register index
`define WR_EE      10            //EE register index
`define WR_HH       9            //HH register index
`define WR_LL       8            //LL register index
`define WR_AA       7            //AA register index
`define WR_FF       6            //FF register index
```

```
`define WR_SP        5            //SP register index
`define WR_TMP       4            //TMP register index
`define WR_IX        3            //IX register index
`define WR_IY        2            //IY register index
`define WR_II        1            //II register index
`define WR_RR        0            //RR register index
```

Listing 6-13. defines.v section for register write control.

The *ALU A* worksheet identifiers are shown in Listing 6-14. I initially considered combining some of the cases outside of the multiplexer. For example the *zer*, *one*, *neg1* and *neg2* identifiers could use two bits to create these fixed values. In parallel the same two bits could select from among the *bit*, *daa*, *int* and *rst* identifiers. This would reduce the number of unique *ALU A* cases to nine instead of fifteen. I decided that the extra complexity didn't really accomplish anything and I settled on the one-hot encoding shown here.

```
/*******************************************************************************************/
/*                                                                                         */
/* ALU input A control: alua_sel                                                           */
/*                                                                                         */
/*******************************************************************************************/
`define ALUA_IDX 13
`define ALUA_RSTVAL 14'h0000      //Reset value for pipeline controls
`define ALUA_ZER    14'h0000      //Select 16'h0000 (default)
`define ALUA_ONE    14'h0001      //Select 16'h0001
`define ALUA_M1     14'h0002      //Select 16'hFFFF
`define ALUA_M2     14'h0004      //Select 16'hFFFE
`define ALUA_HL     14'h0008      //Select HL register
`define ALUA_IX     14'h0010      //Select IX register
`define ALUA_IY     14'h0020      //Select IY register
`define ALUA_PC     14'h0040      //Select PC register
`define ALUA_AA     14'h0080      //Select A register
`define ALUA_BIT    14'h0100      //Select bit select constant
`define ALUA_DAA    14'h0200      //Select decimal adjust constant
`define ALUA_II     14'h0400      //Select I register
`define ALUA_RR     14'h0800      //Select R register
`define ALUA_INT    14'h1000      //Select interrupt address
`define ALUA_RST    14'h2000      //Select restart address

`define AA_ONE       0            //alua one
`define AA_M1        1            //alua -1
```

```
`define AA_M2         2              //alua -2
`define AA_HL         3              //alua hl
`define AA_IX         4              //alua ix
`define AA_IY         5              //alua iy
`define AA_PC         6              //alua pc
`define AA_AA         7              //alua aa
`define AA_BIT        8              //alua bit
`define AA_DAA        9              //alua daa
`define AA_II        10              //alua ii
`define AA_RR        11              //alua rr
`define AA_INT       12              //alua interrupt
`define AA_RST       13              //alua restart
```

Listing 6-14. defines.v section for ALU input A control.

It might have seemed as though the *ALU B* worksheet had many more cases than the *ALU A* worksheet, but in fact that isn't true. There are really only eleven unique sources for the B input to the ALU. It's just that there needs to be a byte shifter on this input to shift the high byte of the source down to the low byte of the ALU input. I use bit 0 of this control field to enable this byte shift function and the remainder of the bits are one-hot selectors for the source register, as shown in Listing 6-15. I do not need to distinguish between a word register and the low byte of the register because the *ALU OP* identifier will always control the byte/word operation for the ALU.

```
/*******************************************************************************************/
/*                                                                                         */
/* ALU input B control: alub_sel                                                           */
/*                                                                                         */
/*******************************************************************************************/
`define ALUB_IDX 12
`define ALUB_RSTVAL 13'h1000         //Reset value for pipeline controls
`define ALUB_AF      13'h1002        //Select A and F registers
`define ALUB_AA      13'h1003        //Select A register
`define ALUB_BC      13'h0004        //Select BC register
`define ALUB_BB      13'h0005        //Select B register
`define ALUB_CC      13'h0004        //Select C register
`define ALUB_DE      13'h0008        //Select DE register
`define ALUB_DD      13'h0009        //Select D register
`define ALUB_EE      13'h0008        //Select E register
`define ALUB_HL      13'h0010        //Select HL register
`define ALUB_HH      13'h0011        //Select H register
`define ALUB_LL      13'h0010        //Select L register
```

```
`define ALUB_IX      13'h0020        //Select IX register
`define ALUB_IXH     13'h0021        //Select IX register high byte
`define ALUB_IXL     13'h0020        //Select IX register low byte
`define ALUB_IY      13'h0040        //Select IY register
`define ALUB_IYH     13'h0041        //Select IY register high byte
`define ALUB_IYL     13'h0040        //Select IY register low byte
`define ALUB_SP      13'h0080        //Select SP register
`define ALUB_SPH     13'h0081        //Select SP register high byte
`define ALUB_DIN     13'h0100        //Select data input register
`define ALUB_DINH    13'h0101        //Select data input register high byte
`define ALUB_IO      13'h0200        //Select i/o address
`define ALUB_TMP     13'h0400        //Select TMP register
`define ALUB_PC      13'h1800        //Select PC register
`define ALUB_PCH     13'h1801        //Select PC register high byte

`define AB_SHR       0               //alub shift right
`define AB_AF        1               //alub af
`define AB_BC        2               //alub bc
`define AB_DE        3               //alub de
`define AB_HL        4               //alub hl
`define AB_IX        5               //alub ix
`define AB_IY        6               //alub iy
`define AB_SP        7               //alub sp
`define AB_DIN       8               //alub din
`define AB_IO        9               //alub io
`define AB_TMP       10              //alub tmp
`define AB_PC        11              //alub pc
`define AB_ADR       12              //alub address pc
```

Listing 6-15. defines.v section for ALU input B control.

The *ALU Op* worksheet is easily the most complicated piece of the design spreadsheet, and it is also likely to be the section of the design that sets the maximum clock frequency. To give more control over the optimization of this section of the design I am going to break it into four separate Verilog modules. I'll use separate modules for the arithmetic operations, the logical operations and the shift/rotate operations. Then the fourth module will select which of the three functional modules to connect to the ALU output.

Partitioning the design this way allows me to dedicate two bits of the control field to select the function unit, and then these bits can be ignored by the function units. This is why there are two sets of `` `define `` statements shown in Listing 6-16. The 8-bit values are used when generating the control field, but the function units only need to use six bits of the control field. I have to be very careful doing this though, because it will be disastrous if there is a difference between the two sets of definitions.

Within the lower six bits of the control field I use bit 0 to select byte operations, and the remaining bits can almost be used as one-hot values. Some of the rarely-used identifiers deviate from this where required.

```
/*******************************************************************************************/
/*                                                                                         */
/* ALU operation control: aluop_sel - 2 MSBs fixed for unit sel                           */
/*                                                                                         */
/*******************************************************************************************/
`define ALUOP_IDX 7
`define ALUOP_RSTVAL 8'b00000000     //Reset Value for pipeline controls
`define ALUOP_ADD    8'b01000000     //ALU math: add
`define ALUOP_BADD   8'b01000001     //ALU math: byte add
`define ALUOP_BDEC   8'b01000011     //ALU math: byte add (decrement)
`define ALUOP_ADS    8'b01000100     //ALU math: add signed byte
`define ALUOP_DAA    8'b01000101     //ALU math: byte add (daa)
`define ALUOP_ADC    8'b01001000     //ALU math: add with carry
`define ALUOP_BADC   8'b01001001     //ALU math: byte add with carry
`define ALUOP_SUB    8'b01010000     //ALU math: subtract
`define ALUOP_BSUB   8'b01010001     //ALU math: subtract
`define ALUOP_SBC    8'b01100000     //ALU math: subtract with carry
`define ALUOP_BSBC   8'b01100001     //ALU math: byte subtract with carry

`define ALUOP_PASS   8'b00000000     //ALU logic: pass b bus
`define ALUOP_BAND   8'b00000011     //ALU logic: byte and
`define ALUOP_BOR    8'b00000101     //ALU logic: byte or
`define ALUOP_BXOR   8'b00001001     //ALU logic: byte or
`define ALUOP_CCF    8'b00010000     //ALU logic: complement carry
`define ALUOP_SCF    8'b00010010     //ALU logic: set carry
`define ALUOP_RLD1   8'b00011000     //ALU logic: rld first step
`define ALUOP_RLD2   8'b00011010     //ALU logic: rld second step
`define ALUOP_RRD1   8'b00011100     //ALU logic: rrd first step
`define ALUOP_RRD2   8'b00011110     //ALU logic: rrd second step
`define ALUOP_APAS   8'b00100000     //ALU logic: pass a bus
```

```
`define ALUOP_RL      8'b10000000     //ALU shft: rotate left
`define ALUOP_RLA     8'b10000001     //ALU shft: rotate left acc
`define ALUOP_RLC     8'b10000010     //ALU shft: rotate left circular
`define ALUOP_RLCA    8'b10000011     //ALU shft: rotate left circular acc
`define ALUOP_RR      8'b10000100     //ALU shft: rotate right
`define ALUOP_RRA     8'b10000101     //ALU shft: rotate right acc
`define ALUOP_RRC     8'b10001000     //ALU shft: rotate right circular
`define ALUOP_RRCA    8'b10001001     //ALU shft: rotate right circular acc
`define ALUOP_SLA     8'b10010000     //ALU shft: shift left arithmetic
`define ALUOP_SRL     8'b10100000     //ALU shft: shift right logical
`define ALUOP_SRA     8'b10101000     //ALU shft: shift right arithmetic

/******************************************************************************************/
/*                                                                                        */
/* ALU operation control: 6 encoded                                                       */
/*                                                                                        */
/******************************************************************************************/
`define AOP_IDX 5
`define AOP_ADD       6'b000000       //ALU math: add
`define AOP_BADD      6'b000001       //ALU math: byte add
`define AOP_BDEC      6'b000011       //ALU math: byte add (decr)
`define AOP_ADS       6'b000100       //ALU math: add signed byte
`define AOP_DAA       6'b000101       //ALU math: byte add (daa)
`define AOP_ADC       6'b001000       //ALU math: add with carry
`define AOP_BADC      6'b001001       //ALU math: byte add with carry
`define AOP_SUB       6'b010000       //ALU math: subtract
`define AOP_BSUB      6'b010001       //ALU math: subtract
`define AOP_SBC       6'b100000       //ALU math: subtract with carry
`define AOP_BSBC      6'b100001       //ALU math: byte subtract with carry

`define AOP_PASS      6'b000000       //ALU logic: pass b bus
`define AOP_BAND      6'b000011       //ALU logic: byte and
`define AOP_BOR       6'b000101       //ALU logic: byte or
`define AOP_BXOR      6'b001001       //ALU logic: byte or
`define AOP_CCF       6'b010000       //ALU logic: complement carry
`define AOP_SCF       6'b010010       //ALU logic: set carry
`define AOP_RLD1      6'b011000       //ALU logic: rld first step
`define AOP_RLD2      6'b011010       //ALU logic: rld second step
`define AOP_RRD1      6'b011100       //ALU logic: rrd first step
`define AOP_RRD2      6'b011110       //ALU logic: rrd second step
`define AOP_APAS      6'b100000       //ALU logic: pass a bus
```

```
`define AOP_RL       6'b000000    //ALU shft: rotate left
`define AOP_RLA      6'b000001    //ALU shft: rotate left acc
`define AOP_RLC      6'b000010    //ALU shft: rotate left circular
`define AOP_RLCA     6'b000011    //ALU shft: rotate left circular acc
`define AOP_RR       6'b000100    //ALU shft: rotate right
`define AOP_RRA      6'b000101    //ALU shft: rotate right acc
`define AOP_RRC      6'b001000    //ALU shft: rotate right circular
`define AOP_RRCA     6'b001001    //ALU shft: rotate right circular acc
`define AOP_SLA      6'b010000    //ALU shft: shift left arithmetic
`define AOP_SRL      6'b100000    //ALU shft: shift right logical
`define AOP_SRA      6'b101000    //ALU shft: shift right arithmetic
```

Listing 6-16. defines.v section for ALU operation control.

The last definitions, in Listing 6-17, correspond to the identifiers in the *Next State* worksheet. There are thirty-two unique identifiers, so I should be able to encode them into a 5-bit control field. It will be grossly inefficient do go this way though, because this state information needs to be decoded many times for each control signal that is generated.

My first thought was to use a one-hot coding for the machine cycle with a separate bit to track the clock within the machine cycle. This would make the control field seventeen bits wide. The disadvantage of this encoding is that the parity of the control field is not constant, which makes detecting illegal states problematic.

After thinking about it for a while I decided to go with the modified one-hot encoding shown here. There are a couple of minor advantages with this encoding. First is that the parity of the control field is always even, so checking for an illegal state due to a single event upset (SEU) is trivial. Second is that every state transition has exactly two bits changing state, so there aren't going to be large differences in the supply current with different state sequences.

```
/****************************************************************************************/
/*                                                                                      */
/* machine state - pseudo-one-hot                                                       */
/*                                                                                      */
/****************************************************************************************/
`define STATE_IDX 31
`define sRST    32'b00000000000000000000000000000000    //reset
`define sDEC1   32'b00000000000000000000000000000011    //decode 1st opcode
`define sIF2B   32'b00000000000000000000000000000101    //fetch 2nd opcode (2)
`define sDEC2   32'b00000000000000000000000000001001    //decode 2nd opcode
```

```
`define sOF1B  32'b00000000000000000000000000010001   //fetch 1st operand (2)
`define sOF2A  32'b00000000000000000000000000100001   //fetch 2nd operand (1)
`define sOF2B  32'b00000000000000000000000001000001   //fetch 2nd operand (2)
`define sIF3A  32'b00000000000000000000000010000001   //fetch 3rd opcode (1)
`define sIF3B  32'b00000000000000000000000100000001   //fetch 3rd opcode (2)
`define sADR1  32'b00000000000000000000001000000001   //address calculate (1)
`define sADR2  32'b00000000000000000000010000000001   //address calculate (2)
`define sRD1A  32'b00000000000000000000100000000001   //read 1st operand (1)
`define sRD1B  32'b00000000000000000001000000000001   //read 1st operand (2)
`define sRD2A  32'b00000000000000000010000000000001   //read 2nd operand (1)
`define sRD2B  32'b00000000000000000100000000000001   //read 2nd operand (2)
`define sWR1A  32'b00000000000000001000000000000001   //write 1st operand (1)
`define sWR1B  32'b00000000000000010000000000000001   //write 1st operand (2)
`define sWR2A  32'b00000000000000100000000000000001   //write 2nd operand (1)
`define sWR2B  32'b00000000000001000000000000000001   //write 2nd operand (2)
`define sBLK1  32'b00000000000010000000000000000001   //block instruction (1)
`define sBLK2  32'b00000000000100000000000000000001   //block instruction (2)
`define sPCA   32'b00000000001000000000000000000001   //PC adjust
`define sPCO   32'b00000000010000000000000000000001   //PC output
`define sIF1A  32'b00000000100000000000000000000001   //fetch 1st opcode (1)
`define sIF1B  32'b00000001000000000000000000000001   //fetch 1st opcode (2)
`define sINTA  32'b00000010000000000000000000000001   //interrupt acknowledge (1)
`define sINTB  32'b00000100000000000000000000000001   //interrupt acknowledge (2)
`define sHLTA  32'b00001000000000000000000000000001   //halt & sleep (1)
`define sHLTB  32'b00010000000000000000000000000001   //halt & sleep (2)
`define sDMA1  32'b00100000000000000000000000000001   //dma transfer (1)
`define sDMA2  32'b01000000000000000000000000000001   //dma transfer (2)
`define sRSTE  32'b10000000000000000000000000000001   //reset exit

`define  RST   32'bxxxxxxxxxxxxxxxxxxxxxxxxxxxxxxx0   //reset
`define  DEC1  32'bxxxxxxxxxxxxxxxxxxxxxxxxxxxxxx11   //decode 1st opcode
`define  IF2B  32'bxxxxxxxxxxxxxxxxxxxxxxxxxxxxx1x1   //fetch 2nd opcode (2)
`define  DEC2  32'bxxxxxxxxxxxxxxxxxxxxxxxxxxxx1xx1   //decode 2nd opcode
`define  OF1B  32'bxxxxxxxxxxxxxxxxxxxxxxxxxxx1xxx1   //fetch 1st operand (2)
`define  OF2A  32'bxxxxxxxxxxxxxxxxxxxxxxxxxx1xxxx1   //fetch 2nd operand (1)
`define  OF2B  32'bxxxxxxxxxxxxxxxxxxxxxxxxx1xxxxx1   //fetch 2nd operand (2)
`define  IF3A  32'bxxxxxxxxxxxxxxxxxxxxxxxx1xxxxxx1   //fetch 3rd opcode (1)
`define  IF3B  32'bxxxxxxxxxxxxxxxxxxxxxxx1xxxxxxx1   //fetch 3rd opcode (2)
`define  ADR1  32'bxxxxxxxxxxxxxxxxxxxxxx1xxxxxxxx1   //address calculate (1)
```

```
`define  ADR2  32'bxxxxxxxxxxxxxxxxxxxxx1xxxxxxxxx1   //address calculate (2)
`define  RD1A  32'bxxxxxxxxxxxxxxxxxxxx1xxxxxxxxxx1   //read 1st operand (1)
`define  RD1B  32'bxxxxxxxxxxxxxxxxxxx1xxxxxxxxxxx1   //read 1st operand (2)
`define  RD2A  32'bxxxxxxxxxxxxxxxxxx1xxxxxxxxxxxx1   //read 2nd operand (1)
`define  RD2B  32'bxxxxxxxxxxxxxxxxx1xxxxxxxxxxxxx1   //read 2nd operand (2)
`define  WR1A  32'bxxxxxxxxxxxxxxxx1xxxxxxxxxxxxxx1   //write 1st operand (1)
`define  WR1B  32'bxxxxxxxxxxxxxxx1xxxxxxxxxxxxxxx1   //write 1st operand (2)
`define  WR2A  32'bxxxxxxxxxxxxxx1xxxxxxxxxxxxxxxx1   //write 2nd operand (1)
`define  WR2B  32'bxxxxxxxxxxxxx1xxxxxxxxxxxxxxxxx1   //write 2nd operand (2)
`define  BLK1  32'bxxxxxxxxxxxx1xxxxxxxxxxxxxxxxxx1   //block instruction (1)
`define  BLK2  32'bxxxxxxxxxxx1xxxxxxxxxxxxxxxxxxx1   //block instruction (2)
`define  PCA   32'bxxxxxxxxxx1xxxxxxxxxxxxxxxxxxxx1   //PC adjust
`define  PCO   32'bxxxxxxxxx1xxxxxxxxxxxxxxxxxxxxx1   //PC output
`define  IF1A  32'bxxxxxxxx1xxxxxxxxxxxxxxxxxxxxxx1   //fetch 1st opcode (1)
`define  IF1B  32'bxxxxxxx1xxxxxxxxxxxxxxxxxxxxxxx1   //fetch 1st opcode (2)
`define  INTA  32'bxxxxxx1xxxxxxxxxxxxxxxxxxxxxxxx1   //interrupt acknowledge (1)
`define  INTB  32'bxxxxx1xxxxxxxxxxxxxxxxxxxxxxxxx1   //interrupt acknowledge (2)
`define  HLTA  32'bxxxx1xxxxxxxxxxxxxxxxxxxxxxxxxx1   //halt & sleep (1)
`define  HLTB  32'bxxx1xxxxxxxxxxxxxxxxxxxxxxxxxxx1   //halt & sleep (2)
`define  DMA1  32'bxx1xxxxxxxxxxxxxxxxxxxxxxxxxxxx1   //dma transfer (1)
`define  DMA2  32'bx1xxxxxxxxxxxxxxxxxxxxxxxxxxxxx1   //dma transfer (2)
`define  RSTE  32'b1xxxxxxxxxxxxxxxxxxxxxxxxxxxxxx1   //reset exit
```

Listing 6-17. defines.v section for the machine state control.

That takes care of the defines.v file. I don't want to give the impression that creating this file is a trivial task of just typing in values. A fair amount of thought goes into selecting the encodings for the control fields, and it is almost always an iterative process. In a number of cases the encodings that I have presented here are not the ones that I started out with. I don't claim that these are the optimum choices either, so feel free to experiment with them yourself.

The hierarchy.v file

The hierarchy.v file contains all of the `` `include `` directives for the design. I used this file as an example in the Verilog section, so you have seen it before. It is shown again in Listing 6-18. I like to use this type of structure so that I only need to `` `include `` one design file in the testbench.

Like the defines.v file, this is not a Verilog file. It is used by the compiler outside of any Verilog module and should never contain anything except the `` `include `` statements and comments. I prefer to include the entire design hierarchy in this file, but it is also possible to nest the contents of this type of file.

```
`include "defines.v"                          /* control signal mnemonics     */
`include "control.v"                          /* processor control            */
`include "datapath.v"                         /* processor data path          */
  `include "alu_log.v"                        /* alu logic unit               */
  `include "alu_math.v"                       /* alu math unit                */
  `include "alu_shft.v"                       /* alu shifter unit             */
  `include "aluamux.v"                        /* alu a input multiplexer      */
  `include "alubmux.v"                        /* alu b input multiplexer      */
  `include "aluout.v"                         /* alu output multiplexer       */
`include "extint.v"                           /* processor external interface */
`include "machine.v"                          /* processor state machine      */
`include "y80_top.v"                          /* cpu top level                */
```

Listing 6-18. hierarchy.v complete file.

The machine.v module

The machine.v module is the main state machine for the CPU. The module is very simple because I prefer to include the next-state information in the control.v module where the logic can be shared with other control signals. Figure 6-1 shows the connection diagram for the machine.v module.

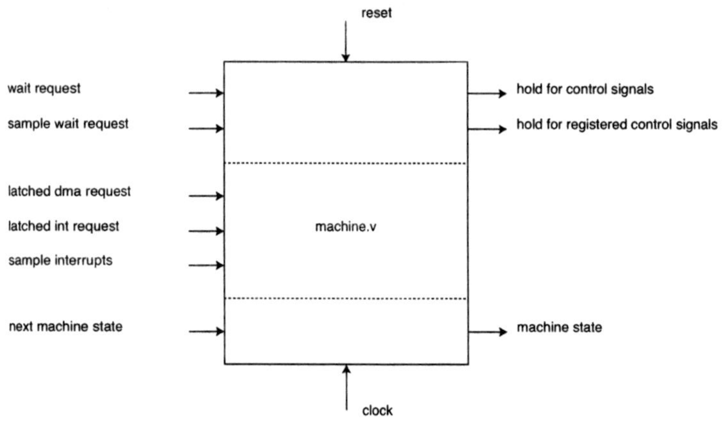

Figure 6-1. Connection diagram for the machine.v module.

Listing 6-19 shows the connections for the machine.v module. Most of the signals are self-explanatory from the comments.

```
module machine (ld_ctrl, state_reg, wait_st, clkc, dmar_reg, intr_reg, ld_inta, ld_wait,
                resetb, state_nxt, wait_req);

  input          clkc;          /* main cpu clock                                    */
  input          dmar_reg;      /* latched dma request                               */
  input          intr_reg;      /* latched interrupt request                         */
  input          ld_inta;       /* load interrupt request                            */
  input          ld_wait;       /* load wait request                                 */
  input          resetb;        /* internal reset                                    */
  input          wait_req;      /* wait request                                      */
  input   [`STATE_IDX:0] state_nxt;    /* next processor state                       */
  output         ld_ctrl;       /* load control register                             */
  output         wait_st;       /* wait state identifier                             */
  output  [`STATE_IDX:0] state_reg;    /* current processor state                    */
```

Listing 6-19. machine.v inputs and outputs.

The `ld_inta` signal is just the *jmp* identifier from the *Load PC* worksheet, that causes the state to divert to either interrupt acknowledge machine cycle or the bus release machine cycle.

The `ld_wait` signal is the sample for the Wait Request input to the CPU. It will be active during the first clock cycle of every read or write machine cycle. The *dec1* and *dec2* states are a little complicated, because they don't always correspond to the first clock of a read machine cycle. So when the *Next State* worksheet has *adr2* or *pco* for the next state after the *dec1* state this signal should not be active. The same rule is true for the *dec2* state.

I have chosen to implement the wait function by holding the current machine state, but this means that the control signals that are active in the current state are going to also be held. This will lead to all sorts of problems, so I need to generate signals to inhibit these control signals. The `ld_ctrl` signal is required for all of the control signals that are registered, while the `wait_st` signal is used by control signals that are not registered. The timing diagram in Figure 6-2 shows the operation of these signals.

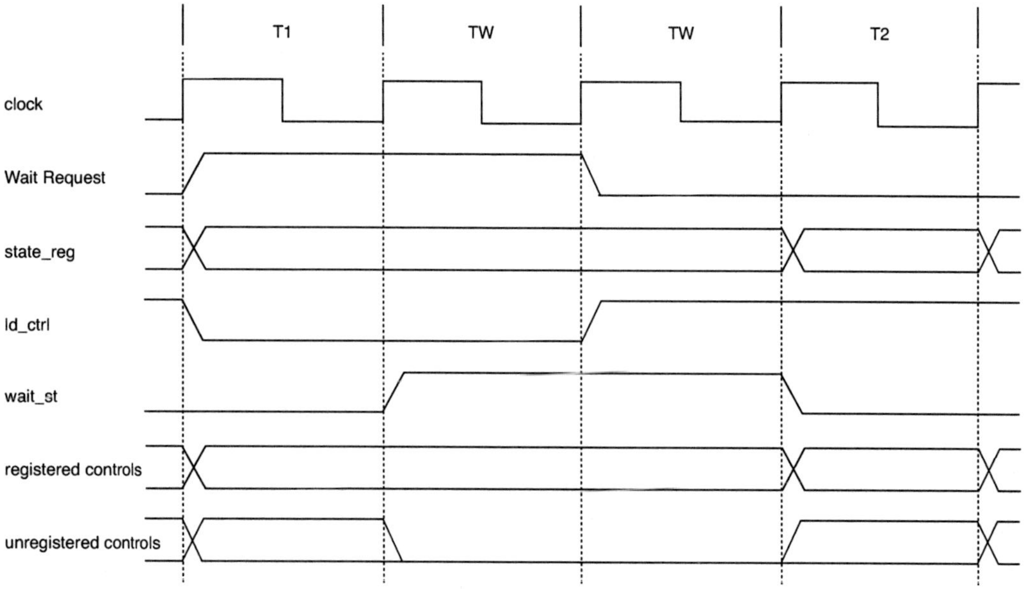

Figure 6-2. Timing of control signal with Wait states.

The Verilog code in Listing 6-20 implements all of these functions.

```
/*****************************************************************************************/
/*                                                                                       */
/* processor state machine                                                               */
/*                                                                                       */
/*****************************************************************************************/
assign ld_ctrl = !ld_wait || !wait_req;

always @ (posedge clkc or negedge resetb) begin
  if (!resetb) wait_st   <= 1'b0;
  else         wait_st   <= !ld_ctrl;
  end
```

```
always @ (posedge clkc or negedge resetb) begin
  if      (!resetb) state_reg <= `sRST;
  else if (ld_ctrl) state_reg <= (ld_inta && dmar_reg) ? `sDMA1 :
                                 (ld_inta && intr_reg) ? `sINTA : state_nxt;
  end
```

Listing 6-20. machine.v processor state machine section.

The extint.v module

The extint.v module creates all of the external interface signals for the CPU. Figure 6-3 shows the connection diagram for this module.

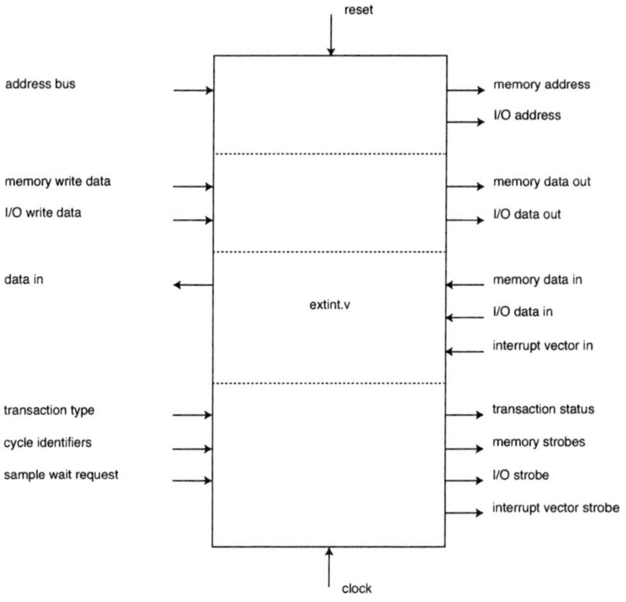

Figure 6-3. Connection diagram for the extint.v module.

The interface for the extint.v module is shown in Listing 6-21. Since the machine cycle time matches the bus cycle time this is also a very simple module. Since I covered the bus interface earlier, only a few of the signals need an explanation.

The `output_inh` signal is used to force the address outputs to all zeros and disable the `mem_tran` signal during Bus Release and Halt machine cycles. This feature is not strictly necessary, but will allow the external multiplexer to be implemented with a logical-OR function if the other bus master uses the same technique. It will also guarantee that the address buses are in a particular state during Halt.

The `halt_nxt` signal has the same timing and creates a Halt transaction status output. I probably should have included both of these status bits in the `tran_sel` control bus, but didn't think of it at the time.

```
module extint (data_in, dma_ack, ftch_tran, halt_tran, iack_tran, io_addr_out, io_data_out,
               io_read, io_strobe, io_tran, ivec_rd, mem_addr_out, mem_data_out, mem_rd,
               mem_tran, mem_wr, reti_tran, t1, addr_reg_in, clkc, dmar_reg,
               dout_io_reg, dout_mem_reg, halt_nxt, if_frst, inta_frst, io_data_in,
               ivec_data_in, ld_dmaa, ld_wait, mem_data_in, output_inh, rd_frst, rd_nxt,
               resetb, reti_nxt, tran_sel, wr_frst);

  input          clkc;          /* main cpu clock                                    */
  input          dmar_reg;      /* latched dma request                               */
  input          halt_nxt;      /* halt cycle identifier                             */
  input          if_frst;       /* first part of fetch cycle identifier              */
  input          inta_frst;     /* first part of intack cycle identifier             */
  input          ld_dmaa;       /* load dma request                                  */
  input          ld_wait;       /* load wait request                                 */
  input          output_inh;    /* disable cpu outputs                               */
  input          rd_frst;       /* first part of read cycle identifier               */
  input          rd_nxt;        /* read cycle identifier                             */
  input          resetb;        /* internal reset                                    */
  input          reti_nxt;      /* reti cycle identifier                             */
  input          wr_frst;       /* first part of write cycle identifier              */
  input    [7:0] dout_io_reg;   /* io data output                                    */
  input    [7:0] dout_mem_reg;  /* mem data output                                   */
  input    [7:0] io_data_in;    /* i/o input data bus                                */
  input    [7:0] ivec_data_in;  /* interrupt vector bus                              */
  input    [7:0] mem_data_in;   /* memory input bus                                  */
  input   [15:0] addr_reg_in;   /* processor logical address bus                     */
  input  [`TTYPE_IDX:0] tran_sel;    /* transaction type select                      */
  output         dma_ack;       /* dma acknowledge                                   */
  output         ftch_tran;     /* instruction fetch transaction                     */
  output         halt_tran;     /* halt transaction                                  */
  output         iack_tran;     /* interrupt acknowledge transaction                 */
  output         io_read;       /* i/o read enable                                   */
```

```
output         io_strobe;     /* i/o data strobe                               */
output         io_tran;       /* i/o transaction                               */
output         ivec_rd;       /* interrupt vector enable                       */
output         mem_rd;        /* memory read enable                            */
output         mem_tran;      /* memory transaction                            */
output         mem_wr;        /* memory write enable                           */
output         reti_tran;     /* return from interrupt transaction             */
output         t1;            /* first clock of transaction                    */
output   [7:0] data_in;       /* data input bus                                */
output   [7:0] io_data_out;   /* i/o output data bus                           */
output   [7:0] mem_data_out;  /* memory output data bus                        */
output  [15:0] io_addr_out;   /* i/o address bus                               */
output  [15:0] mem_addr_out;  /* memory address bus                            */
```

Listing 6-21. extint.v inputs and outputs.

The first section of extint.v is shown in Listing 6-22, and uses the transaction status to do the multiplexing of the input buses. It also inhibits the data output buses during Halt and Bus Release and creates a couple of internal signals.

```
/*****************************************************************************/
/*                                                                           */
/* misc signals & buses                                                      */
/*                                                                           */
/*****************************************************************************/
assign io_data_out  = (out_inh_reg) ? 8'h00 : dout_io_reg;
assign mem_data_out = (out_inh_reg) ? 8'h00 : dout_mem_reg;
assign ld_io_addr   = tran_sel[`TT_IO] || output_inh;
assign ld_mem_addr  = tran_sel[`TT_IAK] || tran_sel[`TT_IDL] || tran_sel[`TT_IF] ||
                      tran_sel[`TT_MEM] || tran_sel[`TT_STK];

always @ (iack_tran or io_tran or io_data_in or ivec_data_in or mem_data_in) begin
  case ({iack_tran, io_tran})
    2'b01:    data_in = io_data_in;
    2'b10:    data_in = ivec_data_in;
    default:  data_in = mem_data_in;
    endcase
  end
```

Listing 6-22. extint.v external bus multiplexing.

The remainder of the extint.v module is straightforward, as shown in Listing 6-23. Notice how the coding relies on the one-hot nature of the `tran_sel` control bus. This coding style makes the Verilog code much more readable. It also makes it very easy to modify the code to generate a `ftch_tran` or `stk_tran` signal if desired.

```
/*****************************************************************************************/
/*                                                                                       */
/* timing generation                                                                     */
/*                                                                                       */
/*****************************************************************************************/
always @ (posedge clkc or negedge resetb) begin
  if (!resetb) begin
    dma_ack      <= 1'b0;
    ftch_tran    <= 1'b0;
    halt_tran    <= 1'b0;
    iack_tran    <= 1'b0;
    io_addr_out  <= 16'h0000;
    io_read      <= 1'b0;
    io_tran      <= 1'b0;
    mem_addr_out <= 16'h0000;
    mem_tran     <= 1'b0;
    out_inh_reg  <= 1'b0;
    reti_tran    <= 1'b0;
    end
  else if (|tran_sel) begin
    dma_ack      <= ld_dmaa && dmar_reg;
    ftch_tran    <= tran_sel[`TT_IF];
    halt_tran    <= halt_nxt;
    iack_tran    <= tran_sel[`TT_IAK];
    if (ld_io_addr) io_addr_out <= (output_inh) ? 16'h0000 : addr_reg_in;
    io_read      <= tran_sel[`TT_IO] && rd_nxt;
    io_tran      <= tran_sel[`TT_IO];
    if (ld_mem_addr) mem_addr_out <= (output_inh) ? 16'h0000 : addr_reg_in;
    mem_tran     <= (tran_sel[`TT_IDL] || tran_sel[`TT_IF] || tran_sel[`TT_MEM] ||
                     tran_sel[`TT_STK]) && !output_inh;
    out_inh_reg  <= output_inh;
    reti_tran    <= reti_nxt;
    end
  end
```

```
always @ (posedge clkc or negedge resetb) begin
  if (!resetb) begin
    io_strobe    <= 1'b0;
    ivec_rd      <= 1'b0;
    mem_rd       <= 1'b0;
    mem_wr       <= 1'b0;
    t1           <= 1'b0;
    end
  else begin
    io_strobe    <= io_tran && (rd_frst || wr_frst);
    ivec_rd      <= iack_tran && inta_frst;
    mem_rd       <= (if_frst || (mem_tran && rd_frst)) && ld_wait;
    mem_wr       <= mem_tran && wr_frst;
    t1           <= |tran_sel && !(halt_nxt || dmar_reg);
    end
  end
```

Listing 6-23. extint.v timing generation.

The aluamux.v module

The aluamux.v module implements ALU input multiplexer specified in the *ALU A* worksheet. The connection diagram for this module is shown in Figure 6-4.

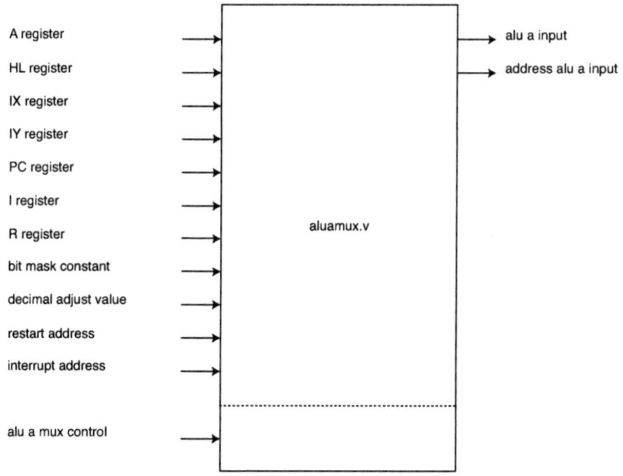

Figure 6-4. Connection diagram for the aluamux.v module.

The interface for the aluamux.v module is shown in Listing 6-24. If you count the number of inputs to the module versus the identifiers in the worksheet you'll notice that some are missing. There is no particular reason to create the constant values of zero, one, negative one and negative two outside of the module, so I'll just implement them inside this module.

One of the reasons that I went with a two-clock machine cycle was to use the regular ALU to do the increment of the PC register. But in the interest of performance, I am going to implement the ALU with a couple of separate paths, one for data and one for addresses. The address calculations that use the ALU require only a fraction of the cases that are otherwise required, so a separate path for the address calculations will be faster. This is why there are two output buses from the aluamux.v module.

```
module aluamux (adda_in, alua_in, alua_reg, aa_reg_out, bit_mask, daa_out, hl_reg_out,
                ii_reg, int_addr, ix_reg, iy_reg, pc_reg, rr_reg, rst_addr);

  input    [7:0] aa_reg_out;     /* a register output                                    */
  input    [7:0] bit_mask;       /* bit mask for bit operations                          */
  input    [7:0] daa_out;        /* daa constant                                         */
  input    [7:0] ii_reg;         /* i register output                                    */
  input    [7:0] rr_reg;         /* r register output                                    */
  input    [7:0] rst_addr;       /* restart address                                      */
  input   [15:0] hl_reg_out;     /* hl register output                                   */
  input   [15:0] int_addr;       /* interrupt address                                    */
  input   [15:0] ix_reg;         /* ix register output                                   */
  input   [15:0] iy_reg;         /* iy register output                                   */
  input   [15:0] pc_reg;         /* pc register output                                   */
  input   [`ALUA_IDX:0] alua_reg;    /* pipelined alu input a mux control                */
  output  [15:0] adda_in;        /* address alu a input bus                              */
  output  [15:0] alua_in;        /* alu a input bus                                      */
```

Listing 6-24. aluamux.v inputs and outputs.

The path for data through the module is shown in Listing 6-25. The multiplexer in this section uses a different Verilog coding style from the examples that I have shown previously. With this coding style the logic synthesis tool gives about 15% better performance. If I had to guess, I would say that this is because the synthesis tool is forced to preserve the individual `alua_in_` signals, which are generated with simple logic. Then these individual signals are combined using more simple logic, resulting in higher performance.

Note that there is no explicit case for selecting an output of all zeros. The all zeros case naturally falls out of this implementation if no other case is selected.

```
/*****************************************************************************************/
/*                                                                                       */
/* alu input a select                                                                    */
/*                                                                                       */
/*****************************************************************************************/
always @ (alua_reg or aa_reg_out or bit_mask or daa_out or ii_reg or int_addr or
          hl_reg_out or ix_reg or iy_reg or pc_reg or rr_reg or rst_addr) begin
  alua_in_0  = 16'h0;
  alua_in_1  = 16'h0;
  alua_in_2  = 16'h0;
  alua_in_3  = 16'h0;
  alua_in_4  = 16'h0;
  alua_in_5  = 16'h0;
  alua_in_6  = 16'h0;
  alua_in_7  = 16'h0;
  alua_in_8  = 16'h0;
  alua_in_9  = 16'h0;
  alua_in_10 = 16'h0;
  alua_in_11 = 16'h0;
  alua_in_12 = 16'h0;
  alua_in_13 = 16'h0;
  if (alua_reg[`AA_ONE]) alua_in_0  = 16'h0001;
  if (alua_reg[`AA_M1])  alua_in_1  = 16'hffff;
  if (alua_reg[`AA_M2])  alua_in_2  = 16'hfffe;
  if (alua_reg[`AA_HL])  alua_in_3  = hl_reg_out;
  if (alua_reg[`AA_IX])  alua_in_4  = ix_reg;
  if (alua_reg[`AA_IY])  alua_in_5  = iy_reg;
  if (alua_reg[`AA_PC])  alua_in_6  = pc_reg;
  if (alua_reg[`AA_AA])  alua_in_7  = {8'h00, aa_reg_out};
  if (alua_reg[`AA_BIT]) alua_in_8  = {8'h00, bit_mask};
  if (alua_reg[`AA_DAA]) alua_in_9  = {8'h00, daa_out};
  if (alua_reg[`AA_II])  alua_in_10 = {8'h00, ii_reg};
  if (alua_reg[`AA_RR])  alua_in_11 = {8'h00, rr_reg};
  if (alua_reg[`AA_INT]) alua_in_12 = int_addr;
  if (alua_reg[`AA_RST]) alua_in_13 = {8'h00, rst_addr};
  end
```

```
always @ (alua_in_0  or alua_in_1  or alua_in_2  or alua_in_3  or alua_in_4  or
          alua_in_5  or alua_in_6  or alua_in_7  or alua_in_8  or alua_in_9  or
          alua_in_10 or alua_in_11 or alua_in_12 or alua_in_13) begin
  alua_in = alua_in_0  | alua_in_1  | alua_in_2  | alua_in_3  | alua_in_4  |
            alua_in_5  | alua_in_6  | alua_in_7  | alua_in_8  | alua_in_9  |
            alua_in_10 | alua_in_11 | alua_in_12 | alua_in_13;
  end
```

Listing 6-25. aluamux.v data multiplexer.

The address path through the module is shown in Listing 6-26. It uses the exact same coding style except that `assign` statements are used instead of a `case` statement as in the previous section. Notice that the address path only requires seven separate cases, while the data path required fourteen.

```
/*******************************************************************************************/
/*                                                                                         */
/* address alu input a select                                                              */
/*                                                                                         */
/*******************************************************************************************/
assign adda_in_0  = (alua_reg[`AA_ONE]) ? 16'h0001           : 16'h0000;
assign adda_in_1  = (alua_reg[`AA_M1])  ? 16'hffff           : 16'h0000;
assign adda_in_2  = (alua_reg[`AA_M2])  ? 16'hfffe           : 16'h0000;
assign adda_in_4  = (alua_reg[`AA_IX])  ? ix_reg             : 16'h0000;
assign adda_in_5  = (alua_reg[`AA_IY])  ? iy_reg             : 16'h0000;
assign adda_in_12 = (alua_reg[`AA_INT]) ? int_addr           : 16'h0000;
assign adda_in_13 = (alua_reg[`AA_RST]) ? {8'h00,  rst_addr} : 16'h0000;

assign adda_in = adda_in_0  | adda_in_1  | adda_in_2  | adda_in_4  | adda_in_5 |
                 adda_in_12 | adda_in_13;
```

Listing 6-26. aluamux.v address multiplexer.

The alubmux.v module

The alubmux.v module implements ALU input multiplexer specified in the *ALU B* worksheet. Figure 6-5 shows the connection diagram for this module.

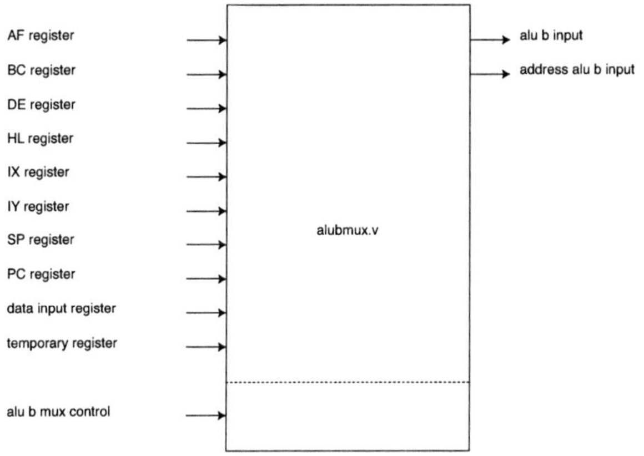

Figure 6-5. Connection diagram for the alubmux.v module.

Listing 6-27 shows the interface for the alubmux.v module. The two ALU input multiplexers ended up being reasonably balanced in terms of complexity.

```
module alubmux (addb_in, alub_in, alub_reg, af_reg_out, bc_reg_out, de_reg_out, din0_reg,
                din1_reg, hl_reg_out, ix_reg, iy_reg, pc_reg, sp_reg, tmp_reg);

  input    [7:0] din0_reg;       /* data input 0 register                              */
  input    [7:0] din1_reg;       /* data input 1 register                              */
  input   [15:0] af_reg_out;     /* af register output                                 */
  input   [15:0] bc_reg_out;     /* bc register output                                 */
  input   [15:0] de_reg_out;     /* de register output                                 */
  input   [15:0] hl_reg_out;     /* hl register output                                 */
  input   [15:0] ix_reg;         /* ix register output                                 */
  input   [15:0] iy_reg;         /* iy register output                                 */
  input   [15:0] pc_reg;         /* pc register output                                 */
  input   [15:0] sp_reg;         /* sp register output                                 */
  input   [15:0] tmp_reg;        /* temporary register output                          */
  input   [`ALUB_IDX:0] alub_reg;   /* pipelined alu input b mux control               */
  output  [15:0] addb_in;        /* address alu b input bus                            */
  output  [15:0] alub_in;        /* alu b input bus                                    */
```

Listing 6-27. alubmux.v inputs and outputs.

The section of alubmux.v in Listing 6-28 is the path for data through the multiplexer. This multiplexer needs to be able to shift the high byte of the input to the low byte. The most efficient way to do this is to put the byte shifter on the output.

```
/*****************************************************************************************/
/*                                                                                       */
/* alu input b select                                                                    */
/*                                                                                       */
/*****************************************************************************************/
 always @ (alub_reg or af_reg_out or bc_reg_out or de_reg_out or hl_reg_out or ix_reg or
          iy_reg or sp_reg or din1_reg or din0_reg or tmp_reg or pc_reg) begin
  alub_mux_1  = 32'h0;
  alub_mux_2  = 32'h0;
  alub_mux_3  = 32'h0;
  alub_mux_4  = 32'h0;
  alub_mux_5  = 32'h0;
  alub_mux_6  = 32'h0;
  alub_mux_7  = 32'h0;
  alub_mux_8  = 32'h0;
  alub_mux_9  = 32'h0;
  alub_mux_10 = 32'h0;
  alub_mux_11 = 32'h0;
  if (alub_reg[`AB_AF])  alub_mux_1  = af_reg_out;
  if (alub_reg[`AB_BC])  alub_mux_2  = bc_reg_out;
  if (alub_reg[`AB_DE])  alub_mux_3  = de_reg_out;
  if (alub_reg[`AB_HL])  alub_mux_4  = hl_reg_out;
  if (alub_reg[`AB_IX])  alub_mux_5  = ix_reg;
  if (alub_reg[`AB_IY])  alub_mux_6  = iy_reg;
  if (alub_reg[`AB_SP])  alub_mux_7  = sp_reg;
  if (alub_reg[`AB_DIN]) alub_mux_8  = {din1_reg, din0_reg};
  if (alub_reg[`AB_IO])  alub_mux_9  = {af_reg_out[15:8], din0_reg};
  if (alub_reg[`AB_TMP]) alub_mux_10 = tmp_reg;
  if (alub_reg[`AB_PC])  alub_mux_11 = pc_reg;
  end
```

```
always @ (alub_mux_1 or alub_mux_2 or alub_mux_3 or alub_mux_4 or alub_mux_5 or
          alub_mux_6 or alub_mux_7 or alub_mux_8 or alub_mux_9 or alub_mux_10 or
          alub_mux_11) begin
  alub_mux = alub_mux_1 | alub_mux_2 | alub_mux_3 | alub_mux_4 | alub_mux_5 |
             alub_mux_6 | alub_mux_7 | alub_mux_8 | alub_mux_9 | alub_mux_10 | alub_mux_11;
  end

assign alub_in  = (alub_reg[`AB_SHR]) ? {alub_mux[15:8], alub_mux[15:8]} : alub_mux;
```

Listing 6-28. alubmux.v data multiplexer.

The address path through the multiplexer is again much simpler, as shown in Listing 6-29. Since the byte shift function is never needed for addresses I can create the output bus directly.

```
/*****************************************************************************************/
/*                                                                                       */
/* address alu input b select                                                            */
/*                                                                                       */
/*****************************************************************************************/
assign addb_mux_2  = (alub_reg[`AB_BC])  ? bc_reg_out                    : 16'h0;
assign addb_mux_3  = (alub_reg[`AB_DE])  ? de_reg_out                    : 16'h0;
assign addb_mux_4  = (alub_reg[`AB_HL])  ? hl_reg_out                    : 16'h0;
assign addb_mux_5  = (alub_reg[`AB_IX])  ? ix_reg                        : 16'h0;
assign addb_mux_6  = (alub_reg[`AB_IY])  ? iy_reg                        : 16'h0;
assign addb_mux_7  = (alub_reg[`AB_SP])  ? sp_reg                        : 16'h0;
assign addb_mux_8  = (alub_reg[`AB_DIN]) ? {din1_reg, din0_reg}          : 16'h0;
assign addb_mux_9  = (alub_reg[`AB_IO])  ? {af_reg_out[15:8], din0_reg} : 16'h0;
assign addb_mux_10 = (alub_reg[`AB_TMP]) ? tmp_reg                       : 16'h0;
assign addb_mux_12 = (alub_reg[`AB_ADR]) ? pc_reg                        : 16'h0;

assign addb_in =  addb_mux_2 | addb_mux_3 | addb_mux_4 | addb_mux_5  | addb_mux_6 |
                  addb_mux_7  | addb_mux_8 |addb_mux_9 | addb_mux_10 | addb_mux_12;
```

Listing 6-29. alubmux.v address multiplexer.

The data outputs from both ALU input multiplexers feed into all three ALU function units, but I am going to implement the address calculations separately. This is mainly because the address calculation really only uses four of the ALU operations, so the logic can be fairly simple.

The alu_math.v module

The alu_math.v module implements all of the add and subtract operations for the ALU, and the connection diagram is shown in Figure 6-6.

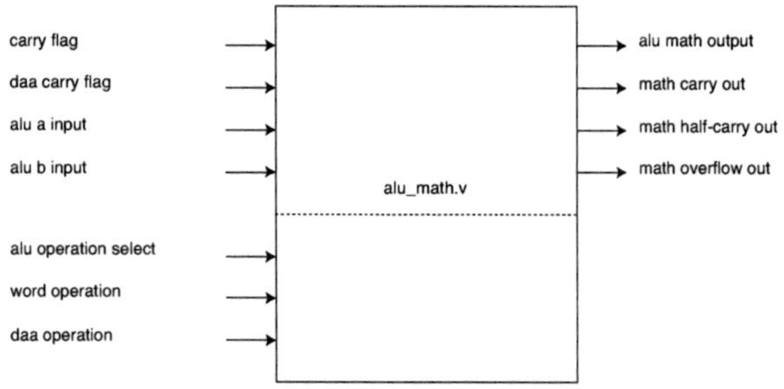

Figure 6-6. Connection diagram for the alu_math.v module.

Most of the inputs to the alu_math.v module are as you would expect, as shown in Listing 6-30. The exceptions are for the Decimal Adjust operation. For this operation it is easiest to generate the carry result in the same logic that generates the adjust value, so this is the dedicated `carry_daa` input to the module.

The `daa_op` signal has the same timing as the `aluop_reg` bus and enables the special Decimal Adjust carry signal. The `word_op` signal also has the same timing as the `aluop_reg` bus and selects the appropriate carry result for the operations.

Notice that the index for the aluop_reg control bus uses the `AOP_IDX mnemonic, which strips off the unit select bits. As I mentioned before, this should improve the performance of the ALU.

```
module alu_math (adder_c, adder_hc, adder_out, adder_ov, alua_in, alub_in, aluop_reg,
                 carry_bit, carry_daa, daa_op, word_op);

  input          carry_bit;      /* carry flag                                    */
  input          carry_daa;      /* carry for daa                                 */
  input          daa_op;         /* daa operation                                 */
  input          word_op;        /* word operation                                */
```

```
input  [15:0] alua_in;       /* alu a input                              */
input  [15:0] alub_in;       /* alu b input                              */
input  [`AOP_IDX:0] aluop_reg;   /* alu operation control subset         */
output         adder_c;      /* alu math carry result                    */
output         adder_hc;     /* alu math half-carry result               */
output         adder_ov;     /* alu math overflow result                 */
output [15:0] adder_out;     /* alu math result                          */
```

Listing 6-30. alu_math.v inputs and outputs.

The first section of the module, shown in Listing 6-31, creates a couple of signals for use inside the module. Conditionally passing the `carry_bit` information to the add/subtract section makes that section much simpler to code. The same is true for the `bsign_ext` bus, which is the sign-extend byte for use when adding a signed byte to a word. Even though this operation is used only for addresses, it needs to also be implemented in this module so that the result can be loaded into the Temporary register.

```
/*****************************************************************************************/
/*                                                                                       */
/* alu math carry input, sign extend                                                     */
/*                                                                                       */
/*****************************************************************************************/
always @ (aluop_reg or carry_bit) begin
  casex (aluop_reg) //synopsys parallel_case
    `AOP_ADC,
    `AOP_BADC,
    `AOP_SBC,
    `AOP_BSBC: alu_cin = carry_bit;
    default:   alu_cin = 1'b0;
    endcase
  end

assign bsign_ext = {alub_in[7],  alub_in[7],  alub_in[7],  alub_in[7],
                    alub_in[7],  alub_in[7],  alub_in[7],  alub_in[7]};
```

Listing 6-31. alu_math.v carry input and sign extend.

The section in Listing 6-32 is the actual math part of the module. I have to implement the logic this way to provide access to the carry result out of each nibble. Notice that I always choose the most common operation as the default case to minimize the decoding necessary for the `aluop_reg` control bus. You can see the advantage of multiplexing the carry input outside of the math unit. I could have just as well done the same thing with the `alub_in` high byte and `bsign_ext`.

```
/*****************************************************************************************/
/*                                                                                       */
/* alu math function unit                                                                */
/*                                                                                       */
/*****************************************************************************************/
always @ (aluop_reg or alua_in or alub_in or alu_cin) begin
  casex (aluop_reg) //synopsys parallel_case
    `AOP_SUB,
    `AOP_BSUB,
    `AOP_SBC,
    `AOP_BSBC: alu0_out = alua_in[3:0] - alub_in[3:0] - alu_cin;
    default:   alu0_out = alua_in[3:0] + alub_in[3:0] + alu_cin;
    endcase
  end

always @ (aluop_reg or alua_in or alub_in or alu0_out) begin
  casex (aluop_reg) //synopsys parallel_case
    `AOP_SUB,
    `AOP_BSUB,
    `AOP_SBC,
    `AOP_BSBC: alu1_out = alua_in[7:4] - alub_in[7:4] - alu0_out[4];
    default:   alu1_out = alua_in[7:4] + alub_in[7:4] + alu0_out[4];
    endcase
  end

always @ (aluop_reg or alua_in or alub_in or alu1_out or bsign_ext) begin
  casex (aluop_reg) //synopsys parallel_case
    `AOP_ADS:   alu2_out = alua_in[11:8] + bsign_ext[11:8] + alu1_out[4];
    `AOP_SUB,
    `AOP_BSUB,
    `AOP_SBC,
    `AOP_BSBC:  alu2_out = alua_in[11:8] - alub_in[11:8] - alu1_out[4];
    default:    alu2_out = alua_in[11:8] + alub_in[11:8] + alu1_out[4];
    endcase
  end
```

```
always @ (aluop_reg or alua_in or alub_in or alu2_out or bsign_ext) begin
  casex (aluop_reg) //synopsys parallel_case
    `AOP_ADS:    alu3_out = alua_in[15:12] + bsign_ext[15:12] + alu2_out[4];
    `AOP_SUB,
    `AOP_BSUB,
    `AOP_SBC,
    `AOP_BSBC:   alu3_out = alua_in[15:12] - alub_in[15:12] - alu2_out[4];
    default:     alu3_out = alua_in[15:12] + alub_in[15:12] + alu2_out[4];
    endcase
  end

assign adder_out = {alu3_out[3:0], alu2_out[3:0], alu1_out[3:0], alu0_out[3:0]};
```

Listing 6-32. alu_math.v math function unit.

The flag generation logic is shown in Listing 6-33. The intermediate carry information flows though the byte/word multiplexer to the module outputs except in the Decimal Adjust case. I use the `word_op` signal rather than decoding the `aluop_reg` control bus because I need to generate this signal outside of this module anyway.

The overflow signal is easiest to generate by directly decoding the `aluop_reg` control bus. Remember that arithmetic overflow for an add operation occurs when the sign of the two operands are the same and the sign of the result is different. Arithmetic overflow for a subtract operation occurs when the signs of the operands are different and the sign of the result is the same as the sign of the subtrahend. This is exactly how I code the operation in Verilog.

```
/*****************************************************************************************/
/*                                                                                       */
/* alu math flag generation                                                              */
/*                                                                                       */
/*****************************************************************************************/
assign adder_c  = (word_op) ? alu3_out[4] :
                  (daa_op)  ? carry_daa   : alu1_out[4];
assign adder_hc = (word_op) ? alu2_out[4] : alu0_out[4];

always @ (aluop_reg or alua_in or alub_in or alu3_out or alu1_out or bsign_ext) begin
  casex (aluop_reg) //synopsys parallel_case
    `AOP_ADC,
    `AOP_ADD:  adder_ov = (!alu3_out[3] &&  alua_in[15] &&  alub_in[15]) ||
                          ( alu3_out[3] && !alua_in[15] && !alub_in[15]);
    `AOP_BADC,
```

```
    `AOP_BADD,
    `AOP_BDEC: adder_ov = (!alu1_out[3] &&  alua_in[7]  &&  alub_in[7]) ||
                          ( alu1_out[3] && !alua_in[7]  && !alub_in[7]);
    `AOP_SBC,
    `AOP_SUB:  adder_ov = (!alu3_out[3] &&  alua_in[15] && !alub_in[15]) ||
                          ( alu3_out[3] && !alua_in[15] &&  alub_in[15]);
    `AOP_BSBC,
    `AOP_BSUB: adder_ov = (!alu1_out[3] &&  alua_in[7]  && !alub_in[7]) ||
                          ( alu1_out[3] && !alua_in[7]  &&  alub_in[7]);
    default:   adder_ov = 1'b0;
    endcase
  end
```

Listing 6-33. alu_math.v math flag generation.

The alu_log.v module

The alu_log.v module implements all of the logical operations for the ALU, and this is also where I implement the two pass-through operations, the four rotate digit operations and the operations on the Carry flag. The connection diagram for this module is shown in Figure 6-7.

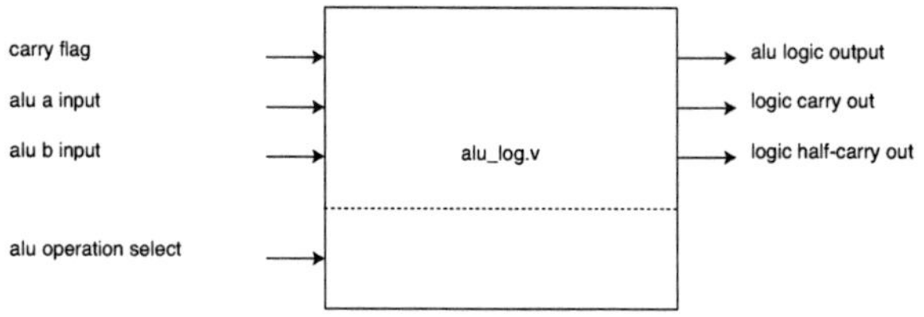

Figure 6-7. Connection diagram for the alu_log.v module.

No special inputs are required for this ALU function unit. The interface for the alu_log.v module is shown in Listing 6-34.

```
module alu_log  (logic_c, logic_hc, logic_out, alua_in, alub_in, aluop_reg, carry_bit);

  input          carry_bit;      /* cpu carry flag                                   */
  input   [15:0] alua_in;        /* alu a input                                      */
  input   [15:0] alub_in;        /* alu b input                                      */
  input   [`AOP_IDX:0] aluop_reg;    /* alu operation control                        */
  output         logic_c;        /* alu logic carry result                           */
  output         logic_hc;       /* alu logic half-carry result                      */
  output [15:0]  logic_out;      /* alu logic result                                 */
```

Listing 6-34. alu_log.v inputs and outputs.

The alu_log.v module itself is simple, with just one section of code, shown in Listing 6-35. The Carry and Half-Carry outputs are only needed for the special carry operations and will be inactive for all other operations. All of the logical operations in the module are straightforward to describe in Verilog after having gone through the effort of creating the design spreadsheet. Even the Rotate Digit operations are trivial to describe when I have the A register on the `alua_in` bus and the Data Input register on the `alub_in` bus.

```
  /*****************************************************************************************/
  /*                                                                                       */
  /* alu logic function                                                                    */
  /*                                                                                       */
  /*****************************************************************************************/
  always @ (aluop_reg or carry_bit) begin
    casex (aluop_reg)
      `AOP_CCF:   logic_c = !carry_bit;
      `AOP_SCF:   logic_c = 1'b1;
      default:    logic_c = 1'b0;
      endcase
    end

  always @ (aluop_reg or carry_bit) begin
    casex (aluop_reg)
      `AOP_BAND:  logic_hc = 1'b1;
      `AOP_CCF:   logic_hc = carry_bit;
      default:    logic_hc = 1'b0;
      endcase
    end
```

```
always @ (aluop_reg or alua_in or alub_in) begin
  casex (aluop_reg)
    `AOP_BAND:  logic_out = {8'h00, alua_in[7:0] & alub_in[7:0]};
    `AOP_BOR:   logic_out = {8'h00, alua_in[7:0] | alub_in[7:0]};
    `AOP_BXOR:  logic_out = {8'h00, alua_in[7:0] ^ alub_in[7:0]};
    `AOP_RLD1:  logic_out = {8'h00, alub_in[3:0],  alua_in[3:0]};
    `AOP_RLD2:  logic_out = {8'h00, alua_in[7:4],  alub_in[7:4]};
    `AOP_RRD1:  logic_out = {8'h00, alua_in[3:0],  alub_in[7:4]};
    `AOP_RRD2:  logic_out = {8'h00, alua_in[7:4],  alub_in[3:0]};
    `AOP_APAS:  logic_out = alua_in;
    `AOP_PASS:  logic_out = alub_in;
    default:    logic_out = 16'h0000;
    endcase
  end
```

Listing 6-35. alu_log.v logic functions.

The alu_shft.v module

The alu_shft.v module implements all of the normal rotate and shift operations for the ALU. I implemented the Rotate Digit operations in the alu_log.v module to balance out the amount of logic in each of the three ALU function units. The connection diagram for the alu_shft.v module is shown in Figure 6-8.

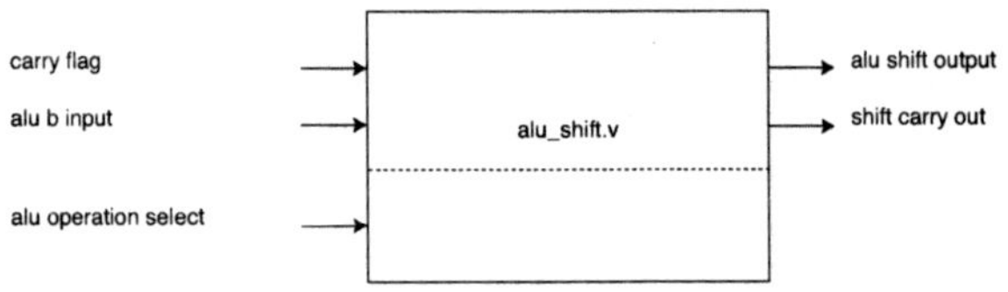

Figure 6-8. Connection diagram for the alu_shft.v module.

The interface for the alu_shft.v module is shown in Listing 6-36.

Like the alu_log.v module, no special inputs are required for this module, and I don't even need the `alua_in` input bus. Only the Carry output is needed because none of the instructions that use these operations affect the Half-Carry flag.

There are no word shift operations, so I won't bother to make this module support anything other than byte-wide inputs and outputs.

```
module alu_shft (shft_c, shft_out, alub_in, aluop_reg, carry_bit);

  input          carry_bit;      /* carry flag input                                  */
  input   [7:0] alub_in;         /* alu b input                                       */
  input  [`AOP_IDX:0] aluop_reg;    /* alu operation control subset                   */
  output         shft_c;         /* alu shifter carry output                          */
  output  [7:0] shft_out;        /* alu shifter output                                */
```

Listing 6-36. alu_shft.v inputs and outputs.

This module also only requires one section for the Verilog code, shown in Listing 6-37. It turns out that the special *rla*, *rlca*, *rra* and *rrca* identifiers are not needed, but I won't bother going back and eliminating them at this point. Keeping them effectively reduces the number of bits required for decoding, so it isn't really a big deal. As in alu_log.v, specifying the operations is straightforward.

The Carry output signal only has three cases, so I could simplify the Verilog code by grouping cases with the same output. I prefer to keep it this way, using the same identifier order that I use in the shifter output generation because that makes it easier to find the `shft_c` value that goes with the corresponding `shft_out` value.

```
/*****************************************************************************************/
/*                                                                                       */
/* alu shifter function                                                                  */
/*                                                                                       */
/*****************************************************************************************/
always @ (aluop_reg or alub_in) begin
  casex (aluop_reg) //synopsys parallel_case
    `AOP_RL,
    `AOP_RLA:   shft_c = alub_in[7];
    `AOP_RLC,
    `AOP_RLCA:  shft_c = alub_in[7];
    `AOP_RR,
    `AOP_RRA:   shft_c = alub_in[0];
    `AOP_RRC,
    `AOP_RRCA:  shft_c = alub_in[0];
    `AOP_SLA:   shft_c = alub_in[7];
```

```
      `AOP_SRA:    shft_c = alub_in[0];
      `AOP_SRL:    shft_c = alub_in[0];
      default:     shft_c = 1'b0;
      endcase
    end

  always @ (aluop_reg or alub_in or carry_bit) begin
    casex (aluop_reg) //synopsys parallel_case
      `AOP_RL,
      `AOP_RLA:    shft_out = {alub_in[6:0], carry_bit};
      `AOP_RLC,
      `AOP_RLCA:   shft_out = {alub_in[6:0], alub_in[7]};
      `AOP_RR,
      `AOP_RRA:    shft_out = {carry_bit, alub_in[7:1]};
      `AOP_RRC,
      `AOP_RRCA:   shft_out = {alub_in[0], alub_in[7:1]};
      `AOP_SLA:    shft_out = {alub_in[6:0], 1'b0};
      `AOP_SRA:    shft_out = {alub_in[7], alub_in[7:1]};
      `AOP_SRL:    shft_out = {1'b0, alub_in[7:1]};
      default:     shft_out = 8'h00;
      endcase
      end
```

Listing 6-37. alu_shft.v shifter functions.

That takes care of the three ALU function units. For all the apparent complexity involved in the ALU it really only requires a few pages of Verilog code to specify. The effort that I put into the design spreadsheet pays off because all of the operations required have been worked out in advance, and it's just a matter of translating the operations into Verilog code.

The aluout.v module

The aluout.v module combines the outputs of the three ALU function units into a single internal data bus. The update values for all of the flags are also created in this module. The connection diagram for this module is shwon in Figure 6-9.

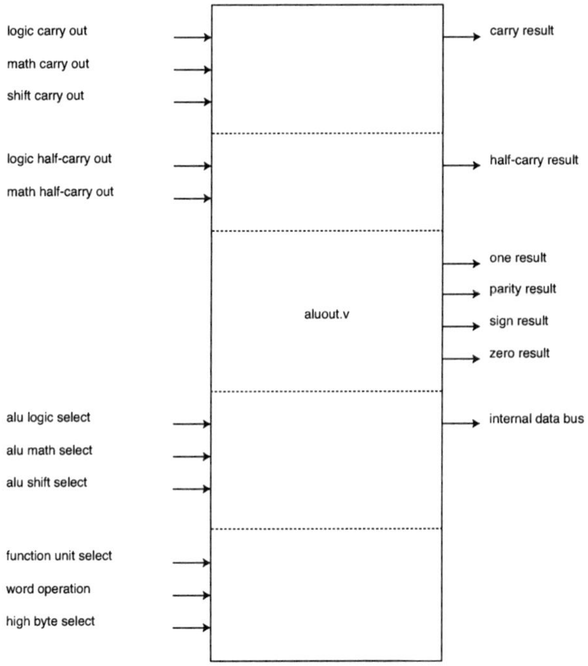

Figure 6-9. Connection diagram for the aluout.v module.

The module interface for aluout.v is shown in Listing 6-38.

There are two new signals used by this module. The `hi_byte` signal is active when the destination for the data bus is one of the registers on the high byte of the data bus. Since I always right-justify the data through the ALU I need to shift the result from the low byte to the high byte for the write back to a register. I could do this operation outside of this module, but I think that it makes more sense to do it here. The `unit_sel` bus is just the two most-significant bits of the ALU operation control field.

```
module aluout (cry_nxt, data_bus, hcar_nxt, one_nxt, par_nxt, sign_nxt, zero_nxt, adder_c,
               adder_hc, adder_out, hi_byte, logic_c, logic_hc, logic_out, shft_c, shft_out,
               unit_sel, word_op);

  input         adder_c;       /* math carry result                                    */
  input         adder_hc;      /* math half-carry result                               */
  input         hi_byte;       /* shift left byte control                              */
  input         logic_c;       /* logic carry result                                   */
  input         logic_hc;      /* logic half-carry result                              */
  input         shft_c;        /* shift carry result                                   */
  input         word_op;       /* word operation                                       */
  input   [1:0] unit_sel;      /* alu function unit select                             */
  input   [7:0] shft_out;      /* shift unit result                                    */
  input  [15:0] adder_out;     /* math unit result                                     */
  input  [15:0] logic_out;     /* logic unit result                                    */
  output        cry_nxt;       /* carry flag next                                      */
  output        hcar_nxt;      /* half-carry flag next                                 */
  output        one_nxt;       /* one flag next                                        */
  output        par_nxt;       /* parity flag next                                     */
  output        sign_nxt;      /* sign flag next                                       */
  output        zero_nxt;      /* zero flag next                                       */
  output [15:0] data_bus;      /* datapath data bus                                    */
```

Listing 6-38. aluout.v inputs and outputs.

The first section of the aluout.v module, shown in Listing 6-39, is where the outputs of the individual ALU function units are combined. The output of the alu_shft.v module is only eight bits so this is where I expand it to sixteen bits. I have made the output of the alu_log.v module the default case because that is also the default case for the `unit_sel` control bus, and I prefer not to mix default cases.

```
/*****************************************************************************************/
/*                                                                                       */
/* alu function unit combination                                                         */
/*                                                                                       */
/*****************************************************************************************/
always @ (unit_sel or adder_out or logic_out or shft_out) begin
  casex (unit_sel)
    2'b01:   alu_result = adder_out;
    2'b1x:   alu_result = {8'h00, shft_out};
    default: alu_result = logic_out;
    endcase
  end
```

Listing 6-39. aluout.v combining the function unit outputs.

The next section of the aluout.v module, shown in Listing 6-40, generates all of the raw results for the flags. I will combine these raw results outside of this module using the various flag control signals.

The Carry flag and Half-Carry flag are created just like the `alu_result` bus is in the previous section. There is no Half-Carry output from the alu_shft.v module, so that is why the Half-Carry description is different.

The `one_nxt` signal is the test for an output value of one. Remember that this case is needed by the block compare instructions because of where the count decrement operation is performed. This test always coincides with a word operation.

The `par_nxt` signal is the test for the parity of the result. This is always a byte operation.

Both the `sign_nxt` and `zero_nxt` signals have different byte and word cases, so this is why the `word_op` signal is needed in this module.

```
/*****************************************************************************************/
/*                                                                                       */
/* alu flag outputs                                                                      */
/*                                                                                       */
/*****************************************************************************************/
always @ (unit_sel or adder_c or logic_c or shft_c) begin
  casex (unit_sel)
    2'b01:   cry_nxt = adder_c;
    2'b1x:   cry_nxt = shft_c;
    default: cry_nxt = logic_c;
    endcase
  end

always @ (unit_sel or adder_hc or logic_hc) begin
  casex (unit_sel)
    2'b01:   hcar_nxt = adder_hc;
    2'b1x:   hcar_nxt = 1'b0;
    default: hcar_nxt = logic_hc;
    endcase
  end

assign one_nxt  = ~|alu_result[7:1] && alu_result[0];
assign par_nxt  = ~^alu_result[7:0];
assign sign_nxt = (word_op) ?  alu_result[15]   :   alu_result[7];
assign zero_nxt = (word_op) ? ~|alu_result[15:0] : ~|alu_result[7:0];
```

Listing 6-40. aluout.v flag outputs.

The last section, shown in Listing 6-41, is just the one line where the byte shift is implemented. If the logic synthesis tool is doing its job properly the lower byte will not go through a multiplexer. Taking care of the byte alignment this way is much easier than trying to keep track of the different alignment cases within all of the ALU operations.

```
/*****************************************************************************************/
/*                                                                                       */
/* alu output left shift                                                                 */
/*                                                                                       */
/*****************************************************************************************/
assign data_bus = (hi_byte) ? {alu_result[7:0], alu_result[7:0]} : alu_result[15:0];
```

Listing 6-41. aluout.v byte shifter.

Now that all of the individual ALU modules are done I can start on the full data path, where all of these modules are instantiated.

The datapath.v module

In addition to instantiating all of the ALU modules, the datapath.v module contains all of the CPU registers, the interrupt logic, the page and instruction registers, and some other bits and pieces. Most of the datapath.v inputs come from the control section, and most of the outputs go to the control section. I showed a preliminary block diagram for datapath.v in Figure 5-21, so I won't show an updated version of it here. The interface for the datapath.v module is shown in Listing 6-42. Nearly all of the signals should be self-explanatory from the accompanying comments, but I'll go over the inputs that are in some way special.

The `clearb` signal is an asynchronous reset signal that is used only during simulation and testing. The original Z80 specification says that only some of the user-visible registers are cleared by reset, and for that I use the normal `resetb` signal. But simulation and testing will be simplified if I can also clear all of the registers without having to go through multiple instructions to get into a completely known state. This is what the `clearb` signal is for.

The `dma_req` signal is the bus request, directly from the top level of the design. All synchronization and sampling for this signal is done inside this module.

In the same way, the `int_req` and `nmi_req` signals are the interrupt request and non-maskable interrupt request. I am going to implement the non-maskable interrupt request a little differently from the original Z80. In the original Z80 design the non-maskable interrupt request was an edge-triggered signal, designed to catch short transient conditions. I don't like to use edge-triggering on anything except a clock, because such circuits are susceptible to noise and decoding glitches, so I am going to sample the `nmi_req` signal with the clock. I will still latch the condition, but the non-maskable interrupt request signal will need to remain active for at least one full clock cycle to be recognized.

The only other special input is the `ivec_rd` signal. Why does a signal from the external bus interface need to enter the datapath.v module? I need something to clear the latched non-maskable interrupt condition, and this signal has exactly the right timing. I am being a little lazy here, because I really should generate a dedicated signal in the control section to do this.

```
module datapath (addr_reg_in, carry_bit, dmar_reg, dout_io_reg, dout_mem_reg, inst_reg,
                 intr_reg, page_reg, par_bit, sign_bit, tflg_reg, vector_int, xhlt_reg,
                 zero_bit, add_sel, alua_sel, alub_sel, aluop_sel, clearb, clkc, cflg_en,
                 data_in, di_ctl, dma_req, do_ctl, ex_af_pls, ex_bank_pls, ex_dehl_inst,
                 hflg_ctl, ief_ctl, imd_ctl, int_req, ivec_rd, ld_ctrl, ld_inst, ld_page,
                 nflg_ctl, nmi_req, page_sel, pc_sel, pflg_ctl, resetb, sflg_en, tflg_ctl,
                 wait_st, wr_addr, zflg_en);

  input          cflg_en;       /* carry flag control                              */
  input          clearb;        /* master (testing) reset                          */
  input          clkc;          /* main cpu clock                                  */
  input          dma_req;       /* dma request                                     */
  input          ex_af_pls;     /* exchange af,af'                                 */
  input          ex_bank_pls;   /* exchange register bank                          */
  input          ex_dehl_inst;  /* exchange de,hl                                  */
  input          int_req;       /* interrupt request                               */
  input          ivec_rd;       /* interrupt vector enable                         */
  input          ld_ctrl;       /* load control register                           */
  input          ld_inst;       /* load instruction register                       */
  input          ld_page;       /* load page register                              */
  input          nmi_req;       /* nmi request                                     */
  input          resetb;        /* internal (user) reset                           */
  input          sflg_en;       /* sign flag control                               */
  input          wait_st;       /* wait state identifier                           */
  input          zflg_en;       /* zero flag control                               */
  input    [3:0] page_sel;      /* instruction decode "page" control               */
  input    [7:0] data_in;       /* read data bus                                   */
```

```
input   [`ADCTL_IDX:0] add_sel;     /* address output mux control          */
input    [`ALUA_IDX:0] alua_sel;    /* alu input a mux control             */
input    [`ALUB_IDX:0] alub_sel;    /* alu input b mux control             */
input   [`ALUOP_IDX:0] aluop_sel;   /* alu operation control               */
input      [`DI_IDX:0] di_ctl;      /* data input control                  */
input      [`DO_IDX:0] do_ctl;      /* data output control                 */
input    [`HFLG_IDX:0] hflg_ctl;    /* half-carry flag control             */
input     [`IEF_IDX:0] ief_ctl;     /* interrupt enable control            */
input     [`IMD_IDX:0] imd_ctl;     /* interrupt mode control              */
input    [`NFLG_IDX:0] nflg_ctl;    /* negate flag control                 */
input   [`PCCTL_IDX:0] pc_sel;      /* program counter source control      */
input    [`PFLG_IDX:0] pflg_ctl;    /* parity/overflow flag control        */
input    [`TFLG_IDX:0] tflg_ctl;    /* temp flag control                   */
input    [`WREG_IDX:0] wr_addr;     /* register write address bus          */
output        carry_bit;      /* carry flag                                */
output        dmar_reg;       /* latched dma request                       */
output        intr_reg;       /* latched interrupt request                 */
output        par_bit;        /* parity flag                               */
output        sign_bit;       /* sign flag                                 */
output        tflg_reg;       /* temporary flag                            */
output        vector_int;     /* int vector enable                         */
output        xhlt_reg;       /* halt exit                                 */
output        zero_bit;       /* zero flag                                 */
output  [3:0] page_reg;       /* instruction decode "page"                 */
output  [7:0] inst_reg;       /* instruction register                      */
output  [7:0] dout_io_reg;    /* i/o write data bus                        */
output  [7:0] dout_mem_reg;   /* memory write data bus                     */
output [15:0] addr_reg_in;    /* processor address bus                     */
```

Listing 6-42. datapath.v inputs and outputs.

There is no particular requirement for the ordering of the sections within the datapath.v module, so I'll just go through them in the order that they appear in the actual code. I typically order sections starting with inputs and work my way through the logic to the outputs, much like I would work left-to-right entering a schematic.

Listing 6-43 contains the synchronization logic for the external bus request and interrupt requests. This is also where the `nmi_req` signal is latched, in the `nmi_hld` register. This register is set when a rising edge is detected on the `nmi_req` input and will be latched until the `ivec_rd` signal is active during the interrupt acknowledge machine cycle.

The valid_dma register is the synchronized bus request. The valid_int register is the synchronized interrupt request, either an enabled maskable interrupt or the non-maskable interrupt. The valid_nmi register distinguishes these two cases.

The valid_xhlt register is the signal used to force an exit from the Halt state. Remember that only an interrupt will cause an exit from the Halt state, while a bus request keeps the CPU in the Halt state.

These synchronized request signals are used in a later section where the interrupts are actually sampled.

```
/*****************************************************************************************/
/*                                                                                       */
/* input synchronization                                                                 */
/*                                                                                       */
/*****************************************************************************************/
always @ (posedge clkc or negedge resetb) begin
  if (!resetb) begin
    nmi_hld     <= 1'b0;
    valid_dma   <= 1'b0;
    valid_int   <= 1'b0;
    valid_nmi   <= 1'b0;
    valid_xhlt  <= 1'b0;
    end
  else begin
    nmi_hld     <= (nmi_req && !valid_nmi) || (!(ivec_rd && nmi_reg) && nmi_hld);
    valid_dma   <= dma_req;
    valid_int   <= nmi_req || nmi_hld || ((&ief_ctl[1:0] || ief1_reg) && int_req);
    valid_nmi   <= nmi_req || nmi_hld;
    valid_xhlt  <= !dma_req && (nmi_req || nmi_hld || (ief1_reg && int_req));
    end
  end
```

Listing 6-43. datapath.v external input synchronization.

Listing 6-44 contains the interrupt enable flags and the interrupt mode registers. I have chosen the encoding for the ief_ctl control bus to make it easy to implement the required functionality directly, without using the signals symbolically.

I pre-decode the interrupt mode registers `imd2_reg` and `imd1_reg` to simplify the timing analysis. These registers are used to create the interrupt branch location in a later section. This also makes it easy to generate the `vector_int` signal that is used in the control section to select the state sequence after the interrupt acknowledge machine cycle.

```
/*****************************************************************************************/
/*                                                                                       */
/* interrupt mode and enables                                                            */
/*                                                                                       */
/*****************************************************************************************/
always @ (posedge clkc or negedge resetb) begin
  if (!resetb) begin
    ief1_reg   <= 1'b0;
    ief2_reg   <= 1'b0;
    imd1_reg   <= 1'b0;
    imd2_reg   <= 1'b0;
    end
  else begin
    if (|ief_ctl[2:1]) ief1_reg <= (ief_ctl[1]) ? ief_ctl[0]  : (ief_ctl[0] && ief2_reg);
    if (|ief_ctl[2:1]) ief2_reg <= (ief_ctl[1]) ? ief_ctl[0]  :
                                   (ief_ctl[0]) ? ief2_reg    : (nmi_reg && ief1_reg);
    if (|imd_ctl)      imd1_reg <= imd_ctl[1] && !imd_ctl[0];
    if (|imd_ctl)      imd2_reg <= &imd_ctl;
    end
  end

assign vector_int = imd2_reg && !nmi_reg;
```

Listing 6-44. datapath.v interrupt mode and enables.

The `ld_dmar` and `ld_intr` signals in Listing 6-45 are the enables for the sampling of the bus request and the interrupt requests respectively. The `` `PC_DMA `` and `` `PC_INT `` cases are only active during clock cycles where a wait state is not possible, so they do not need to be conditioned with the `wait_st` information. But the normal interrupt sample occurs during the *if1a* state, which can be extended by wait states, so this case has to be conditioned with the `wait_st` information.

The `dmar_reg` signal is active while a bus request is pending, and this is the highest priority exception case. The `intr_reg` signal is active when an interrupt request is pending without a bus request. Both of these signals were used in the machine.v module to implement the modification to the normal state sequence. They will also be used in the control module.

The nmi_reg signal will be needed to create the interrupt branch address. The xhlt_reg signal will be needed in the control section to force an exit of the halt sequence because of an interrupt. Remember that this signal should not be active for a bus request.

```
/*****************************************************************************************/
/*                                                                                       */
/* interrupt pending                                                                     */
/*                                                                                       */
/*****************************************************************************************/
always @ (pc_sel or wait_st) begin
  case (pc_sel)
    `PC_DMA,                                             /* dma xfer dma sample         */
    `PC_INT:  ld_dmar = 1'b1;                            /* block inst dma sample       */
    `PC_NILD: ld_dmar = !wait_st;                        /* inst end dma sample         */
    default:  ld_dmar = 1'b0;
    endcase
  end

always @ (pc_sel or wait_st) begin
  case (pc_sel)
    `PC_INT:  ld_intr = 1'b1;                            /* block inst int sample       */
    `PC_NILD: ld_intr = !wait_st;                        /* inst end int sample         */
    default:  ld_intr = 1'b0;
    endcase
  end

always @ (posedge clkc or negedge resetb) begin
  if (!resetb) begin
    dmar_reg <= 1'b0;
    intr_reg <= 1'b0;
    nmi_reg  <= 1'b0;
    xhlt_reg <= 1'b0;
    end
  else begin
    if (ld_dmar) dmar_reg <= valid_dma;
    if (ld_intr) intr_reg <= !valid_dma && (valid_nmi || (iefl_reg && valid_int));
    if (ld_intr) nmi_reg  <= !valid_dma &&  valid_nmi;
    if (ld_intr) xhlt_reg <= !valid_dma &&  valid_xhlt;
    end
  end
```

Listing 6-45. datapath.v interrupt pending.

Listing 6-46 is where the register bank selects are created, along with the main register write enables. The first register write enable is for the PC register, with the `ld_pc` signal. I described the three cases in the *Load PC* worksheet section, so the only new thing here is conditioning the different cases with the `wait_st` information to prevent multiple loads of the PC register during a Wait state.

The two bank select controls, `alt_af_reg` and `alt_bnk_reg`, are toggled by signals that I'll generate in the control section. These signals will be active during the *if1b* state so they do not need to be conditioned by the `wait_st` or `ld_ctrl` signal.

The `ex_dehl_reg` signal is a registered control signal, so it needs to use the `ld_ctrl` version of the Wait state information. This signal will be active during the *if1b* state of the exchange instruction, and is used to control the multiplexing required to write two registers simultaneously.

I could implement the F register as individual flip-flops with individual write enables, and it might even be more efficient to do it that way, but instead I'm going to implement it as a normal byte-wide register. I think that it makes the code easier to understand, especially because of the complications due to the alternate bank function. So the special `ld_flag` signal will be active when writing to any flag, and I'll use a multiplexer to select which flags should be affected.

Finally, the `ld_regf` signal is the master write enable for the registers. Remember that I used one bit in the register write control bus as the write enable, which makes generating this signal easy.

```
/*****************************************************************************/
/*                                                                           */
/* register control                                                          */
/*                                                                           */
/*****************************************************************************/
always @ (pc_sel or dmar_reg or intr_reg or valid_dma or valid_int or wait_st) begin
  case (pc_sel)
    `PC_LD:    ld_pc = !wait_st;                        /* load PC unconditionally      */
    `PC_NILD:  ld_pc = !((iefl_reg && valid_int) || valid_nmi || valid_dma) && !wait_st;
    `PC_NILD2: ld_pc = !(intr_reg || dmar_reg) && !wait_st;     /* if no latched int      */
    default:   ld_pc = 1'b0;
    endcase
  end

always @ (posedge clkc or negedge resetb) begin
  if (!resetb) begin
    alt_af_reg  <= 1'b0;
    alt_bnk_reg <= 1'b0;
    ex_dehl_reg <= 1'b0;
```

```
    end
  else begin
    alt_af_reg  <= ex_af_pls   ^ alt_af_reg;
    alt_bnk_reg <= ex_bank_pls ^ alt_bnk_reg;
    ex_dehl_reg <= ex_dehl_inst && ld_ctrl;
    end
  end

assign ld_flag = (sflg_en || zflg_en || |hflg_ctl || |pflg_ctl || |nflg_ctl ||
                  cflg_en) && !wait_st;
assign ld_regf = wr_addr[`WR_REG] && !wait_st;
```

Listing 6-46. datapath.v register control.

Next comes the register interface section in Listing 6-47. The normal source for the data for all of the registers is the internal data bus, but the F register also needs the path to update the individual flags that I mentioned previously. Similarly, the DE register needs a special path so that I can do the exchange with the HL register in a single clock cycle.

The individual enables for the register writes are simple with the encoding for the `wr_addr` bus that I have chosen. All I need is the master write enable, `ld_regf`, the appropriate `wr_addr` bit, and the bank enable where appropriate. The timing is controlled by the master write enable and all of the decoding is embedded within the `wr_addr` encoding.

The bank information is also required on the register outputs, and that multiplexing is done in this section. I also assign some descriptive names for the accumulator, flag register and some of the individual flags.

The last thing generated in this section is the `hi_byte` signal that controls the byte shifter on the output of the ALU. The encoding of the `wr_addr` bus again makes the decoding straightforward.

```
/*****************************************************************************************/
/*                                                                                       */
/* cpu register interface                                                                */
/*                                                                                       */
/*****************************************************************************************/
assign ff_reg_in    = (ld_flag)     ? new_flags : data_bus[7:0];
assign de_reg_in    = (ex_dehl_reg) ? hl_reg_out : data_bus;
```

```
assign ld_m_aa =   ld_regf && wr_addr[`WR_AA] && !alt_af_reg;
assign ld_m_ff = ((ld_regf && wr_addr[`WR_FF]) || ld_flag) && !alt_af_reg;
assign ld_m_bb =   ld_regf && wr_addr[`WR_BB] && !alt_bnk_reg;
assign ld_m_cc =   ld_regf && wr_addr[`WR_CC] && !alt_bnk_reg;
assign ld_m_dd =   ld_regf && wr_addr[`WR_DD] && !alt_bnk_reg;
assign ld_m_ee =   ld_regf && wr_addr[`WR_EE] && !alt_bnk_reg;
assign ld_m_hh =   ld_regf && wr_addr[`WR_HH] && !alt_bnk_reg;
assign ld_m_ll =   ld_regf && wr_addr[`WR_LL] && !alt_bnk_reg;
assign ld_a_aa =   ld_regf && wr_addr[`WR_AA] &&  alt_af_reg;
assign ld_a_ff = ((ld_regf && wr_addr[`WR_FF]) || ld_flag) &&  alt_af_reg;
assign ld_a_bb =   ld_regf && wr_addr[`WR_BB] &&  alt_bnk_reg;
assign ld_a_cc =   ld_regf && wr_addr[`WR_CC] &&  alt_bnk_reg;
assign ld_a_dd =   ld_regf && wr_addr[`WR_DD] &&  alt_bnk_reg;
assign ld_a_ee =   ld_regf && wr_addr[`WR_EE] &&  alt_bnk_reg;
assign ld_a_hh =   ld_regf && wr_addr[`WR_HH] &&  alt_bnk_reg;
assign ld_a_ll =   ld_regf && wr_addr[`WR_LL] &&  alt_bnk_reg;
assign ld_sp   =   ld_regf && wr_addr[`WR_SP];
assign ld_ix   =   ld_regf && wr_addr[`WR_IX];
assign ld_iy   =   ld_regf && wr_addr[`WR_IY];
assign ld_ii   =   ld_regf && wr_addr[`WR_II];
assign ld_rr   =   ld_regf && wr_addr[`WR_RR];
assign ld_tmp  =   ld_regf && wr_addr[`WR_TMP];

assign af_reg_out = (alt_af_reg)  ? {a_aa_reg, a_ff_reg} : {m_aa_reg, m_ff_reg};
assign bc_reg_out = (alt_bnk_reg) ? {a_bb_reg, a_cc_reg} : {m_bb_reg, m_cc_reg};
assign de_reg_out = (alt_bnk_reg) ? {a_dd_reg, a_ee_reg} : {m_dd_reg, m_ee_reg};
assign hl_reg_out = (alt_bnk_reg) ? {a_hh_reg, a_ll_reg} : {m_hh_reg, m_ll_reg};
assign aa_reg_out = af_reg_out[15:8];
assign ff_reg_out = af_reg_out[7:0];
assign carry_bit  = af_reg_out[0];
assign par_bit    = af_reg_out[2];
assign sign_bit   = af_reg_out[7];
assign zero_bit   = af_reg_out[6];
assign hi_byte    = (wr_addr[`WR_AA] && !wr_addr[`WR_FF]) ||
                    (wr_addr[`WR_BB] && !wr_addr[`WR_CC]) ||
                    (wr_addr[`WR_DD] && !wr_addr[`WR_EE]) ||
                    (wr_addr[`WR_HH] && !wr_addr[`WR_LL]) ||
                     wr_addr[`WR_II] || wr_addr[`WR_RR];
```

Listing 6-47. datapath.v cpu register interface.

Listing 6-48 contains the actual CPU registers. Only a few of the registers are affected by the normal `resetb` signal, so I use the special `clearb` signal to clear the others for simulation and testing. If the partial-reset feature of the original Z80 isn't required, users can tie these two input signals together.

This is where the special input path for the Temporary register is implemented. Without this special path I would need an extra machine cycle during the interrupt acknowledge sequence to move the vector into this register. plus a special ALU operation to combine the I register and the vector.

```
/*****************************************************************************************/
/*                                                                                       */
/* cpu registers                                                                         */
/*                                                                                       */
/*****************************************************************************************/
always @ (posedge clkc or negedge clearb) begin
  if (!clearb) begin
    m_aa_reg <= 8'h00;
    m_ff_reg <= 8'h00;
    m_bb_reg <= 8'h00;
    m_cc_reg <= 8'h00;
    m_dd_reg <= 8'h00;
    m_ee_reg <= 8'h00;
    m_hh_reg <= 8'h00;
    m_ll_reg <= 8'h00;
    a_aa_reg <= 8'h00;
    a_ff_reg <= 8'h00;
    a_bb_reg <= 8'h00;
    a_cc_reg <= 8'h00;
    a_dd_reg <= 8'h00;
    a_ee_reg <= 8'h00;
    a_hh_reg <= 8'h00;
    a_ll_reg <= 8'h00;
    ix_reg   <= 16'h0000;
    iy_reg   <= 16'h0000;
    end
  else begin
    if (ld_m_aa) m_aa_reg <= data_bus[15:8];
```

```
      if (ld_m_ff) m_ff_reg <= ff_reg_in;
      if (ld_m_bb) m_bb_reg <= data_bus[15:8];
      if (ld_m_cc) m_cc_reg <= data_bus[7:0];
      if (ld_m_dd) m_dd_reg <= de_reg_in[15:8];
      if (ld_m_ee) m_ee_reg <= de_reg_in[7:0];
      if (ld_m_hh) m_hh_reg <= data_bus[15:8];
      if (ld_m_ll) m_ll_reg <= data_bus[7:0];
      if (ld_a_aa) a_aa_reg <= data_bus[15:8];
      if (ld_a_ff) a_ff_reg <= ff_reg_in;
      if (ld_a_bb) a_bb_reg <= data_bus[15:8];
      if (ld_a_cc) a_cc_reg <= data_bus[7:0];
      if (ld_a_dd) a_dd_reg <= de_reg_in[15:8];
      if (ld_a_ee) a_ee_reg <= de_reg_in[7:0];
      if (ld_a_hh) a_hh_reg <= data_bus[15:8];
      if (ld_a_ll) a_ll_reg <= data_bus[7:0];
      if (ld_ix)   ix_reg   <= data_bus;
      if (ld_iy)   iy_reg   <= data_bus;
      end
    end

  always @ (posedge clkc or negedge resetb) begin
    if (!resetb) begin
      ii_reg  <= 8'h00;
      pc_reg  <= 16'h0000;
      rr_reg  <= 8'h00;
      sp_reg  <= 16'h0000;
      tmp_reg <= 16'h0000;
      end
    else begin
      if (ld_ii)  ii_reg  <= data_bus[15:8];
      if (ld_pc)  pc_reg  <= data_bus;
      if (ld_rr)  rr_reg  <= data_bus[15:8];
      if (ld_sp)  sp_reg  <= data_bus;
      if (ld_tmp) tmp_reg <= (ivec_rd) ? {ii_reg, data_in} : data_bus;
      end
    end
```

Listing 6-48. datapath.v cpu registers.

The Temporary flag in Listing 6-49, called `tflg_reg`, is only used by the block instructions. This is an example where I do treat the control field symbolically to select between the different cases, mainly because there is no advantage to using a special encoding.

The block compare case is somewhat strange because of the way the terminal count is signaled. For this instruction the PV flag is cleared to signal that the count is complete, and this is the `!ff_reg_out[2]` term. In this case the `alu_zero` signal is signaling the result of the compare. In the other case where the `alu_zero` signal is used it is signaling that the count is complete.

```
/*****************************************************************************************/
/*                                                                                       */
/* temporary flag                                                                        */
/*                                                                                       */
/*****************************************************************************************/
assign ld_tflg = |tflg_ctl && !wait_st;

always @ (tflg_ctl or alu_one or alu_zero or ff_reg_out) begin
  casex (tflg_ctl)
    `TFLG_1:  tflg_nxt = alu_one;                      /* blk set if done (next xfr)   */
    `TFLG_Z:  tflg_nxt = alu_zero;                     /* blk set if done (this xfr)   */
    `TFLG_B:  tflg_nxt = alu_zero || !ff_reg_out[2];   /* blk cp set if done or match  */
    default:  tflg_nxt = 1'b0;
    endcase
  end

always @ (posedge clkc or negedge resetb) begin
  if       (!resetb) tflg_reg <= 1'b0;
  else if (ld_tflg) tflg_reg <= tflg_nxt;
  end
```

Listing 6-49. datapath.v temporary flag.

There is nothing special about the Data Input and Data Output registers in Listing 6-50. The load control signals need to be conditioned with the `wait_st` signal, and the control fields are used directly to take advantage of the encoding I am using. I thought about clearing these registers in the case of a Halt transaction or bus request, but decided that just masking the outputs in the extint.v module would be cheaper to implement.

```
/*****************************************************************************************/
/*                                                                                       */
/* data input and data output registers                                                  */
/*                                                                                       */
/*****************************************************************************************/
assign ld_dout_io   = do_ctl[1] && !wait_st;
assign ld_dout_mem  = do_ctl[2] && !wait_st;

always @ (posedge clkc or negedge resetb) begin
  if (!resetb) begin
    din0_reg     <= 8'h00;
    din1_reg     <= 8'h00;
    dout_io_reg  <= 8'h00;
    dout_mem_reg <= 8'h00;
    end
  else begin
    if (di_ctl[0])   din0_reg     <= data_in;
    if (di_ctl[1])   din1_reg     <= data_in;
    if (ld_dout_io)  dout_io_reg  <= data_bus[7:0];
    if (ld_dout_mem) dout_mem_reg <= (do_ctl[0]) ? data_bus[15:8]  : data_bus[7:0];
    end
  end
```

Listing 6-50. datapath.v data input and data output registers.

Listing 6-51 shows the instruction and page registers. The instruction register, `inst_reg`, is just another register. There is no need to condition the load control signal with the `wait_st` signal or the `ld_ctrl` signal because this register is only loaded in the *if1b*, *if2b* or *if3b* states.

The page register, `page_reg`, is another matter though. This register should change at the end of the clock cycle where the load is enabled, so it can be thought of as a registered control bus. This is why the `ld_ctrl` signal is used to condition the load enable signal for this register instead of the `wait_st` signal.

```
/*****************************************************************************************/
/*                                                                                       */
/* instruction and page registers                                                        */
/*                                                                                       */
/*****************************************************************************************/
always @ (posedge clkc or negedge resetb) begin
  if       (!resetb) inst_reg <= 8'h00;
  else if (ld_inst) inst_reg <= data_in;
  end

always @ (posedge clkc or negedge resetb) begin
  if                 (!resetb) page_reg <= 4'b0000;
  else if (ld_page && ld_ctrl) page_reg <= page_sel;
  end
```

Listing 6-51. datapath.v instruction and page registers.

The registered control buses and signals in Listing 6-52 need the same timing as the `page_reg` signals do, so the `ld_ctrl` signal is also used as the load enable here. This is where I pre-decode and register the *daa* case, the *bdec* case and the word operation case to use in the ALU.

```
/*****************************************************************************************/
/*                                                                                       */
/* alu control pipeline registers                                                        */
/*                                                                                       */
/*****************************************************************************************/
always @ (aluop_sel) begin
  case (aluop_sel)
    `ALUOP_DAA:  daa_sel = 1'b1;
    default:     daa_sel = 1'b0;
    endcase
  end
```

```
always @ (aluop_sel) begin
  case (aluop_sel)
    `ALUOP_BDEC: decr_sel = 1'b1;
    default:     decr_sel = 1'b0;
    endcase
  end

always @ (aluop_sel) begin
  case (aluop_sel) //synopsys parallel_case
    `ALUOP_ADC,
    `ALUOP_ADD,
    `ALUOP_PASS,
    `ALUOP_SBC,
    `ALUOP_SUB:  word_sel = 1'b1;
    default:     word_sel = 1'b0;
    endcase
  end

always @ (posedge clkc or negedge resetb) begin
  if (!resetb) begin
    addsel_reg <= `ADD_RSTVAL;
    alua_reg   <= `ALUA_RSTVAL;
    alub_reg   <= `ALUB_RSTVAL;
    aluop_reg  <= `ALUOP_RSTVAL;
    daa_op     <= 1'b0;
    decr_op    <= 1'b0;
    word_op    <= 1'b0;
    end
  else if (ld_ctrl) begin
    addsel_reg <= add_sel;
    alua_reg   <= alua_sel;
    alub_reg   <= alub_sel;
    aluop_reg  <= aluop_sel;
    daa_op     <= daa_sel;
    decr_op    <= decr_sel;
    word_op    <= word_sel;
    end
  end
```

Listing 6-52. datapath.v alu control pipeline registers.

I create the bit mask for the ALU directly from the instruction register according to Table 6-1. The "one high" value will be used for the bit test and bit set instructions, while the "one low" value will be used for the bit reset instructions.

inst_reg	bit_mask
00000xx - 00111xx	00000001 - 10000000 (one high)
01000xx - 01111xx	00000001 - 10000000 (one high)
10000xx - 10111xx	11111110 - 01111111 (one low)
11000xx - 11111xx	00000001 - 10000000 (one high)

Table 6-1. Creating the bit mask values.

Listing 6-53 shows the logic to create the bit manipulation constant. I could save some power by only enabling this `bit_mask` generator using the appropriate Page register values. I'll leave this as an exercise for the reader.

```
/*******************************************************************************************/
/*                                                                                         */
/* bit manipulation constant generator                                                     */
/*                                                                                         */
/*******************************************************************************************/
assign bit7     = (inst_reg[7] && !inst_reg[6]) ^ (inst_reg[5:3] == 3'b111);
assign bit6     = (inst_reg[7] && !inst_reg[6]) ^ (inst_reg[5:3] == 3'b110);
assign bit5     = (inst_reg[7] && !inst_reg[6]) ^ (inst_reg[5:3] == 3'b101);
assign bit4     = (inst_reg[7] && !inst_reg[6]) ^ (inst_reg[5:3] == 3'b100);
assign bit3     = (inst_reg[7] && !inst_reg[6]) ^ (inst_reg[5:3] == 3'b011);
assign bit2     = (inst_reg[7] && !inst_reg[6]) ^ (inst_reg[5:3] == 3'b010);
assign bit1     = (inst_reg[7] && !inst_reg[6]) ^ (inst_reg[5:3] == 3'b001);
assign bit0     = (inst_reg[7] && !inst_reg[6]) ^ (inst_reg[5:3] == 3'b000);
assign bit_mask = {bit7, bit6, bit5, bit4, bit3, bit2, bit1, bit0};
```

Listing 6-53. datapath.v bit manipulation constant generator.

There is probably a much better way to describe the logic required for the Decimal Adjust constant and Decimal Adjust Carry flag value in Verilog than is shown in Listing 6-54. But sometimes "better" is the enemy of "good enough", and this works even if it is ugly. But do not use this as an example of how to code in Verilog.

```
/*****************************************************************************************/
/*                                                                                       */
/* decimal adjust accumulator constant generator                                         */
/*                                                                                       */
/*****************************************************************************************/
assign daa_l1 = !ff_reg_out[1] && !ff_reg_out[4] &&
                (!aa_reg_out[3] || (aa_reg_out[3] && !aa_reg_out[2] && !aa_reg_out[1]));
assign daa_l2 = !ff_reg_out[1] && !ff_reg_out[4] &&
                (aa_reg_out[3] && (aa_reg_out[2] || aa_reg_out[1]));
assign daa_l3 = !ff_reg_out[1] &&  ff_reg_out[4] && (!aa_reg_out[3] && !aa_reg_out[2]);
assign daa_l4 =  ff_reg_out[1] && !ff_reg_out[4] &&
                (!aa_reg_out[3] || (aa_reg_out[3] && !aa_reg_out[2] && !aa_reg_out[1]));
assign daa_l5 =  ff_reg_out[1] &&  ff_reg_out[4] &&
                ((!aa_reg_out[3] && aa_reg_out[2] && aa_reg_out[1]) || aa_reg_out[3]);
assign daa_h1 = !ff_reg_out[0] && (aa_reg_out[7] && (aa_reg_out[6] || aa_reg_out[5]));
assign daa_h2 =  ff_reg_out[0] &&
                (!aa_reg_out[7] && !aa_reg_out[6] && (!aa_reg_out[5] || !aa_reg_out[4]));
assign daa_h3 = !ff_reg_out[0] &&
                (aa_reg_out[7] && (aa_reg_out[6] || aa_reg_out[5] || aa_reg_out[4]));
assign daa_h4 =  ff_reg_out[0] && (!aa_reg_out[7] && !aa_reg_out[6]);
assign daa_h5 =  ff_reg_out[0] &&
                ((aa_reg_out[6] && aa_reg_out[5] && aa_reg_out[4]) || aa_reg_out[7]);
assign daa_h6 = !ff_reg_out[0] &&
                ((!aa_reg_out[6] && !aa_reg_out[5] && !aa_reg_out[4]) || !aa_reg_out[7]);
assign daa_h7 =  ff_reg_out[0] && ((aa_reg_out[6] && aa_reg_out[5]) || aa_reg_out[7]);

assign daa1    = daa_l2 || daa_l3 || daa_l5;
assign daa2    = daa_l2 || daa_l3;
assign daa3    = daa_l5;
assign daa4    = daa_l5 && (daa_h6 || daa_h7);
assign daa5    = (daa_l1 && (daa_h1 || daa_h2)) || (daa_l2 && (daa_h2 || daa_h3)) ||
                 (daa_l3 && (daa_h1 || daa_h4)) || (daa_l4 && daa_h5) ||
                 (daa_l5 && daa_h6);
```

```
assign daa6   = (daa_l1 && (daa_h1 || daa_h2)) || (daa_l2 && (daa_h2 || daa_h3)) ||
                (daa_l3 && (daa_h1 || daa_h4)) || (daa_l5 && daa_h6);
assign daa7   = (daa_l4 && daa_h5) || (daa_l5 && (daa_h6 || daa_h7));

assign daa_out   = {daa7, daa6, daa5, daa4, daa3, daa2, daa1, 1'b0};
assign carry_daa = (daa_l1 && (daa_h1 || daa_h2)) || (daa_l2 && (daa_h2 || daa_h3)) ||
                   (daa_l3 && (daa_h1 || daa_h4)) || (daa_l4 && daa_h5) ||
                   (daa_l5 && daa_h7);
```

Listing 6-54. datapath.v decimal adjust accumulator constant generator.

Listing 6-55 creates the two final constants needed by the ALU. The restart address is created directly from the instruction register, while the interrupt address is a function of the interrupt mode and the type of interrupt pending.

```
/*****************************************************************************************/
/*                                                                                       */
/* interrupt/restart address generator                                                   */
/*                                                                                       */
/*****************************************************************************************/
assign rst_addr = {2'b00, inst_reg[5:3], 3'b000};

always @ (nmi_reg or imd2_reg or imd1_reg or din0_reg or din1_reg) begin
  casex ({nmi_reg, imd2_reg, imd1_reg})
    3'b001:  int_addr = 16'h0038;
    3'b010:  int_addr = {din1_reg, din0_reg};
    3'b1xx:  int_addr = 16'h0066;
    default: int_addr = 16'h0000;
    endcase
  end
```

Listing 6-55. datapath.v interrupt/restart address generator.

Listing 6-56 instantiates the two input multiplexers for the ALU. As I mentioned in previous sections, I always like to use the "dot notation" when instantiating modules, and I always try to use the same signal names across a module interface.

```
/*****************************************************************************************/
/*                                                                                       */
/* alu input selects                                                                     */
/*                                                                                       */
/*****************************************************************************************/
aluamux AMUX ( .adda_in(adda_in), .alua_in(alua_in), .alua_reg(alua_reg),
               .aa_reg_out(aa_reg_out), .bit_mask(bit_mask), .daa_out(daa_out),
               .hl_reg_out(hl_reg_out), .ii_reg(ii_reg), .int_addr(int_addr),
               .ix_reg(ix_reg), .iy_reg(iy_reg), .pc_reg(pc_reg), .rr_reg(rr_reg),
               .rst_addr(rst_addr) );

alubmux BMUX ( .addb_in(addb_in), .alub_in(alub_in), .alub_reg(alub_reg),
               .af_reg_out(af_reg_out), .bc_reg_out(bc_reg_out), .de_reg_out(de_reg_out),
               .din0_reg(din0_reg), .din1_reg(din1_reg), .hl_reg_out(hl_reg_out),
               .ix_reg(ix_reg), .iy_reg(iy_reg), .pc_reg(pc_reg), .sp_reg(sp_reg),
               .tmp_reg(tmp_reg) );
```

Listing 6-56. datapath.v instantiating the alu input selects.

Instantiating the ALU function units and ALU output multiplexer requires some compromises with regard to signal names across the module boundary, as shown in Listing 6-57. First, the ALU function units do not use the full `aluop_reg` width. Second, the aluout.v module uses two bits of the `aluop_reg` control bus for the unit select control.

```
/*****************************************************************************************/
/*                                                                                       */
/* function units                                                                        */
/*                                                                                       */
/*****************************************************************************************/
alu_log  ALULOG  ( .logic_c(logic_c), .logic_hc(logic_hc), .logic_out(logic_out),
                   .alua_in(alua_in), .alub_in(alub_in), .aluop_reg(aluop_reg[`AOP_IDX:0]),
                   .carry_bit(carry_bit) );
```

```
alu_math ALUMATH ( .adder_c(adder_c), .adder_hc(adder_hc), .adder_out(adder_out),
                   .adder_ov(adder_ov), .alua_in(alua_in), .alub_in(alub_in),
                   .aluop_reg(aluop_reg[`AOP_IDX:0]), .carry_bit(carry_bit),
                   .carry_daa(carry_daa), .daa_op(daa_op), .word_op(word_op) );

alu_shft ALUSHFT ( .shft_c(shft_c), .shft_out(shft_out), .alub_in(alub_in[7:0]),
                   .aluop_reg(aluop_reg[`AOP_IDX:0]), .carry_bit(carry_bit) );

aluout   ALUOUT  ( .cry_nxt(cry_nxt), .data_bus(data_bus), .hcar_nxt(hcar_nxt),
                   .one_nxt(one_nxt), .par_nxt(par_nxt), .sign_nxt(sign_nxt),
                   .zero_nxt(zero_nxt), .adder_c(adder_c), .adder_hc(adder_hc),
                   .adder_out(adder_out), .hi_byte(hi_byte), .logic_c(logic_c),
                   .logic_hc(logic_hc), .logic_out(logic_out), .shft_c(shft_c),
                   .shft_out(shft_out), .unit_sel(aluop_reg[7:6]), .word_op(word_op) );
```

Listing 6-57. datapath.v instantiating the alu function units.

In Listing 6-58 I take the raw flag outputs from the ALU and create the values to load into the F register. The Carry, Half-Carry, Negate and Parity/Overflow flags need to be modified or created from the raw flag outputs, but I create place-holders for the other flags also in case I've overlooked something. The final step is to create the byte-wide valuc for the parallel load of the F register.

```
/*****************************************************************************************/
/*                                                                                       */
/* flag generation                                                                       */
/*                                                                                       */
/*****************************************************************************************/
assign alu_carry = decr_op ^ cry_nxt;
assign alu_hcar  = (hflg_ctl[1]) ? hflg_ctl[0] : (decr_op ^ hcar_nxt);
assign alu_neg   = (nflg_ctl[1]) ? nflg_ctl[0] : sign_nxt;
assign alu_one   = one_nxt;
assign alu_sign  = sign_nxt;
assign alu_zero  = zero_nxt;

always @ (pflg_ctl or adder_ov or ief2_reg or par_nxt or zero_nxt) begin
  case (pflg_ctl)
    `PFLG_V: alu_ovflo = adder_ov;
    `PFLG_1: alu_ovflo = 1'b1;
    `PFLG_P: alu_ovflo = par_nxt;
```

```
      `PFLG_B: alu_ovflo = !zero_nxt;
      `PFLG_F: alu_ovflo = ief2_reg;
      default: alu_ovflo = 1'b0;
      endcase
    end

  assign new_flags[7] = (sflg_en)    ? alu_sign  : ff_reg_out[7];
  assign new_flags[6] = (zflg_en)    ? alu_zero  : ff_reg_out[6];
  assign new_flags[5] =                            ff_reg_out[5];
  assign new_flags[4] = (|hflg_ctl) ? alu_hcar  : ff_reg_out[4];
  assign new_flags[3] =                            ff_reg_out[3];
  assign new_flags[2] = (|pflg_ctl) ? alu_ovflo : ff_reg_out[2];
  assign new_flags[1] = (|nflg_ctl) ? alu_neg   : ff_reg_out[1];
  assign new_flags[0] = (cflg_en)    ? alu_carry : ff_reg_out[0];
```

Listing 6-58. datapath.v flag generation.

The final section of the datapath.v module, shown in Listing 6-59, is the ALU and output multiplexer for the address. Only four possible operations are used to calculate an address, so this ALU is significantly simpler than the one for the data. Then the final step is the multiplexer for the address special cases. Even though this should not be a slow path because of the reduced ALU complexity, I still code this multiplexer for the maximum speed.

```
  /*******************************************************************************************/
  /*                                                                                         */
  /* address alu                                                                             */
  /*                                                                                         */
  /*******************************************************************************************/
  assign bsign_ext = {addb_in[7],  addb_in[7],  addb_in[7],  addb_in[7],
                      addb_in[7],  addb_in[7],  addb_in[7],  addb_in[7]};

  always @ (aluop_reg or adda_in or addb_in or bsign_ext) begin
    case (aluop_reg)
      `ALUOP_ADS:  adda_out = adda_in + {bsign_ext[15:8], addb_in[7:0]};
      `ALUOP_ADD:  adda_out = adda_in + addb_in;
      `ALUOP_APAS: adda_out = adda_in;
      default:     adda_out = addb_in;
      endcase
    end
```

```
assign addr_alu = (addsel_reg[`AD_ALU]) ? adda_out   : 16'h0000;
assign addr_hl  = (addsel_reg[`AD_HL])  ? hl_reg_out : 16'h0000;
assign addr_pc  = (addsel_reg[`AD_PC])  ? pc_reg     : 16'h0000;
assign addr_sp  = (addsel_reg[`AD_SP])  ? sp_reg     : 16'h0000;

assign addr_reg_in = addr_alu | addr_hl | addr_pc | addr_sp;
```

Listing 6-59. datapath.v address alu.

The control.v module

The control.v module is the last piece of the design. With about fifty pages of Verilog code it is also the largest, so I am not going to present the entire module here. I will present excerpts from all of the different sections of the module, but it is up to you, the reader, to fill in the rest. All of the information required to complete the control.v module is in the design spreadsheet. The connection diagram for the control.v module is shown in Figure 6-10.

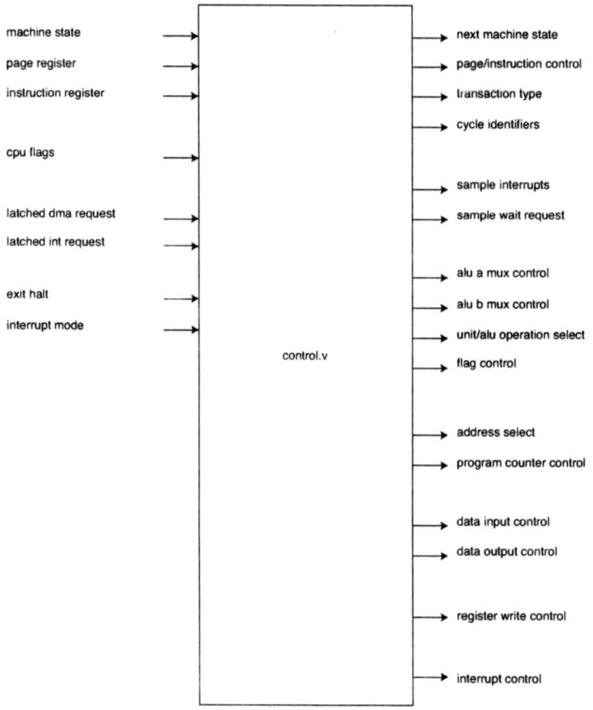

Figure 6-10. Connection diagram for the control.v module.

The interface for the control.v module is shown in Listing 6-60. Every signal here has been presented before, so there should be no need to explain them again. But you are probably wondering why there are only a dozen inputs to this module, and where the clock and reset signal are.

The control.v module is purely combinational logic. I partition the design this way out of habit, and you are free to do it differently. In several microprocessor designs that I have done in the past this section of logic was implemented in either a Read-Only Memory (ROM) or a Programmable Logic Array (PLA). Both of these technologies use regular structures to implement logic and do not contain storage elements, which is why I got in the habit of using this type of partitioning.

```
module control (add_sel, alua_sel, alub_sel, aluop_sel, cflg_en, di_ctl, do_ctl, ex_af_pls,
                ex_bank_pls, ex_dehl_inst, halt_nxt, hflg_ctl, ief_ctl, if_frst, inta_frst,
                imd_ctl, ld_dmaa, ld_inst, ld_inta, ld_page, ld_wait, nflg_ctl, output_inh,
                page_sel, pc_sel, pflg_ctl, rd_frst, rd_nxt, reti_nxt, sflg_en, state_nxt,
                tflg_ctl, tran_sel, wr_addr, wr_frst, zflg_en, carry_bit, dmar_reg, inst_reg,
                intr_reg, page_reg, par_bit, sign_bit, state_reg, tflg_reg, vector_int,
                xhlt_reg, zero_bit);

  input          carry_bit;      /* carry flag                                       */
  input          dmar_reg;       /* latched dma request                              */
  input          intr_reg;       /* latched interrupt request                        */
  input          par_bit;        /* parity flag                                      */
  input          sign_bit;       /* sign flag                                        */
  input          tflg_reg;       /* temporary flag                                   */
  input          vector_int;     /* int vector enable                                */
  input          xhlt_reg;       /* halt exit                                        */
  input          zero_bit;       /* zero flag                                        */
  input    [3:0] page_reg;       /* instruction decode "page"                        */
  input    [7:0] inst_reg;       /* instruction register                             */
  input    [`STATE_IDX:0] state_reg;      /* current processor state                 */
  output         cflg_en;        /* carry flag control                               */
  output         ex_af_pls;      /* exchange af,af'                                  */
  output         ex_bank_pls;    /* exchange register bank                           */
  output         ex_dehl_inst;   /* exchange de,hl                                   */
  output         halt_nxt;       /* halt cycle next                                  */
  output         if_frst;        /* ifetch first cycle                               */
  output         inta_frst;      /* intack first cycle                               */
  output         ld_dmaa;        /* load dma request                                 */
  output         ld_inst;        /* load instruction register                        */
  output         ld_inta;        /* load interrupt request                           */
  output         ld_page;        /* load page register                               */
  output         ld_wait;        /* load wait request                                */
```

```
output         output_inh;    /* disable cpu outputs                        */
output         rd_frst;       /* read first cycle                           */
output         rd_nxt;        /* read cycle identifier                      */
output         reti_nxt;      /* reti identifier                            */
output         sflg_en;       /* sign flag control                          */
output         wr_frst;       /* write first cycle                          */
output         zflg_en;       /* zero flag control                          */
output  [3:0]  page_sel;      /* instruction decode "page" control          */
output [`ADCTL_IDX:0] add_sel;      /* address output mux control           */
output  [`ALUA_IDX:0] alua_sel;     /* alu input a mux control              */
output  [`ALUB_IDX:0] alub_sel;     /* alu input b mux control              */
output [`ALUOP_IDX:0] aluop_sel;    /* alu operation control                */
output    [`DI_IDX:0] di_ctl;       /* data input control                   */
output    [`DO_IDX:0] do_ctl;       /* data output control                  */
output  [`HFLG_IDX:0] hflg_ctl;     /* half-carry flag control              */
output   [`IEF_IDX:0] ief_ctl;      /* interrupt enable control             */
output   [`IMD_IDX:0] imd_ctl;      /* interrupt mode control               */
output  [`NFLG_IDX:0] nflg_ctl;     /* negate flag control                  */
output [`PCCTL_IDX:0] pc_sel;       /* program counter source control       */
output  [`PFLG_IDX:0] pflg_ctl;     /* parity/overflow flag control         */
output [`STATE_IDX:0] state_nxt;    /* next processor state                 */
output  [`TFLG_IDX:0] tflg_ctl;     /* temp flag control                    */
output [`TTYPE_IDX:0] tran_sel;     /* transaction type select              */
output  [`WREG_IDX:0] wr_addr;      /* register write address bus           */
```

Listing 6-60. control.v inputs and outputs.

Throughout this module the primary `case` statement uses the main machine state register, `state_reg`, while the dependent `case` statements use the page register and instruction register to select the required control field value. This arrangement makes it easy to transfer the appropriate instruction codes directly from the *Internal Code* columns in the design spreadsheet to the text editor used to create the Verilog code.

In the design spreadsheet a worksheet is first sorted alphabetically by column. Since each column corresponds to a particular clock cycle each sort result corresponds to one entry in the primary `case` statement. This sort (of the entire worksheet) will arrange the identifiers in that column alphabetically. Selecting the instruction codes corresponding to each sorted identifier gives the entries required for the dependent `case` statements. Creating the control.v module from the design spreadsheet is that simple.

Several of the sections in this module are not explicitly specified in the design spreadsheet, so I will cover these sections completely, which should illustrate the requirements for the remainder of the module.

Listing 6-61 generates the individual control signals that are required for the exchange bank instructions and the special exchange of the DE register and the HL register. There is obviously a less verbose way of generating these signals, but I prefer to use a uniform format in the control.v module.

Notice that all three of these signals are generated during one specific clock cycle, and only for one specific instruction. This is the simplest case for generating a signal in the control.v module.

Also notice that the `ex_dehl_inst` signal only decodes the instruction register. This is because the page register is not yet valid during the *dec1* state. This will be the case for all signals generated during the *dec1* state, and requires some editing of the instruction identifier from the design spreadsheet.

```
/*****************************************************************************************/
/*                                                                                       */
/* exchange instruction control                                                          */
/*                                                                                       */
/*****************************************************************************************/
always @ (inst_reg or page_reg or state_reg) begin
  casex (state_reg)
    `IF1B: begin
      case ({page_reg, inst_reg})
        12'b000000001000: ex_af_pls = 1'b1;
        default:          ex_af_pls = 1'b0;
        endcase
      end
    default:              ex_af_pls = 1'b0;
    endcase
  end

always @ (inst_reg or page_reg or state_reg) begin
  casex (state_reg)
    `IF1B: begin
      case ({page_reg, inst_reg})
        12'b000011011001: ex_bank_pls = 1'b1;
        default:          ex_bank_pls = 1'b0;
        endcase
      end
```

```
      default:                ex_bank_pls = 1'b0;
      endcase
    end

  always @ (inst_reg or page_reg or state_reg) begin
    casex (state_reg)
      `DEC1: begin
        casex (inst_reg)
          8'b11101011:        ex_dehl_inst = 1'b1;
          default:            ex_dehl_inst = 1'b0;
          endcase
        end
      default:                ex_dehl_inst = 1'b0;
      endcase
    end
```

Listing 6-61. control.v exchange instruction control.

The interrupt control section, shown in Listing 6-62, controls the interrupt flags and the selection of the interrupt mode. The mnemonics from the defines.v file make the code much more readable.

I am not going to implement the normal Z80 Interrupt Mode 0, so why is there an identifier for that instruction? This identifier will cause both the `imd1_reg` and `imd2_reg` registers in the datapath.v module to be cleared. This in turn will select the default case for the `int_addr` bus for a normal interrupt, which is all zeros. This value causes a jump to memory address 0x0000 after the interrupt acknowledge, so even though I am not implementing the normal Interrupt Mode 0 operation the CPU will still accept an interrupt in this mode.

```
  /*****************************************************************************************/
  /*                                                                                       */
  /* interrupt control                                                                     */
  /*                                                                                       */
  /*****************************************************************************************/
  always @ (inst_reg or page_reg or state_reg) begin
    casex (state_reg)
      `IF1B: begin
        casex ({page_reg, inst_reg})
          12'b000011110011: ief_ctl = `IEF_0;
          12'b000011111011: ief_ctl = `IEF_1;
          12'b0001xxxxxxxx: ief_ctl = `IEF_NMI;
          12'b1xxx01000101: ief_ctl = `IEF_RTN;
```

```
        default:            ief_ctl = `IEF_NUL;
        endcase
      end
    default:                ief_ctl = `IEF_NUL;
    endcase
  end

always @ (inst_reg or page_reg or state_reg) begin
  casex (state_reg)
    `IF1B: begin
      casex ({page_reg, inst_reg})
        12'b1xxx01000110: imd_ctl = `IMD_0;
        12'b1xxx01010110: imd_ctl = `IMD_1;
        12'b1xxx01011110: imd_ctl = `IMD_2;
        default:          imd_ctl = `IMD_NUL;
        endcase
      end
    default:              imd_ctl = `IMD_NUL;
    endcase
  end
```

Listing 6-62. control.v interrupt control.

Listing 6-63 creates the signals required by the external interface to generate the different external timing signals. The `if_frst`, `inta_frst`, `rd_frst` and `wr_frst` signals are active during the first clock cycle of the corresponding machine cycle and are used to create strobe signals.

In the case of the `if_frst` signal this isn't the whole story though. Remember that the *dec1* and *dec2* states do not always correspond to the first clock cycle of an instruction fetch or operand fetch transaction. In those cases no read strobe should be generated. I could include all of those cases here and inhibit the `if_frst` signal as appropriate. That would be redundant though, because I am going to need to include exactly that information in the next section where I control the sampling of the Wait request signal. This is why the `ld_wait` signal conditions the `if_frst` signal in the extint.v module.

If you look closely at how the `inta_frst` signal is generated, you may wonder why the *rste* state is included here. After all, this state is used just once, when exiting reset, and has nothing to do with an interrupt acknowledge. It turns out the logic synthesis tools will usually try to help the designer and trim "unused" flip-flops from the design. I don't want this to happen, so this is an easy way to keep the flip-flop that signals this state. It is also possible to embed synthesis directives inside Verilog comment lines, which is another way to achieve the same result.

The `rd_nxt` signal is a special case, required because of the type of control signals used for the I/O bus. Recall that the I/O bus uses a read transaction identifier, called `io_read`, that is active for the entire transaction. To meet this timing I need to signal that the next clock cycle is a read machine cycle, which is what the `rd_nxt` signal does.

```
/*****************************************************************************************/
/*                                                                                       */
/* identifiers to create timing signals                                                  */
/*                                                                                       */
/*****************************************************************************************/
always @ (state_reg) begin
  casex (state_reg) //synopsys parallel_case
    `DEC1,
    `DEC2,
    `OF2A,
    `IF3A,
    `IF1A:                if_frst = 1'b1;
    default:              if_frst = 1'b0;
    endcase
  end

always @ (state_reg) begin
  casex (state_reg) //synopsys parallel_case
    `INTA,
    `RSTE:                inta_frst = 1'b1;
    default:              inta_frst = 1'b0;
    endcase
  end

always @ (inst_reg or page_reg or state_nxt) begin
  casex (state_nxt) //synopsys parallel_case
    `RD1A,
    `RD2A:                rd_nxt = 1'b1;
    default:              rd_nxt = 1'b0;
    endcase
  end

always @ (inst_reg or page_reg or state_reg) begin
  casex (state_reg) //synopsys parallel_case
    `RD1A,
```

```
      `RD2A:                  rd_frst = 1'b1;
      default:                rd_frst = 1'b0;
      endcase
    end

  always @ (state_reg) begin
    casex (state_reg) //synopsys parallel_case
      `WR1A,
      `WR2A:                  wr_frst = 1'b1;
      default:                wr_frst = 1'b0;
      endcase
    end
```

Listing 6-63. control.v identifiers to create timing signals.

Listing 6-64 generates the `ld_wait` signal that is used to sample the external `wait_req` input. The necessary conditions for generating this signal are derived from information in the *Next State* worksheet. If the next state in the *dec1* column is *adr2* or *pco* the `wait_req` input should not be sampled, because this is not a memory read machine cycle. The same rule is true for the *dec2* state.

The instruction code identifiers for the *dec1* case require several manual edits. The first edit is to remove the page register from the identifier. This is a simple substitution of `8'b` for all of the `12'b0000` in the original identifiers transferred from the worksheet.

The second required edit is a little more involved, where the *rrr* register field in the identifiers is replaced with three separate values that cover the seven possible values for this field. The `110` case is not valid for this field so I replace each line containing *rrr* with three lines containing `0xx`, `x0x` and `xx1`.

The final required edit expands the `11xxx000` identifier of the Conditional Return instruction into the eight individual cases with the appropriate flag selection. Remember that for this instruction the next state is either *if1b* or *adr2*, and the `wait_req` should only be sampled in the case of *if1b*.

I have done some hand editing of the instruction code identifiers under the *dec2* case. After transferring the instruction code identifiers from the *Next State* worksheet, I edited the identifiers to use don't cares wherever possible. I was able to reduce the number of identifiers from the original forty down to the nine shown in the Verilog code. Normally there is little advantage in doing this, because it is something that the logic synthesis tool will do automatically. This manual editing does lead to more compact Verilog code, but it is easy to make mistakes and I do not recommend the practice.

The *dec1* and *dec2* cases are unique as far as the default case. Normally I prefer to have the signal inactive for the default case, but in this instance the signal needs to be active much more often than not. So in an effort to reduce the logic required, I'll reverse my normal style.

```
/*****************************************************************************************/
/*                                                                                       */
/* wait sample                                                                           */
/*                                                                                       */
/*****************************************************************************************/
always @ (inst_reg or page_reg or state_reg or carry_bit or par_bit or
          sign_bit or zero_bit) begin
  casex (state_reg) //synopsys parallel_case
    `DEC1: begin
      casex (inst_reg) //synopsys parallel_case
        8'b00000010,
        8'b00001010,
        8'b00010010,
        8'b00011010,
        8'b00110100,
        8'b00110101,
        8'b011100xx,
        8'b0111010x,
        8'b01110111,
        8'b010xx110,
        8'b01x0x110,
        8'b01xx1110,
        8'b10000110,
        8'b10001110,
        8'b10010110,
        8'b10011110,
        8'b10100110,
        8'b10101110,
        8'b10110110,
        8'b10111110,
        8'b11001001,
        8'b11100011,
        8'b11xx0001,
        8'b11xx0101,
        8'b11xxx111,
```

```
        8'b01110110,
        8'b11101001:       ld_wait = 1'b0;
        8'b11000000:       ld_wait =   zero_bit;
        8'b11001000:       ld_wait =  !zero_bit;
        8'b11010000:       ld_wait =  carry_bit;
        8'b11011000:       ld_wait = !carry_bit;
        8'b11100000:       ld_wait =    par_bit;
        8'b11101000:       ld_wait =   !par_bit;
        8'b11110000:       ld_wait =   sign_bit;
        8'b11111000:       ld_wait =  !sign_bit;
        default:           ld_wait = 1'b1;
        endcase
      end
    `DEC2: begin
      casex ({page_reg, inst_reg}) //synopsys parallel_case
        12'b0010xxxxx110,
        12'b010x11100001,
        12'b010x11100011,
        12'b010x11100101,
        12'b1xxx0100x101,
        12'b1xxx0110x111,
        12'b1xxx01xxx00x,
        12'b1xxx101xx0xx,
        12'b010x11101001: ld_wait = 1'b0;
        default:           ld_wait = 1'b1;
        endcase
      end
    `OF2A,
    `IF3A,
    `RD1A,
    `RD2A,
    `WR1A,
    `WR2A,
    `IF1A,
    `INTA:                 ld_wait = 1'b1;
    default:               ld_wait = 1'b0;
    endcase
  end
```

Listing 6-64. control.v wait sample control.

The final special section in Listing 6-65 controls the loading of the instruction register and the page register. The `ld_inst` signal is simple, because the instruction register should be loaded during the second clock of every instruction fetch machine cycle.

The `page_sel` and `ld_page` signals are also straightforward, mainly because the page register does not need to be loaded on a machine cycle boundary. This delay is the reason that only the instruction register should be used for decoding during the *dec1* state. I could load the page register with all zeros prior to the *dec1* state, but there is really no need to do so. The shorter instruction code values used during the *dec1* state will mean less logic anyway.

```
/*******************************************************************************************/
/*                                                                                         */
/* instruction register and page register control                                          */
/*                                                                                         */
/*******************************************************************************************/
always @ (inst_reg or page_reg or state_reg) begin
  casex (state_reg) //synopsys parallel_case
    `IF2B,
    `IF3B,
    `IF1B:                 ld_inst = 1'b1;
    default:               ld_inst = 1'b0;
    endcase
  end

always @ (inst_reg or page_reg or state_reg) begin
  casex (state_reg)
    `DEC1: begin
      case (inst_reg)
        8'b11001011:       page_sel = `CB_PAGE;
        8'b11011101:       page_sel = `DD_PAGE;
        8'b11101101:       page_sel = `ED_PAGE;
        8'b11111101:       page_sel = `FD_PAGE;
        default:           page_sel = `MAIN_PG;
        endcase
      end
    `DEC2: begin
      casex ({page_reg, inst_reg})
        12'bx10011001011: page_sel = `DDCB_PG;
        12'bx10111001011: page_sel = `FDCB_PG;
        default:           page_sel = `MAIN_PG;
        endcase
      end
```

```
      `INTA:                 page_sel = `INTR_PG;
      `DMA1:                 page_sel = `DMA_PG;
      default:               page_sel = `MAIN_PG;
      endcase
    end

  always @ (inst_reg or page_reg or state_reg) begin
    casex (state_reg) //synopsys parallel_case
      `DEC1:                 ld_page = 1'b1;
      `DEC2: begin
        casex ({page_reg, inst_reg})
          12'bx10x11001011: ld_page = 1'b1;
          default:           ld_page = 1'b0;
          endcase
        end
      `INTA,
      `DMA1:                 ld_page = 1'b1;
      default:               ld_page = 1'b0;
      endcase
    end
```

Listing 6-65. control.v instruction register and page register control.

Most of the remainder of the sections in the control.v module correspond directly to worksheets in the design spreadsheet, so I will only cover the first few lines and some special cases here.

Listing 6-66 implements the *Next State* worksheet, to create the `state_nxt` control field. Creating this control field requires all of the inputs to the control.v module. Shown below are the first few lines from this section.

```
  /*******************************************************************************************/
  /*                                                                                         */
  /*  next state control                                                                     */
  /*                                                                                         */
  /*******************************************************************************************/
  always @ (inst_reg or page_reg or state_reg or carry_bit or dmar_reg or intr_reg or
            par_bit or sign_bit or tflg_reg or vector_int or xhlt_reg or zero_bit) begin
    casex (state_reg) //synopsys parallel_case
      `DEC1: begin
        casex (inst_reg) //synopsys parallel_case
          8'b00000010,
```

```
8'b00001010,
8'b00010010,
8'b00011010,
8'b00110100,
8'b00110101,
8'b011100xx,
8'b0111010x,
8'b01110111,
8'b010xx110,
8'b0110x110,
8'b01111110,
8'b10000110,
8'b10001110,
8'b10010110,
8'b10011110,
8'b10100110,
8'b10101110,
8'b10110110,
8'b10111110,
8'b11001001,
8'b11100011,
8'b11xx0001,
8'b11xx0101,
8'b11xxx111:       state_nxt = `sADR2;
.
.
.
```

Listing 6-66. control.v start of next state control.

Listing 6-67 is the end of the section that creates the `state_nxt` control field, where I have to include the cases from the Special Case worksheet. I also have to remember to implement the exit from the reset state and think about what to use for the `default` case. If all of the Verilog code in this section is correct it will not be possible to go through the default case, so I will go ahead and use it for the reset state.

```
        .
        .
        .
    `PCA:                    state_nxt = `sPCO;
    `PCO: begin
      casex ({page_reg, inst_reg})
        12'b000001110110: state_nxt = `sHLTA;
        default:          state_nxt = `sIF1A;
        endcase
      end
    `HLTA:                   state_nxt = `sHLTB;
    `HLTB:                   state_nxt = (xhlt_reg) ? `sIF1A : `sHLTA;
    `IF1A:                   state_nxt = `sIF1B;
    `IF1B:                   state_nxt = `sDEC1;
    `INTA:                   state_nxt = `sINTB;
    `INTB:                   state_nxt = (vector_int) ? `sADR1 : `sWR1A;
    `DMA1:                   state_nxt = `sDMA2;
    `DMA2:                   state_nxt = (dmar_reg) ? `sDMA1 : `sIF1A;
    `RSTE:                   state_nxt = `sIF1A;
    default:                 state_nxt = `sRSTE;
    endcase
  end
```

Listing 6-67. control.v end of next state control.

The control.v module continues in the same order of the design spreadsheet. The `tran_sel` control field implements the contents of the *Tran Type* worksheet, and the first part of this section is shown in Listing 6-68. This is another case where all of the inputs to the control.v module are required.

```
/*****************************************************************************************/
/*                                                                                       */
/*  transaction type control                                                             */
/*                                                                                       */
/*****************************************************************************************/
always @ (inst_reg or page_reg or state_reg or carry_bit or dmar_reg or intr_reg or
          par_bit or sign_bit or tflg_reg or vector_int or xhlt_reg or zero_bit) begin
  casex (state_reg) //synopsys parallel_case
    `IF2B:                tran_sel = `TRAN_IF;
    `OF1B: begin
      casex ({page_reg, inst_reg}) //synopsys parallel_case
        12'b000000010000,
        12'b000000011000,
        12'b000011010011,
        12'b000011011011,
        12'b010x00110100,
        12'b010x00110101,
        12'b010x011100xx,
        12'b010x0111010x,
        12'b010x01110111,
        12'b010x010xx110,
        12'b010x0110x110,
        12'b010x01111110,
        12'b010x10000110,
        12'b010x10001110,
        12'b010x10010110,
        12'b010x10011110,
        12'b010x10100110,
        12'b010x10101110,
        12'b010x10110110,
        12'b010x10111110: tran_sel = `TRAN_IDL;
        12'b000000100000: tran_sel = (  zero_bit) ? `TRAN_IF : `TRAN_IDL;
        12'b000000101000: tran_sel = ( !zero_bit) ? `TRAN_IF : `TRAN_IDL;
        12'b000000110000: tran_sel = ( carry_bit) ? `TRAN_IF : `TRAN_IDL;
        12'b000000111000: tran_sel = (!carry_bit) ? `TRAN_IF : `TRAN_IDL;
        12'b000000110110: tran_sel = `TRAN_MEM;
        default:          tran_sel = `TRAN_IF;
        endcase
```

```
      end
        .
        .
        .
```

Listing 6-68. control.v start of transaction type control.

At the end of the `tran_sel` section I again need to implement the special cases, and this is shown in Listing 6-69. The *if1b* section here is worth noting. I could have implemented this same set of cases for the `state_nxt` section, but I instead implemented the interrupt and bus request cases directly in the machine.v module. There isn't really an advantage one way or the other, but putting the code in machine.v reminds me that these are exception cases for the state sequence.

```
        .
        .
        .
    `PC0: begin
      casex ({page_reg, inst_reg})
        12'b000001110110: tran_sel = `TRAN_IDL;
        default:          tran_sel = `TRAN_IF;
        endcase
      end
    `IF1B: begin
      casex ({page_reg, inst_reg}) //synopsys parallel_case
        12'b1xxx01000101,
        12'b1xxx01001101,
        12'b000011110011,
        12'b0001xxxxxxxx: tran_sel = `TRAN_IF;
        default:          tran_sel = (dmar_reg) ? `TRAN_IDL :
                                     (intr_reg) ? `TRAN_IAK : `TRAN_IF;
        endcase
      end
    `HLTB:                tran_sel = (xhlt_reg)    ? `TRAN_IF  : `TRAN_IDL;
    `INTB:                tran_sel = (vector_int) ? `TRAN_IDL : `TRAN_MEM;
    `DMA2:                tran_sel = (dmar_reg)    ? `TRAN_IDL : `TRAN_IF;
    `RSTE:                tran_sel = `TRAN_IF;
    default:              tran_sel = `TRAN_RSTVAL;
    endcase
  end
```

Listing 6-69. control.v end of transaction type control.

They are not directly part of the Tran Type worksheet, but the signals in Listing 6-70 are the special cases for the transaction type. The `halt_nxt` signal activates the top-level `halt_tran` output, while the `reti_nxt` signal does the same for the `reti_tran` output.

```
/*****************************************************************************************/
/*                                                                                       */
/*  special transaction identifiers                                                      */
/*                                                                                       */
/*****************************************************************************************/
always @ (inst_reg or page_reg or state_reg or xhlt_reg) begin
  casex (state_reg)
    `PC0,
    `HLTB: begin
      casex ({page_reg, inst_reg})
        12'b000001110110: halt_nxt = !xhlt_reg;
        default:          halt_nxt = 1'b0;
        endcase
      end
    default:              halt_nxt = 1'b0;
    endcase
  end

always @ (inst_reg or page_reg or state_reg) begin
  casex (state_reg)
    `RD2B: begin
      casex ({page_reg, inst_reg})
        12'b1xxx01001101: reti_nxt = 1'b1;
        default:          reti_nxt = 1'b0;
        endcase
      end
    default:              reti_nxt = 1'b0;
    endcase
  end
```

Listing 6-70. control.v special transaction identifiers.

The output_inh signal is created next, because it requires essentially the same information as the tran_sel control bus. This is shown in Listing 6-71. Remember that I use this signal to inhibit the outputs during the Halt machine cycles and the Bus Release machine cycles. I could have just as easily used the tran_sel control bus directly, but I prefer to keep a uniform coding style within the control.v module.

```
/*****************************************************************************************/
/*                                                                                       */
/*  output inhibit                                                                       */
/*                                                                                       */
/*****************************************************************************************/
always @ (inst_reg or page_reg or state_reg or dmar_reg or xhlt_reg) begin
  casex (state_reg)
    `IF1B: begin
      casex ({page_reg, inst_reg}) //synopsys parallel_case
        12'b1xxx01000101,
        12'b1xxx01001101,
        12'b000011110011,
        12'b0001xxxxxxxx: output_inh = 1'b0;
        default:          output_inh = dmar_reg;
        endcase
      end
    `DMA2:                output_inh = dmar_reg;
    `PC0,
    `HLTB: begin
      casex ({page_reg, inst_reg})
        12'b000001110110: output_inh = !xhlt_reg;
        default:          output_inh = 1'b0;
        endcase
      end
    default:              output_inh = 1'b0;
    endcase
  end
```

Listing 6-71. control.v output inhibit generation.

Listing 6-72 implements the *Pre-address* worksheet, creating the `add_sel` control bus. This first section illustrates all four possibilities for the `add_sel` signals. Note that the cases for the Conditional Return instructions need to be manually created from the instruction code identifiers in the worksheet. As usual, the special cases need to be manually entered at the end of this section.

```
/*****************************************************************************************/
/*                                                                                       */
/*  address output control                                                               */
/*                                                                                       */
/*****************************************************************************************/
always @ (inst_reg or page_reg or state_reg or carry_bit or par_bit or sign_bit or
          vector_int or zero_bit) begin
  casex (state_reg) //synopsys parallel_case
    `DEC1: begin
      casex (inst_reg) //synopsys parallel_case
        8'b00000010,
        8'b00001010,
        8'b00010010,
        8'b00011010,
        8'b11101001,
        8'b11xx0101,
        8'b11xxx111:      add_sel = `ADD_ALU;
        8'b00110100,
        8'b00110101,
        8'b00110110,
        8'b011100xx,
        8'b0111010x,
        8'b01110111,
        8'b010xx110,
        8'b0110x110,
        8'b01111110,
        8'b10000110,
        8'b10001110,
        8'b10010110,
        8'b10011110,
        8'b10100110,
        8'b10101110,
        8'b10110110,
        8'b10111110:      add_sel = `ADD_HL;
        8'b11000000:      add_sel = ( !zero_bit) ? `ADD_SP : `ADD_PC;
        8'b11001000:      add_sel = (  zero_bit) ? `ADD_SP : `ADD_PC;
        8'b11010000:      add_sel = (!carry_bit) ? `ADD_SP : `ADD_PC;
```

```
        8'b11011000:        add_sel = ( carry_bit) ? `ADD_SP : `ADD_PC;
        8'b11100000:        add_sel = (  !par_bit) ? `ADD_SP : `ADD_PC;
        8'b11101000:        add_sel = (   par_bit) ? `ADD_SP : `ADD_PC;
        8'b11110000:        add_sel = ( !sign_bit) ? `ADD_SP : `ADD_PC;
        8'b11111000:        add_sel = (  sign_bit) ? `ADD_SP : `ADD_PC;
        8'b11xx0001,
        8'b11100011,
        8'b11001001:        add_sel = `ADD_SP;
        default:            add_sel = `ADD_PC;
        endcase
      end
        .
        .
        .
    `IF1A:                  add_sel = `ADD_PC;
    `INTA:                  add_sel = (vector_int) ? `ADD_PC : `ADD_ALU;
    `DMA1:                  add_sel = `ADD_PC;
    default:                add_sel = `ADD_RSTVAL;
    endcase
  end
```

Listing 6-72. control.v address output control.

The `pc_sel` control bus is created from the *Load PC* worksheet, and is shown in Listing 6-73 This section is fairly complex, because the value needs to be specified for every instruction in every state where this control bus is active. The special cases at the end of this section are much simpler than in previous sections.

```
/*****************************************************************************************/
/*                                                                                       */
/*  program counter control                                                              */
/*                                                                                       */
/*****************************************************************************************/
always @ (inst_reg or page_reg or state_reg or carry_bit or par_bit or sign_bit or
          tflg_reg or zero_bit) begin
  casex (state_reg) //synopsys parallel_case
    `DEC1: begin
      casex (inst_reg) //synopsys parallel_case
        8'b00000000,
        8'b00000111,
        8'b00001000,
```

```
        8'b00001111,
        8'b00010111,
        8'b00011111,
        8'b00100111,
        8'b00101111,
        8'b00110111,
        8'b00111111,
        8'b000xx10x,
        8'b0010x10x,
        8'b0011110x,
        8'b00xx0011,
        8'b00xx1001,
        8'b00xx1011,
        8'b010xx0xx,
        8'b0110x0xx,
        8'b011110xx,
        8'b010xx10x,
        8'b0110x10x,
        8'b0111110x,
        8'b010xx111,
        8'b0110x111,
        8'b01111111,
        8'b10xxx0xx,
        8'b10xxx10x,
        8'b10xxx111,
        8'b11011001,
        8'b11101011,
        8'b11111001,
        8'b11111011:      pc_sel = `PC_NILD;
        8'b01110110,
        8'b11xxx111:      pc_sel = `PC_NUL;
        .
        .
        .
    `HLTA:                pc_sel = `PC_INT;
    `DMA1:                pc_sel = `PC_DMA;
    default:              pc_sel = `PC_NUL;
    endcase
  end
```

Listing 6-73. control.v Program Counter control.

The enables for the exception cases are mostly specified in the *if1b* column of the *Load PC* worksheet, but they are not part of the `pc_sel` control bus. Listing 6-74 creates these signals, which sample the Interrupt requests and the Bus Request. Note that besides sampling the Bus Request at the end of most instructions, I also need to sample this signal during the Halt state and the Bus Release state.

```
/*****************************************************************************/
/*                                                                           */
/*  interrupt ack and dma ack                                                */
/*                                                                           */
/*****************************************************************************/
always @ (inst_reg or page_reg or state_reg) begin
  casex (state_reg) //synopsys parallel_case
    `IF1B: begin
      casex ({page_reg, inst_reg}) //synopsys parallel_case
        12'b1xxx01000101,
        12'b1xxx01001101,
        12'b000011110011,
        12'b0001xxxxxxxx: ld_inta = 1'b0;
        default:          ld_inta = 1'b1;
        endcase
      end
    default:              ld_inta = 1'b0;
    endcase
  end

always @ (inst_reg or page_reg or state_reg) begin
  casex (state_reg) //synopsys parallel_case
    `IF1B: begin
      casex ({page_reg, inst_reg}) //synopsys parallel_case
        12'b1xxx01000101,
        12'b1xxx01001101,
        12'b000011110011,
        12'b0001xxxxxxxx: ld_dmaa = 1'b0;
        default:          ld_dmaa = 1'b1;
        endcase
      end
```

```
    `HLTB,
    `DMA2:                   ld_dmaa = 1'b1;
    default:                 ld_dmaa = 1'b0;
    endcase
  end
```

Listing 6-74. control.v Interrupt Acknowledge and Bus Acknowledge control.

The controls for the Data Input register and the Data Output register share the *DinDout* worksheet, but they are specified separately in the control.v module. Control for the Data Input register is shown in Listing 6-75. The `di_ctl` control bus entry during the Interrupt Acknowledge machine cycle isn't strictly necessary, because I directly load the Temporary register with the interrupt vector. But it's there in case I have overlooked something.

```
/*****************************************************************************************/
/*                                                                                       */
/*  data input register control                                                          */
/*                                                                                       */
/*****************************************************************************************/
always @ (inst_reg or page_reg or state_reg) begin
  casex (state_reg) //synopsys parallel_case
    `OF1B:                   di_ctl = `DI_DI10;
    `OF2B: begin
      casex ({page_reg, inst_reg}) //synopsys parallel_case
        12'b010000110110,
        12'b010100110110: di_ctl = `DI_DI0;
        default:          di_ctl = `DI_DI1;
        endcase
      end
    `RD1B:                   di_ctl = `DI_DI0;
    `RD2B: begin
      casex ({page_reg, inst_reg}) //synopsys parallel_case
        12'b000000101010,
        12'b000011001001,
        12'b010x00101010,
        12'b010x11100001,
        12'b010x11100011,
        12'b000011100011,
        12'b1xxx01000101,
        12'b1xxx01001101,
```

```
          12'b1xxx01xx1011,
          12'b000011xxx000,
          12'b000011xx0001,
          12'b0001xxxxxxxx: di_ctl = `DI_DI1;
          default:          di_ctl = `DI_DI0;
          endcase
        end
      `INTB:                di_ctl = `DI_DI0;
      default:              di_ctl = `DI_NUL;
      endcase
    end
```

Listing 6-75. control.v Data Input register control.

The `do_ctl` section is simple, as shown in Listing 6-76. The Data Output register is only loaded for Write machine cycles, and there are only a few different cases, with stack writes requiring the high byte of the register and I/O instructions using the I/O Data Output register.

```
/*****************************************************************************************/
/*                                                                                       */
/*  data output register control                                                         */
/*                                                                                       */
/*****************************************************************************************/
always @ (inst_reg or page_reg or state_reg) begin
  casex (state_reg) //synopsys parallel_case
    `WR1A: begin
      casex ({page_reg, inst_reg}) //synopsys parallel_case
        12'b000011001101,
        12'b010x11100101,
        12'b000011xxx100,
        12'b000011xx0101,
        12'b000011xxx111,
        12'b0001xxxxxxxx: do_ctl = `DO_MSB;
        12'b1xxx10100011,
        12'b1xxx10101011,
        12'b1xxx10110011,
        12'b1xxx10111011: do_ctl = `DO_IO;
        default:          do_ctl = `DO_LSB;
        endcase
      end
```

```
    `WR2A: begin
      casex ({page_reg, inst_reg}) //synopsys parallel_case
        12'b000000100010,
        12'b010x00100010,
        12'b010x11100011,
        12'b000011100011,
        12'b1xxx01xx0011: do_ctl = `DO_MSB;
        12'b000011010011,
        12'b1xxx0x0xx001,
        12'b1xxx0x10x001,
        12'b1xxx0x111001,
        12'b1xxx10100011,
        12'b1xxx10101011,
        12'b1xxx10110011,
        12'b1xxx10111011: do_ctl = `DO_IO;
        default:          do_ctl = `DO_LSB;
        endcase
      end
    default:              do_ctl = `DO_NUL;
    endcase
  end
```

Listing 6-76. control.v Data Output register control.

The *ALU Op* worksheet is implemented in the `aluop_sel` section in Listing 6-77. This section isn't really that complex as long as I carefully choose the default case for each state. Taking advantage of the don't-care values in unused states helps simplify the Verilog code.

```
/*****************************************************************************************/
/*                                                                                       */
/*  alu operation control                                                                */
/*                                                                                       */
/*****************************************************************************************/
always @ (inst_reg or page_reg or state_reg or carry_bit or par_bit or sign_bit or
          zero_bit) begin
  casex (state_reg) //synopsys parallel_case
    `DEC1: begin
```

```
    casex (inst_reg) //synopsys parallel_case
      8'b00xx0011,
      8'b00xx1001,
      8'b00xx1011,
      8'b11100011,
      8'b11xx0101,
      8'b11xxx111:      aluop_sel = `ALUOP_ADD;
      8'b10001xxx:      aluop_sel = `ALUOP_BADC;
      8'b00010000,
      8'b00xxx100,
      8'b10000xxx:      aluop_sel = `ALUOP_BADD;
      8'b10100xxx:      aluop_sel = `ALUOP_BAND;
      8'b00xxx101:      aluop_sel = `ALUOP_BDEC;
      8'b10110xxx:      aluop_sel = `ALUOP_BOR;
      8'b10011xxx:      aluop_sel = `ALUOP_BSBC;
      8'b10010xxx,
      8'b10111xxx:      aluop_sel = `ALUOP_BSUB;
      8'b00101111,
      8'b10101xxx:      aluop_sel = `ALUOP_BXOR;
      8'b00111111:      aluop_sel = `ALUOP_CCF;
      8'b00100111:      aluop_sel = `ALUOP_DAA;
      8'b00010111:      aluop_sel = `ALUOP_RLA;
      8'b00000111:      aluop_sel = `ALUOP_RLCA;
      8'b00011111:      aluop_sel = `ALUOP_RRA;
      8'b00001111:      aluop_sel = `ALUOP_RRCA;
      8'b00110111:      aluop_sel = `ALUOP_SCF;
      default:          aluop_sel = `ALUOP_PASS;
      endcase
    end
      .
      .
      .
  `INTB:                aluop_sel = `ALUOP_PASS;
  default:              aluop_sel = `ALUOP_ADD;
  endcase
end
```

Listing 6-77. control.v ALU operation control.

Not surprisingly, the `alua_sel` section, which implements the *ALU A* worksheet, is much simpler than the `aluop_sel` section, as shown in Listing 6-78. This is because this ALU input is not used for a number of common ALU operations like *pass*. For most states there are only two or three different options required.

```
/*****************************************************************************************/
/*                                                                                       */
/*  alu a input control                                                                  */
/*                                                                                       */
/*****************************************************************************************/
always @ (inst_reg or page_reg or state_reg or carry_bit or par_bit or sign_bit or
         tflg_reg or zero_bit) begin
  casex (state_reg) //synopsys parallel_case
    `DEC1: begin
      casex (inst_reg) //synopsys parallel_case
        8'b10000xxx,
        8'b10001xxx,
        8'b10010xxx,
        8'b10011xxx,
        8'b10100xxx,
        8'b10101xxx,
        8'b10110xxx,
        8'b10111xxx:      alua_sel = `ALUA_AA;
        8'b00100111:      alua_sel = `ALUA_DAA;
        8'b00xx1001:      alua_sel = `ALUA_HL;
        8'b00010000,
        8'b00101111,
        8'b00xxx101,
        8'b00xx1011,
        8'b11xx0101,
        8'b11xxx111:      alua_sel = `ALUA_M1;
        default:          alua_sel = `ALUA_ONE;
        endcase
      end
        .
        .
        .
    `INTA:                alua_sel = `ALUA_M1;
    default:              alua_sel = `ALUA_ONE;
    endcase
```

Listing 6-78. control.v ALU A input control.

The `alub_sel` section, which implements the *ALU B* worksheet, is just the opposite. This is shown in Listing 6-79. In fact it is more complex than the `aluop_sel` section. This is because of all of the identifiers like *rrr* that must be expanded into the individual register selects.

Expanding all of the identifiers into the individual register selects requires a fair amount of time and is prone to error. But the alternative, which would separate out the individual identifiers in the entire design spreadsheet, is unattractive to me.

```
/*****************************************************************************************/
/*                                                                                       */
/*  alu b input control                                                                  */
/*                                                                                       */
/*****************************************************************************************/
always @ (inst_reg or page_reg or state_reg or carry_bit or par_bit or sign_bit or
          zero_bit) begin
  casex (state_reg) //synopsys parallel_case
    `DEC1: begin
      casex (inst_reg) //synopsys parallel_case
        8'b00000111,
        8'b00001111,
        8'b00010111,
        8'b00011111,
        8'b00100111,
        8'b00101111:        alub_sel = `ALUB_AA;
        8'b00010000:        alub_sel = `ALUB_BB;
        8'b00000010,
        8'b00001010:        alub_sel = `ALUB_BC;
        8'b00010010,
        8'b00011010,
        8'b11101011:        alub_sel = `ALUB_DE;
        8'b11101001,
        8'b11111001:        alub_sel = `ALUB_HL;
        8'b01xxx000,
        8'b10xxx000:        alub_sel = `ALUB_BB;
        8'b01xxx001,
        8'b10xxx001:        alub_sel = `ALUB_CC;
        8'b01xxx010,
        8'b10xxx010:        alub_sel = `ALUB_DD;
        8'b01xxx011,
        8'b10xxx011:        alub_sel = `ALUB_EE;
        8'b01xxx100,
        8'b10xxx100:        alub_sel = `ALUB_HH;
```

```
        8'b01xxx101,
        8'b10xxx101:        alub_sel = `ALUB_LL;
        8'b01xxx111,
        8'b10xxx111:        alub_sel = `ALUB_AA;
        8'b0000010x:        alub_sel = `ALUB_BB;
        8'b0000110x:        alub_sel = `ALUB_CC;
        8'b0001010x:        alub_sel = `ALUB_DD;
        8'b0001110x:        alub_sel = `ALUB_EE;
        8'b0010010x:        alub_sel = `ALUB_HH;
        8'b0010110x:        alub_sel = `ALUB_LL;
        8'b0011110x:        alub_sel = `ALUB_AA;
        8'b00000011,
        8'b00001001,
        8'b00001011:        alub_sel = `ALUB_BC;
        8'b00010011,
        8'b00011001,
        8'b00011011:        alub_sel = `ALUB_DE;
        8'b00100011,
        8'b00101001,
        8'b00101011:        alub_sel = `ALUB_HL;
        8'b00110011,
        8'b00111001,
        8'b00111011:        alub_sel = `ALUB_SP;
        8'b11xx0101,
        8'b11xxx111:        alub_sel = `ALUB_SP;
        default:            alub_sel = `ALUB_PC;
        endcase
      end
        .
        .
        .
    `INTA:                  alub_sel = `ALUB_SP;
    `INTB:                  alub_sel = `ALUB_PCH;
    default:                alub_sel = `ALUB_PC;
    endcase
  end
```

Listing 6-79. control.v ALU B input control.

The *Register Wr* worksheet is implemented in the `wr_addr` control bus, shown in Listing 6-80. Although there are register identifiers in this worksheet that need to be expanded, there are not that many cases to deal with. In addition, all of the identifiers to be expanded occur in the *if1b* state. The `wr_addr` control field performs both the select function and the enable function, so this is one case where the default value must be the idle or inactive condition.

```
/*****************************************************************************************/
/*                                                                                       */
/*  register write control                                                               */
/*                                                                                       */
/*****************************************************************************************/
always @ (inst_reg or page_reg or state_reg or carry_bit or par_bit or sign_bit or
          vector_int or zero_bit) begin
  casex (state_reg) //synopsys parallel_case
    `OF1B: begin
      casex ({page_reg, inst_reg}) //synopsys parallel_case
        12'b000000010000: wr_addr = `WREG_BB;
        default:          wr_addr = `WREG_NUL;
        endcase
      end
    `OF2B: begin
      casex ({page_reg, inst_reg}) //synopsys parallel_case
        12'b000011001101: wr_addr = `WREG_SP;
        12'b000011000100: wr_addr = ( !zero_bit) ? `WREG_SP : `WREG_NUL;
        12'b000011001100: wr_addr = (  zero_bit) ? `WREG_SP : `WREG_NUL;
        12'b000011010100: wr_addr = (!carry_bit) ? `WREG_SP : `WREG_NUL;
        12'b000011011100: wr_addr = ( carry_bit) ? `WREG_SP : `WREG_NUL;
        12'b000011100100: wr_addr = (  !par_bit) ? `WREG_SP : `WREG_NUL;
        12'b000011101100: wr_addr = (   par_bit) ? `WREG_SP : `WREG_NUL;
        12'b000011110100: wr_addr = ( !sign_bit) ? `WREG_SP : `WREG_NUL;
        12'b000011111100: wr_addr = (  sign_bit) ? `WREG_SP : `WREG_NUL;
        default:          wr_addr = `WREG_NUL;
        endcase
      end
    `IF3B:                wr_addr = `WREG_TMP;
        .
        .
        .
```

```
      `INTB:                wr_addr = (vector_int) ? `WREG_TMP : `WREG_SP;
      default:              wr_addr = `WREG_NUL;
      endcase
    end
```

Listing 6-80. control.v register write control.

The sflg_en signal implements the *S Flag* worksheet, and is shown in Listing 6-81. The Sign flag is only set in the *wr2a* and *if1b* states, so this section is fairly simple. This is an enable signal, so the inactive state must always be inactive.

```
/*****************************************************************************************/
/*                                                                                       */
/*  s flag control                                                                       */
/*                                                                                       */
/*****************************************************************************************/
always @ (inst_reg or page_reg or state_reg) begin
  casex (state_reg) //synopsys parallel_case
    `WR2A: begin
      casex ({page_reg, inst_reg}) //synopsys parallel_case
        12'b000000110100,
        12'b000000110101,
        12'b001000000xxx,
        12'b001000001xxx,
        12'b001000010xxx,
        12'b001000011xxx,
        12'b001000100xxx,
        12'b001000101xxx,
        12'b001000111xxx,
        12'b010x00110100,
        12'b010x00110101,
        12'b011x00010110,
        12'b011x00000110,
        12'b011x00011110,
        12'b011x00001110,
        12'b011x00100110,
        12'b011x00101110,
        12'b011x00111110: sflg_en = 1'b1;
        default:          sflg_en = 1'b0;
        endcase
      end
```

```
        .
        .
        .
    default:                sflg_en = 1'b0;
    endcase
  end
```

Listing 6-81. control.v Sign flag control.

Listing 6-82 shows the `zflg_en` signal, which implements the *Z Flag* worksheet. The Zero flag is used by a number of instructions, so generating the `zflg_en` signal is a little more complicated. This is an enable signal, so the inactive state must always be inactive.

```
/*****************************************************************************************/
/*                                                                                       */
/*  z flag control                                                                       */
/*                                                                                       */
/*****************************************************************************************/
always @ (inst_reg or page_reg or state_reg) begin
  casex (state_reg) //synopsys parallel_case
    `RD1A,
    `RD2A: begin
      casex ({page_reg, inst_reg}) //synopsys parallel_case
        12'b1xxx10100010,
        12'b1xxx10100011,
        12'b1xxx10101010,
        12'b1xxx10101011,
        12'b1xxx10110010,
        12'b1xxx10110011,
        12'b1xxx10111010,
        12'b1xxx10111011: zflg_en = 1'b1;
        default:          zflg_en = 1'b0;
        endcase
      end
        .
        .
        .
    default:                zflg_en = 1'b0;
    endcase
  end
```

Listing 6-82. control.v Zero flag control.

The *H Flag* worksheet is implemented with the `hflg_ctl` control bus, as shown in Listing 6-83. Remember that the Half-Carry flag must be set and cleared in addition to the normal function. This is the reason for a control bus rather than a simple enable.

```
/*******************************************************************************************/
/*                                                                                         */
/*  h flag control                                                                         */
/*                                                                                         */
/*******************************************************************************************/
always @ (inst_reg or page_reg or state_reg) begin
  casex (state_reg) //synopsys parallel_case
    `WR2A: begin
      casex ({page_reg, inst_reg}) //synopsys parallel_case
        12'b001000000xxx,
        12'b001000001xxx,
        12'b001000010xxx,
        12'b001000011xxx,
        12'b001000100xxx,
        12'b001000101xxx,
        12'b001000111xxx,
        12'b011x00010110,
        12'b011x00000110,
        12'b011x00011110,
        12'b011x00001110,
        12'b011x00100110,
        12'b011x00101110,
        12'b011x00111110,
        12'b1xxx01100111,
        12'b1xxx01101111: hflg_ctl = `HFLG_0;
        12'b000000110100,
        12'b000000110101,
        12'b010x00110100,
        12'b010x00110101: hflg_ctl = `HFLG_H;
        default:          hflg_ctl = `HFLG_NUL;
        endcase
      end
        .
        .
        .
```

```
      default:                hflg_ctl = `HFLG_NUL;
      endcase
    end
```

Listing 6-83. control.v Half-Carry flag control.

Listing 6-84 shows the pflg_en signal, which implements the *PV Flag* worksheet. The Parity/Overflow flag has the most different uses of any of the flags, but it is not used by that many instructions. If you look closely at the cases for the *rd1a* and *rd2a* states you'll see that the eight individual cases could be replaced by a single line with a little editing.

```
/*******************************************************************************************/
/*                                                                                         */
/*  pv flag control                                                                        */
/*                                                                                         */
/*******************************************************************************************/
always @ (inst_reg or page_reg or state_reg) begin
  casex (state_reg) //synopsys parallel_case
    `RD1A,
    `RD2A: begin
      casex ({page_reg, inst_reg}) //synopsys parallel_case
        12'b1xxx10100000,
        12'b1xxx10100001,
        12'b1xxx10101000,
        12'b1xxx10101001,
        12'b1xxx10110000,
        12'b1xxx10110001,
        12'b1xxx10111000,
        12'b1xxx10111001: pflg_ctl = `PFLG_B;
        default:          pflg_ctl = `PFLG_NUL;
        endcase
      end
        .
        .
        .
    default:              pflg_ctl = `PFLG_NUL;
    endcase
  end
```

Listing 6-84. control.v Parity/Overflow flag control.

The nflg_en signal implements the *N Flag* worksheet, and is shown in Listing 6-85. This is another case where the code could be reduced with a little editing.

```
/*****************************************************************************************/
/*                                                                                       */
/*  n flag control                                                                       */
/*                                                                                       */
/*****************************************************************************************/
always @ (inst_reg or page_reg or state_reg) begin
  casex (state_reg) //synopsys parallel_case
    `WR1A,
    `WR2A: begin
      casex ({page_reg, inst_reg}) //synopsys parallel_case
        12'b1xxx10100010,
        12'b1xxx10100011,
        12'b1xxx10101010,
        12'b1xxx10101011,
        12'b1xxx10110010,
        12'b1xxx10110011,
        12'b1xxx10111010,
        12'b1xxx10111011: nflg_ctl = `NFLG_S;
        default:          nflg_ctl = `NFLG_NUL;
        endcase
      end
        .
        .
        .
    default:              nflg_ctl = `NFLG_NUL;
    endcase
  end
```

Listing 6-85. control.v Negate flag control.

The *C Flag* worksheet is implemented with the `cflg_en` signal, shown in Listing 6-86. Surprisingly, the Carry flag is used by the fewest instructions of any of the flags..

```
/*****************************************************************************************/
/*                                                                                       */
/*  c flag control                                                                       */
/*                                                                                       */
/*****************************************************************************************/
always @ (inst_reg or page_reg or state_reg) begin
  casex (state_reg) //synopsys parallel_case
    `WR2A: begin
      casex ({page_reg, inst_reg}) //synopsys parallel_case
        12'b001000000xxx,
        12'b001000001xxx,
        12'b001000010xxx,
        12'b001000011xxx,
        12'b001000100xxx,
        12'b001000101xxx,
        12'b001000111xxx,
        12'b011x00000110,
        12'b011x00001110,
        12'b011x00010110,
        12'b011x00011110,
        12'b011x00100110,
        12'b011x00101110,
        12'b011x00111110: cflg_en = 1'b1;
        default:          cflg_en = 1'b0;
        endcase
      end
        .
        .
        .
    default:              cflg_en = 1'b0;
    endcase
  end
```

Listing 6-86. control.v Carry flag control.

The `tflg_ctl` control bus implements the *T Flag* worksheet. The Temporary flag is only used by a handful of instructions, so in a couple of cases it can be controlled independent of the instruction. The entire section controlling the Temporary flag is shown in Listing 6-87.

```
/*****************************************************************************************/
/*                                                                                       */
/* temporary flag control                                                                */
/*                                                                                       */
/*****************************************************************************************/
always @ (inst_reg or page_reg or state_reg) begin
  casex (state_reg) //synopsys parallel_case
    `OF1B:                 tflg_ctl = `TFLG_Z;
    `RD1A,
    `RD2A: begin
      casex ({page_reg, inst_reg})
        12'b1xxx10100011,
        12'b1xxx10101011,
        12'b1xxx10110011,
        12'b1xxx10111011: tflg_ctl = `TFLG_1;
        default:           tflg_ctl = `TFLG_Z;
        endcase
      end
    `BLK1:                 tflg_ctl = `TFLG_B;
    default:               tflg_ctl = `TFLG_NUL;
    endcase
  end
```

Listing 6-87. control.v Temporary flag control.

That takes care of all of the individual modules. Now we just need to put the design together.

The y80_top.v module

The y80_top.v module is not necessarily the ultimate top-level module. This is because it is usually necessary to instantiate special I/O cells and clock buffers specific to the technology used for the implementation. I am not going to target the design to a specific technology here, so this will serve as the top-level module for now. Listing 6-88 shows the interface for the top-level module.

```
module y80_top (dma_ack, halt_tran, iack_tran, io_addr_out, io_data_out, io_read, io_strobe,
                io_tran, ivec_rd, mem_addr_out, mem_data_out, mem_rd, mem_tran, mem_wr,
                reti_tran, t1, clearb, clkc, dma_req, int_req, io_data_in, ivec_data_in,
                mem_data_in, nmi_req, resetb, wait_req);

  input          clearb;        /* master (test) reset                              */
  input          clkc;          /* main cpu clock                                   */
  input          dma_req;       /* dma request                                      */
  input          int_req;       /* interrupt request                                */
  input          nmi_req;       /* nmi request                                      */
  input          resetb;        /* internal (user) reset                            */
  input          wait_req;      /* wait request                                     */
  input   [7:0]  io_data_in;    /* i/o input data bus                               */
  input   [7:0]  ivec_data_in;  /* interrupt vector bus                             */
  input   [7:0]  mem_data_in;   /* memory input bus                                 */
  output         dma_ack;       /* dma acknowledge                                  */
  output         halt_tran;     /* halt transaction                                 */
  output         iack_tran;     /* interrupt acknowledge transaction                */
  output         io_read;       /* i/o read enable                                  */
  output         io_tran;       /* i/o transaction                                  */
  output         io_strobe;     /* i/o data strobe                                  */
  output         ivec_rd;       /* interrupt vector enable                          */
  output         mem_rd;        /* memory read enable                               */
  output         mem_tran;      /* memory transaction                               */
  output         mem_wr;        /* memory write enable                              */
  output         reti_tran;     /* return from interrupt transaction                */
  output         t1;            /* first clock of transaction                       */
  output  [7:0]  io_data_out;   /* i/o output data bus                              */
  output  [7:0]  mem_data_out;  /* memory output data bus                           */
  output [15:0]  io_addr_out;   /* i/o address bus                                  */
  output [15:0]  mem_addr_out;  /* memory address bus                               */
```

Listing 6-88. y80_top.v inputs and outputs.

The body of this module is just the instantiation of the extint.v, machine.v, control.v and datapath.v modules. Since signal names do not change across any of these module boundaries, I won't bother to show the Verilog code here.

Now that the design portion of the project is done, I am about halfway finished. That's because the verification phase of the project typically requires just as much time as does the design phase. I am not going to go through the verification phase in nearly as much detail as I did for the design phase, because that would probably double the size of this book. Instead, I'll briefly go over the techniques that I use in a Verilog testbench, and provide the testbench for you to use to verify your version of the design.

7. Debug, Verification and Testing

Introduction

No design is going to be perfect once you finish typing the Verilog code. That's where the debug phase comes in. For a CPU debug is often considered "done" when the machine fetches its first instruction in the simulation, but in reality the debug phase continues in parallel with the verification phase, often all the way to production.

Verification involves checking that every instruction behaves properly, for all data values, and independent of anything that happened prior to or during the instruction. While there are formal methods that can be used to verify a logic design, in practice this is a nearly impossible task. All you can really do is verify a subset of data values and a subset of boundary conditions. I'll discuss some ways to choose what to check shortly.

Testing isn't nearly as important as it used to be, because these days most ASIC designs use Built-In-Self-Test (BIST). But there are times where it is still useful to do functional testing, so I'll discuss how to prepare for this briefly also.

Debug, verification and testing are all done in the Verilog simulator using a dedicated piece of Verilog code called a testbench. Debug and verification do not really impose many constraints on how the testbench works. But any simulation that you do for testing will later be transferred to a real tester, so if you will be doing functional testing it is important to take this into account when creating the testbench.

Debug Requirements

There isn't a lot that you can do in the design or testbench to assist with debugging. Most of what makes debugging less painful is in the simulator that you choose to use.

The very first debug task is to get the Verilog to compile, which only means that all of the syntax errors have been eliminated. If you are lucky enough to use an editor that supports Verilog syntax checking this step can be trivial. But if you're like me and use a regular text editor this is going to be an iterative process. My simulator only reports the first ten errors before aborting, but that isn't really a problem, because I don't recommend trying to fix more than a few errors at a time.

- **When debugging don't try to correct more than a couple of errors at once.**

Often the most difficult part of debugging is trying to get the design to exit the reset state. This is particularly true when it is not possible to force every flip-flop to a known state. This is why I always try to include a special reset input for just this purpose.

Try to resist using an internally-generated reset signal. The most annoying debugging problem I ever encountered involved an internal reset signal that needed to be delayed until any current bus transaction completed. This meant that the state machines that controlled bus transactions could not be affected directly by the external reset. This lead to a nasty circular problem when first starting up the simulation, because all of these state machines started up in an unknown state. I ended up getting around the unknowns at startup by using a timer than basically timed out after the longest machine cycle would have finished to enable the reset to take effect.

I tend to use an asynchronous reset signal in my designs, primarily because this type of reset does not require a clock to be present to initialize flip-flops. But other designers swear by a synchronous reset, often because it makes the timing analysis easier. I don't like to compromise a design to account for tool limitations, but feel free to choose whichever style makes the most sense to you.

- **Whenever possible provide a master reset to initialize all flip-flops.**

It will of course be different for each ISA, but once the CPU can fetch instructions the first thing that you need to get working are instructions to read and write memory. In the case of this design I need the Push and Pop instructions working so that I can load data into registers and write results back out over the write data bus.

- **Once instruction fetches are working concentrate on data reads and writes.**

Once the CPU can fetch instructions and read and write memory the verification phase begins.

Verification Requirements

Verification should never be an ad hoc process. As soon as the CPU exits reset and at least one read and write operation are working it's time to create a verification checklist. The design spreadsheet is an ideal place to do this. In fact, most of the information about what needs to be verified is already present in the *Operation* worksheet.

- **Make a list of everything you plan to verify before you start the verification. Then recognize that you will probably have to add to the list as you go through the verification.**

The level of detail in the verification checklist is a function of what kind of verification you are going to do. Designing in Verilog makes some things correct by construction. For example, in the address ALU shown below the `ALUOP_ADD` operation is always going to properly add the `adda_in` and `addb_in` binary values, so I shouldn't need to verify more than a few different input values.

But verifying the `ALUOP_ADS` operation is a little more complicated. What if there was a typo in the index for the `bsign_ext` variable? What if there was a typo in one of the indexes where this variable is generated? These types of potential errors in the Verilog description of the logic, shown in Listing 7-1, need to be considered in the verification checklist.

```
assign bsign_ext = {addb_in[7],  addb_in[7],  addb_in[7],  addb_in[7],
                    addb_in[7],  addb_in[7],  addb_in[7],  addb_in[7]};

always @ (aluop_reg or adda_in or addb_in or bsign_ext) begin
  case (aluop_reg)
    `ALUOP_ADS:  adda_out = adda_in + {bsign_ext[15:8], addb_in[7:0]};
    `ALUOP_ADD:  adda_out = adda_in + addb_in;
    `ALUOP_APAS: adda_out = adda_in;
    default:     adda_out = addb_in;
    endcase
  end
```

Listing 7-1. How do I check for typos in this code?

Usually this means carefully choosing the appropriate cases for the data used by an operation. In this particular case, where the operation is only used for the indexed addressing mode, I need to vary the address and offset that I use to verify different instructions with this addressing mode. Alternatively, I can comprehensively test different combinations of address and offset for one instruction, knowing that the operation will then be correct for all instructions.

- **Think carefully about the data cases you need to verify. A shotgun approach is likely to miss something.**

Verification should never be done interactively. In other words, every verification test that you do should be repeatable at any time in the future. Fixing one bug can easily break something that you have already verified as working, and you must have a way to test this.

- **Make all simulations repeatable. In essence, your real goal here is to create a regression test for the design.**

It is obviously critical to test all of the special corner cases, like interrupts and bus requests, but I always try to make sure that everything else is working before attempting to verify special cases. Interrupts and bus requests potentially affect any and every instruction, so it is important to have a regression test for instructions before attempting exception cases.

- **Completely verify the instruction set before attempting things like interrupts.**

If your design includes peripheral functions in addition to the CPU it's usually a waste of time to try to debug the peripherals until the CPU is fully verified. After all, if you can't trust that the processor is executing the instructions correctly, how can you isolate a problem?

- **Completely verify the CPU before attempting to verify peripheral functions.**

Often a design will include special cells for memories, I/O buffers, clock buffers, oscillators or Phase-Locked Loops (PLLs). The models for these different functions need to be correct for a simulation to work properly, and these models are usually supplied by whoever designed the special cells. In my experience you should never assume that these models are perfect. If the simulation doesn't seem right, go through the model to convince yourself that it is correct.

- **Models of special cells are not always correct. Verify the models for yourself when in doubt.**

If you are going to need to do a functional test of the design after it has been implemented the time to think about that is during the verification phase, to save any duplicated effort.

Testing Requirements

Functional testing is fundamentally different from verification. During verification you are working with correctly functioning logic, but the goal of functional testing is to uncover incorrectly functioning logic. The usual assumption is that functional testing should uncover signals that are stuck High or stuck Low. A second assumption is that these stuck-at faults occur in isolation.

To test for this type of fault every signal should be both controllable and observable. Controllable means that the signal can be forced to a specific state as a result of external stimulus. Observable means that an incorrect value on a signal will result in a different output from the device under test.

- **If you can't observe it, you can't test it.**

For a design of this complexity controllability and observability for flip-flops are fairly easy to guarantee. For example, the PC register can be loaded with a Jump instruction and the result will be immediately visible on the address bus. The remainder of the CPU registers are similar. Even the buried registers like the machine state and pipeline registers are both controllable and observable.

Logic other than registers can be a little more complicated though. For example, to cover all of the possible cases for a single bit of an adder requires checking all eight possible combinations of the three inputs (don't forget the carry-in). This might seem like a lot of cases to cover for a 16-bit adder, but remember that you can usually check a lot of the bits simultaneously with the right data values.

- **Test multiple cases at the same time. Remember, for this kind of testing it's only important to know that an error exists, not exactly what the error is.**

Even though it may not be strictly necessary, I always try to do all of my simulations with functional testing in mind. In my experience, when people start writing software for a new CPU the tendency is to always blame the hardware when something isn't working right. If the simulation already covers the case that the software folks are complaining about it will be much easier to isolate the real problem.

The Testbench

The testbench presented here is fairly basic, although it does attempt to provide enough coverage to be used for a functional test. The testbench uses fixed timing with a 100nS cycle time for the clock, although it should be straightforward to modify this timing if necessary.

I have not attempted to thoroughly verify setup, hold and delay times in the testbench, but the read data bus is generated with a setup time and a hold time to illustrate how this can be done. In a similar fashion, the output data is sampled with a known delay from the rising edge of the clock.

The code fragment in Listing 7-2 shows the start of the testbench. I start off by setting the timescale for the simulation. This sets the time unit and precision for the remainder of the simulation. Normally a time unit of one percent of the clock cycle time is sufficient. I usually use a precision of one percent of the time step.

Then the version is selected and all of the source files are included. Note that the testbench has no inputs or outputs, because this is the entire system for the simulation. All of the inputs to the CPU use the `reg` data type so that I can control the timing of the inputs.

```
`timescale 1ns / 10ps                             /* set time scale              */
`include "version.v"                              /* select version              */
`include "hierarchy.v"                            /* include sources             */

module top_levl;

  wire         DMA_ACK;                           /* dma acknowledge             */
  wire         HALT_TRAN;                         /* halt transaction            */
  wire         IACK_TRAN;                         /* int ack transaction         */
  wire         IO_READ;                           /* i/o read/write status       */
  wire         IO_STROBE;                         /* i/o strobe                  */
  wire         IO_TRAN;                           /* i/o transaction             */
  wire         IVEC_RD;                           /* int vector read strobe      */
  wire         MEM_RD;                            /* mem read strobe             */
  wire         MEM_TRAN;                          /* mem transaction             */
  wire         MEM_WR;                            /* mem write strobe            */
  wire         RETI_TRAN;                         /* reti transaction            */
  wire         T1;                                /* first clock of transaction  */
  wire  [7:0]  IO_DATA_OUT;                       /* i/o data output bus         */
  wire  [7:0]  MEM_DATA_OUT;                      /* mem data output bus         */
  wire [15:0]  IO_ADDR;                           /* i/o address bus             */
  wire [15:0]  MEM_ADDR;                          /* mem address bus             */

  reg          CLEARB;                            /* master (test) reset         */
  reg          CLKC;                              /* clock                       */
  reg          DMA_REQ;                           /* dma request                 */
  reg          INT_REQ;                           /* interrupt request           */
  reg          NMI_REQ;                           /* non-maskable interrupt req  */
  reg          RESETB;                            /* internal (user) reset       */
  reg          WAIT_REQ;                          /* wait request                */
  reg   [7:0]  IO_DATA_IN;                        /* i/o data input bus          */
  reg   [7:0]  IVEC_DATA_IN;                      /* vector input bus            */
  reg   [7:0]  MEM_DATA_IN;                       /* mem data input bus          */
```

Listing 7-2. The start of the testbench.

The section of code in Listing 7-3 shows the testbench implementation of the memory for the CPU. It is important to remember that the testbench does not need to behave like a normal system with a read/write memory. In fact, for what I am trying to accomplish in the testbench implementing normal memory operation would be counterproductive.

The `rdmem` read memory contains the code that the CPU will execute, as well as data to be read by the CPU and interrupt vectors. The `wrmem` write memory contains data to compare to any data written by the CPU while executing the code loaded into the read memory. This allows the testbench to be self-contained, so that there is no need to inspect the simulation results cycle-by-cycle.

The only restriction on the write memory is that any given memory location can only be written with one data value. This memory organization makes the testbench behave just like a piece of Automatic Test Equipment (ATE) would when testing the finished design.

```
/*******************************************************************************************/
/*                                                                                         */
/* read memory and write data compare memory                                               */
/*                                                                                         */
/*******************************************************************************************/
reg   [7:0] rdmem [0:65535];
reg   [7:0] wrmem [0:65535];

wire  [7:0] wr_data = (MEM_TRAN) ? wrmem[MEM_ADDR] :
                      (IO_TRAN)  ? wrmem[IO_ADDR]  : 8'hxx;

wire  [7:0] rd_data    = rdmem[MEM_ADDR];
wire  [7:0] iord_data = rdmem[IO_ADDR];

always @ (posedge TREF6) begin
  IO_DATA_IN    <= (IO_TRAN && IO_READ && IO_STROBE && !WAIT_REQ) ? iord_data : 8'hxx;
  MEM_DATA_IN   <= (MEM_TRAN && MEM_RD && !WAIT_REQ) ? rd_data : 8'hxx;
  end

always @ (posedge TREF6) begin
  IVEC_DATA_IN <= (IACK_TRAN && IVEC_RD && !WAIT_REQ) ? rd_data : 8'hxx;
  end
```

```
always @ (posedge TREF0) begin
  IO_DATA_IN    <= 8'hxx;
  MEM_DATA_IN   <= 8'hxx;
  IVEC_DATA_IN <= 8'hxx;
  end
```

Listing 7-3. top_levl.v read memory and write data compare memory.

I'll get to the details of the timing shortly, but all of the data provided to the CPU by the testbench is asserted shortly before where it should be sampled by the CPU and then de-asserted shortly after this point. At all other times the data input buses are `8'xx`, so that if the data is sampled on the wrong clock edge this error will show up in the simulation.

I usually instantiate the design fairly early in the testbench, even though the order makes absolutely no difference. Listing 7-4 shows the instantiation. Every input and output must be connected to the testbench. Otherwise why have them?

```
/*****************************************************************************************/
/*                                                                                       */
/* instantiate the design                                                                */
/*                                                                                       */
/*****************************************************************************************/
y80_top Y80 ( .dma_ack(DMA_ACK), .halt_tran(HALT_TRAN), .iack_tran(IACK_TRAN),
             .io_addr_out(IO_ADDR), .io_data_out(IO_DATA_OUT), .io_read(IO_READ),
             .io_strobe(IO_STROBE), .io_tran(IO_TRAN), .ivec_rd(IVEC_RD),
             .mem_addr_out(MEM_ADDR), .mem_data_out(MEM_DATA_OUT), .mem_rd(MEM_RD),
             .mem_tran(MEM_TRAN), .mem_wr(MEM_WR), .reti_tran(RETI_TRAN), .t1(T1),
             .clearb(CLEARB), .clkc(CLKC), .dma_req(DMA_REQ), .int_req(INT_REQ),
             .io_data_in(IO_DATA_IN), .ivec_data_in(IVEC_DATA_IN),
             .mem_data_in(MEM_DATA_IN), .nmi_req(NMI_REQ), .resetb(RESETB),
             .wait_req(WAIT_REQ) );
```

Listing 7-4. top_levl.v instantiating the design.

Listing 7-5 shows the main timing generator for the testbench. I could just generate the clock directly, but deriving it from a higher-frequency reference clock gives me edges that I can use to trigger events in the testbench with precise timing relationships relative to the clock.

```
/*****************************************************************************************/
/*                                                                                       */
/* timing generator                                                                      */
/*                                                                                       */
/*****************************************************************************************/
initial begin
  TREF0 = 1;
  CLKC  = 1;
  end

always begin
  #10 TREF0 <= 1'b0;
      TREF1 <= 1'b1;
  #10 TREF1 <= 1'b0;
      TREF2 <= 1'b1;
  #10 TREF2 <= 1'b0;
      TREF3 <= 1'b1;
  #10 TREF3 <= 1'b0;
      TREF4 <= 1'b1;
  #10 TREF4 <= 1'b0;
      TREF5 <= 1'b1;
  #10 TREF5 <= 1'b0;
      TREF6 <= 1'b1;
  #10 TREF6 <= 1'b0;
      TREF7 <= 1'b1;
  #10 TREF7 <= 1'b0;
      TREF8 <= 1'b1;
  #10 TREF8 <= 1'b0;
      TREF9 <= 1'b1;
  #10 TREF9 <= 1'b0;
      TREF0 <= 1'b1;
  end

always @ (posedge TREF3) CLKC = 0;
always @ (posedge TREF8) CLKC = 1;
```

Listing 7-5. top_levl.v timing generator.

Remember that `reg` variables normally start off unknown in Verilog. This can present a problem with clocks, so they should always be initialized by the testbench. That is why `TREF0` and `CLKC` are both initialized in this section.

The timing diagram in Figure 7-1 shows the relationships for the different parts of the testbench. The choice of ten equal timing reference signals is fairly arbitrary. If you need more granularity feel free to use more, and there is no particular reason that the reference signals need to be equally spaced.

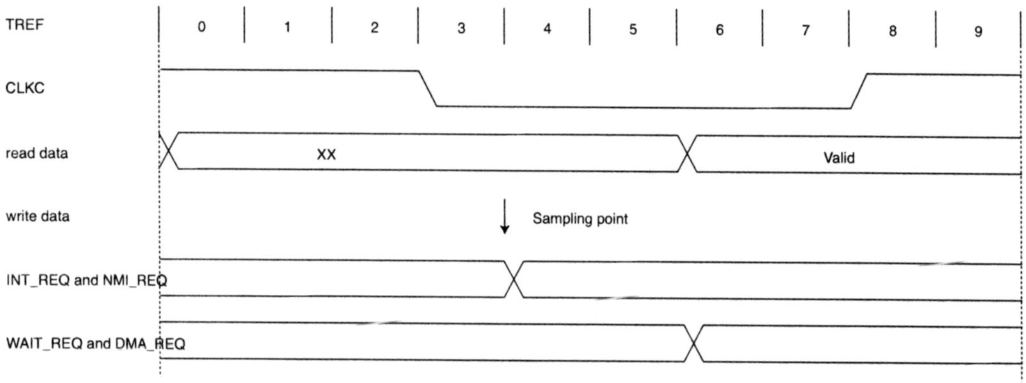

Figure 7-1. Testbench master timing.

All of the inputs to the CPU should start off with a defined value, especially the resets. This is done in Listing 7-6. Always initialize the resets inactive so that there will be a transition on the signal to trigger their use in all of the `always` blocks in the Verilog.

```
/*****************************************************************************************/
/*                                                                                       */
/* initialize input signals                                                              */
/*                                                                                       */
/*****************************************************************************************/
initial begin
  CLEARB    = 1;
  DMA_REQ   = 0;
  INT_REQ   = 0;
  NMI_REQ   = 0;
  RESETB    = 1;
  WAIT_REQ  = 0;
  end
```

Listing 7-6. top_levl.v input signal initialization.

Testbench variables do not have to use synthesizable constructs, so I just initialize them using an `initial` block, shown in Listing 7-7. I'll go over what these testbench variables do in the sections where they are generated. You'll notice that I have used blocking assignment statements in these `initial` blocks. Because these statements are executed only at the start of a simulation, it doesn't really matter if you use blocking or non-blocking statements here. The same is true for the majority of the testbench.

```
/*****************************************************************************************/
/*                                                                                       */
/* initialize testbench variables                                                        */
/*                                                                                       */
/*****************************************************************************************/
initial begin
  breq_mach    = 6'b000000;
  CMP_ERR_L    = 16'h0000;
  CLR_INT      = 0;
  CLR_NMI      = 0;
  DISABLE_BREQ = 1;
  DISABLE_INT  = 1;
  DISABLE_WAIT = 1;
  INT_TYPE     = 0;
  PAT_DONE     = 0;
  TRIG_INT     = 0;
  TRIG_NMI     = 0;
  end
```

Listing 7-7. top_levl.v testbench variable initialization.

Listing 7-8 shows a couple of tasks that I use in the testbench to perform a reset. I usually like keep all tasks in a separate file and `` `include `` the file near the top of the testbench. Since there are only two tasks needed in this testbench I have just implemented them directly.

Verilog tasks are like subroutines that can include timing. Verifying a processor design rarely requires more than a few tasks, but whenever peripheral functions are involved the number of tasks can skyrocket. I have used Verilog tasks to check I/O port values, to force values on input pins, to do serial port transfers, and even to do full Ethernet frame transfers.

To make tasks independent of timing it is important to avoid using absolute delays. I have to use two `wait` statements per clock cycle to keep from falling directly through these statements. The higher-frequency timing generator allows full control of where signal edges occur relative to the clock for the CPU.

```
/*****************************************************************************************/
/*                                                                                       */
/* reset and clear task                                                                  */
/*                                                                                       */
/*****************************************************************************************/
task resettask;
  begin
    wait(TREF6);
    RESETB   = 0;
    wait(TREF0);
    wait(TREF6);
    wait(TREF0);
    wait(TREF6);
    RESETB   = 1;
    CLR_INT  = 1;
    CLR_NMI  = 1;
    wait(TREF0);
    PAT_DONE = 0;
    end
  endtask

task cleartask;
  begin
    wait(TREF6);
    CLEARB   = 0;
    RESETB   = 0;
    wait(TREF0);
    wait(TREF6);
    wait(TREF0);
    wait(TREF6);
```

```
    CLEARB   = 1;
    RESETB   = 1;
    CLR_INT  = 1;
    CLR_NMI  = 1;
    wait(TREF0);
    PAT_DONE = 0;
    end
  endtask
```

Listing 7-8. top_levl.v reset and clear task definitions.

One of the most important features of a testbench is the ability to log errors. In this testbench I only log errors that occur during writes to memory or I/O addresses. This is shown in Listing 7-9. Most of the control signal outputs from the CPU are only checked indirectly, so it is still important to visually inspect the different types of bus transactions looking for errors. A more sophisticated testbench would check every bus transaction for proper signals and timing.

```
/*****************************************************************************************/
/*                                                                                       */
/* error log                                                                             */
/*                                                                                       */
/*****************************************************************************************/
always @ (posedge TREF4) begin
  if (MEM_WR)                  CMP_ERR_L = CMP_ERR_L + (MEM_DATA_OUT != wr_data);
  if (!IO_READ && IO_STROBE) CMP_ERR_L = CMP_ERR_L + (IO_DATA_OUT  != wr_data);
  end
```

Listing 7-9. top_levl.v testbench error log.

The `CMP_ERR_L` variable should be either traced or displayed for the entire simulation. Whenever the variable increments there has been a data mismatch that needs to be investigated.

Partitioning is just as important in the test patterns as it is in the design. But once I partition the tests into multiple test patterns I need a way to signal that the current test pattern is complete. I usually do this by picking a specific address to go to at the end of every individual test pattern. The testbench can then be used to detect a fetch from this address and trigger the testbench to load a new test pattern into the testbench memory. This is the function of the PAT_DONE testbench signal, shown in Listing 7-10.

```
/*******************************************************************************************/
/*                                                                                         */
/* end-of-pattern detect                                                                   */
/*                                                                                         */
/*******************************************************************************************/
always @ (posedge TREF4) begin
  PAT_DONE  = (MEM_ADDR[15:0] == 16'h00c3);
  end
```

Listing 7-10. top_levl.v end-of-pattern detector.

Between each individual test pattern I always do a reset, so that there is no dependence on the order of the patterns. I also clear the error counter at the end of each test pattern.

Interrupts are asynchronous events, and more advanced simulation features allow for randomly generated interrupts. Since in this design the interface to the interrupt machine cycle sequence is quite rigid I don't consider it necessary to test for the proper handling of an interrupt after each and every instruction. Instead, I will generate an interrupt request at specific times in the test patterns to verify proper operation.

There are a couple of methods that I have used to generate interrupt requests in the past. With complex designs I will usually have a separate "drive" file that is loaded along with the test pattern. This file contains timing information with output sample values and input drive values, and runs in parallel with the CPU executing the instructions in the test pattern. I use this type of file when the CPU contains peripheral functions that have their own inputs and outputs, because it allows me to verify the proper operation of the peripherals in conjunction with the CPU.

In this design, with only a CPU present, I am going to use a simpler method of generating interrupts. Listing 7-11 shows how an interrupt is generated when a specific range of addresses is detected.

This interrupt generation function is disabled by the testbench variable DISABLE_INT so that I am free to use any address when not checking interrupts. In a similar fashion the breq_mach variable, which generates bus requests within the testbench, disables this interrupt generation function. The breq_mach term creates a simultaneous Bus Request and Interrupt Request, allowing me to verify that the proper priority resolution takes place. I use another address range to clear the interrupt request.

In this way I can generate an interrupt request for any instruction that I want by executing the instruction within a specific range of addresses. The Non-Maskable Interrupt is generated the same way, using a different address range. Since the interrupt triggers are not a function of the type of bus cycle even a memory read or write to the special address will trigger an interrupt.

```
/*****************************************************************************************/
/*                                                                                       */
/* interrupt/nmi request generator                                                       */
/*                                                                                       */
/*****************************************************************************************/
always @ (posedge TREF4) begin
  TRIG_INT = !((MEM_ADDR[15:13] == 3'b110) && (MEM_ADDR[8:0] == 9'h0ff)) ||
             DISABLE_INT || |breq_mach;
  TRIG_NMI = !((MEM_ADDR[15:13] == 3'b110) && (MEM_ADDR[8:0] == 9'h1ff)) ||
             DISABLE_INT || |breq_mach;
  CLR_INT  = (MEM_ADDR[15:13] == 3'b111);
  CLR_NMI  = (MEM_ADDR[15:13] == 3'b111);
  if (T1) INT_TYPE = MEM_ADDR[8];
  end

always @ (negedge TRIG_NMI) begin
  NMI_REQ = 1;
  end

always @ (posedge CLR_NMI) begin
  NMI_REQ = 0;
  end

always @ (negedge TRIG_INT) begin
  INT_REQ = 1;
  end
```

```
always @ (posedge CLR_INT) begin
  wait(TREF0);
  wait(TREF4);
  wait(TREF0);
  wait(TREF4);
  INT_REQ = 0;
  end
```

Listing 7-11. top_levl.v Interrupt/NMI Request generator.

Since the Address Bus is forced to zero during Halt transactions, this technique cannot be used to generate the interrupt necessary to exit the Halt state. To do this I need the testbench code in Listing 7-12.

When a Halt transaction is detected this code waits for ten clock cycles and then generates an interrupt. The ten clock cycle delay allows enough time for the testbench bus request generator to insert a Bus Request, verifying that feature of thc Halt state.

The `INT_TYPE` variable is set according to the last address prior to the Bus Release, allowing me to control the type of interrupt used to force an exit from the Halt state. Then there is another delay before the interrupt request is de-asserted to make sure that the interrupt has been seen.

The remainder of the code covers the special case where a maskable interrupt will not cause an exit from the Halt state if that interrupt is disabled. In this case I need to generate a Non-Maskable Interrupt to exit the Halt state and continue the testing.

```
/*****************************************************************************************/
/*                                                                                       */
/* interrupt request generator (during Halt)                                             */
/*                                                                                       */
/*****************************************************************************************/
integer j;

always @ (posedge HALT_TRAN) begin
  for (j=0; j < 10; j=j+1) begin
    wait (TREF6);
    wait (TREF0);
    end
  wait (TREF6);
```

```
    INT_REQ = HALT_TRAN && !INT_TYPE;
    NMI_REQ = HALT_TRAN &&  INT_TYPE;
    wait (TREF0);
    for (j=0; j < 12; j=j+1) begin
      wait (TREF6);
      wait (TREF0);
      end
    INT_REQ = 0;
    NMI_REQ = 0;
    wait (TREF6);
    wait (TREF0);
    wait (TREF6);
    NMI_REQ = HALT_TRAN && !INT_TYPE;
    wait (TREF0);
    wait (TREF6);
    wait (TREF0);
    NMI_REQ = 0;
    end
```

Listing 7-12. top_levl.v Interrupt Request during Halt generator.

Next comes the generator for the `WAIT_REQ` input, shown in Listing 7-13. I am not doing anything fancy here, like choosing different numbers of Wait states for memory and I/O or varying the number of Wait states. This is a global two-clock Wait state generator, enabled when the `DISABLE_WAIT` testbench variable is Low. I will set this variable Low and then run the entire set of test patterns to verify that the Wait states work properly.

```
/*******************************************************************************************/
/*                                                                                         */
/* wait request generator                                                                  */
/*                                                                                         */
/*******************************************************************************************/
always @ (posedge CLKC) begin
  wait_dly <= T1;
  end

always @ (posedge TREF6) WAIT_REQ = !DISABLE_WAIT && (T1 || wait_dly);
always @ (posedge TREF9) WAIT_REQ = 1'b0;
```

Listing 7-13. top_levl.v Wait Request generator.

You might be wondering why the `wait_dly` (and `breq_mach`) variables in the testbench are lower case. I do this to remind myself that these variables use `CLKC` timing, as opposed to using `TREF` timing. The `CLKC` signal is used because these variables are generated based on outputs from the CPU.

The timing diagram in Figure 7-2 shows the operation of the Wait state generator. Rather than assert the `WAIT_REQ` input for the entire clock cycle, I have chosen to implement a basic setup and hold check for this input. I control the setup time using the `TREF6` master clock edge. In the same fashion, the hold time is set by the `TREF9` master clock edge.

For a complete test of the setup and hold times I would need to check both rising and falling edges on the `WAIT_REQ` signal around the `CLKC` edge. This would require slightly more complex assertion and de-assertion conditions, as shown in the last trace.

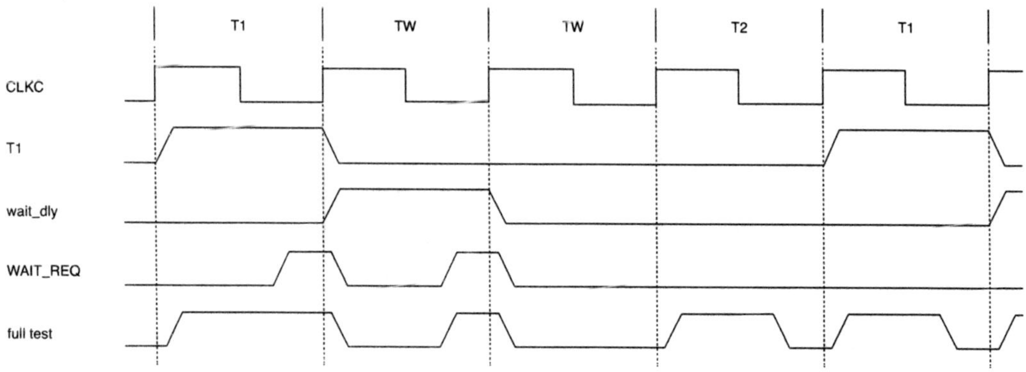

Figure 7-2. Testbench Wait Request timing.

Generating the Bus Request signal is an extension of the technique used to generate the WAIT_REQ input. This is shown in Listing 7-14. In this case the DMA_REQ signal needs to be active for more than the two clocks present in the case of the WAIT_REQ signal. This is because there is a dummy instruction fetch machine cycle (the *if1a* and *if1b* states) prior to starting the Bus Release machine cycles. I have not bothered to implement the hold time check that I used with the WAIT_REQ signal, but it is easy to do.

```
/*****************************************************************************************/
/*                                                                                       */
/* bus request generator                                                                 */
/*                                                                                       */
/*****************************************************************************************/
always @ (posedge CLKC) begin
  breq_mach <= (DISABLE_BREQ) ? 6'b000000 :
               (T1)           ? 6'b000001 : {breq_mach[4:0], wait_dly};
  end

always @ (posedge TREF6) DMA_REQ = !DISABLE_BREQ &&
                         (T1 || |breq_mach[2:0] || (HALT_TRAN && |breq_mach));
```

Listing 7-14. top_levl.v Bus Request generator.

The timing diagram in Figure 7-3 shows the normal (non-Halt) case for the DMA_REQ signal. Decoding the three least-significant bits of the breq_mach variable leads to three Bus Release machine cycles, which will be sufficient to verify proper operation. In the case where the bus is requested during the Halt state the entire width of the breq_mach variable is decoded to make sure that the CPU has actually entered the Halt state before the DMA_REQ signal is de-asserted.

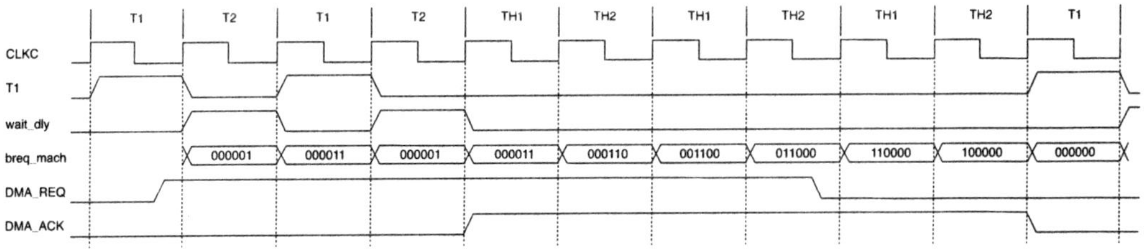

Figure 7-3. Testbench Bus Request timing.

When the Bus Request state machine is enabled the `DMA_REQ` signal is asserted more often than not, basically leading to one instruction executed between each request. This is a quick-and-dirty way to verify that there are no instruction dependencies relative to the Bus Request.

The final section of the testbench loads and executes the different test patterns. Table 7-1 shows the different Verilog Memory (.vm) files that are loaded into the testbench memory.

Files to be loaded into a Verilog memory model need to be in a particular format, but this format is easy to create from a file in Intel Hex format. I use a simple BASIC program to translate between these two formats.

All of these test patterns are written in Assembly language, with particular care taken to make sure that the observed values are toggling, that only the appropriate register is affected, and so on. The patterns are then assembled[7] into an Intel Hex format file, translated into the Verilog memory format, and used in the simulation.

Memory File	Function
setup_hl.vm	Initialization pattern that loads the HL register.
blank_xx.vm	Initialize memory with all unknowns
int_ops.vm	Interrupt modes, interrupt enable and disable, special cases.
int_opsd.vm	Compare data for the int_ops pattern
int_opss.vm	Compare data for the int_ops pattern when testing Bus Request
alu_ops.vm	Data manipulation instructions.
alu_opsd.vm	Compare data for the alu_ops pattern
dat_mov.vm	Load and store operations, push and pop
dat_movd.vm	Compare data for the dat_mov pattern
bit_ops.vm	Bit test, set and clear.
bit_opsd.vm	Compare data for the bit_ops pattern
jmp_ops.vm	Jumps, Calls, Returns and Restart.
jmp_opsd.vm	Compare data for the jmp_ops pattern
io_ops.vm	I/O instructions, block instructions.
io_opsd.vm	Compare data for the io_ops pattern

Table 7-1. Memory files used by the testbench.

A Verilog memory model is loaded from a file using the `$readmemh` system task. There are couple of important things to remember about this system task. First, this system task executes in zero simulation time, so it is completely transparent to the logic that is being simulated (the CPU in this case). Second, only the locations specified in the file will be updated, and all previous contents are unaffected.

Both of these facts have implications in the testbench. The zero simulation time means that it is possible to reload the memory on the fly without disturbing a simulation in progress. This means that I can reload the memory without resetting the CPU if necessary. I do not use this feature in this testbench but I have used it with other designs. In this testbench I will always execute the `resettask` task at the start of a test pattern to make sure that I am starting from a known condition.

To make sure that there is no carry-over from one pattern to the next, I always load both the read memory and the write memory with all unknowns before loading a new test pattern. This is where the blank_xx.vm memory file is used. Having unknowns in all of the unused memory locations will guarantee that the simulation will blow up if an instruction or data fetch is attempted outside of where it is supposed to happen. In the same way the `CMP_ERR_L` variable will go unknown if the CPU attempts to write to an unexpected address.

The setup_hl.vm pattern is a short little program that the CPU executes to load the HL register with a known value at the very start of the simulation. Without this little setup program the contents of the HL register would be unknown at this point, because the HL register is not affected by reset. I need the HL register in a known state to be able to distinguish startup from the RST 0 instruction.

There needs to be some mechanism for the test pattern to signal to the testbench that the pattern is complete and it is okay to load the next pattern into memory. This is what the `PAT_DONE` signal is used for. Both the `resettask` and `cleartask` tasks clear the `PAT_DONE` variable, while all of the test patterns set this variable upon completion. Ultimately the state of this variable is what controls the simulation.

Listing 7-15 shows part of the code that performs the load and execute of the test patterns. In this first section I execute all of the test patterns without Wait states and without Bus Requests. Then the remainder of this section (which isn't shown here) reruns the entire set of tests two more times, once with Wait states enabled and once with Bus Requests enabled.

```
/*****************************************************************************************/
/*                                                                                       */
/* run the test patterns                                                                 */
/*                                                                                       */
/*****************************************************************************************/
initial begin
  $readmemh("setup_hl.vm", rdmem);
  cleartask;
  wait (PAT_DONE);

  DISABLE_INT = 0;                                       /* interrupt generator on       */
```

```
resettask;
CMP_ERR_L = 16'h0000;
PAT_CNT   = 4'h1;
$readmemh("blank_xx.vm", rdmem);
$readmemh("blank_xx.vm", wrmem);
$readmemh("int_ops.vm",  rdmem);
$readmemh("int_opsd.vm", wrmem);
wait (PAT_DONE);

DISABLE_INT  = 1;                       /* interrupt generator off       */

resettask;
CMP_ERR_L = 16'h0000;
PAT_CNT   = 4'h2;
$readmemh("blank_xx.vm", rdmem);
$readmemh("blank_xx.vm", wrmem);
$readmemh("alu_ops.vm", rdmem);
$readmemh("alu_opsd.vm", wrmem);
wait (PAT_DONE);

resettask;
CMP_ERR_L = 16'h0000;
PAT_CNT   = 4'h3;
$readmemh("blank_xx.vm", rdmem);
$readmemh("blank_xx.vm", wrmem);
$readmemh("dat_mov.vm", rdmem);
$readmemh("dat_movd.vm", wrmem);
wait (PAT_DONE);

resettask;
CMP_ERR_L = 16'h0000;
PAT_CNT   = 4'h4;
$readmemh("blank_xx.vm", rdmem);
$readmemh("blank_xx.vm", wrmem);
$readmemh("bit_ops.vm", rdmem);
$readmemh("bit_opsd.vm", wrmem);
wait (PAT_DONE);
```

```
resettask;
CMP_ERR_L = 16'h0000;
PAT_CNT   = 4'h5;
$readmemh("blank_xx.vm", rdmem);
$readmemh("blank_xx.vm", wrmem);
$readmemh("jmp_ops.vm", rdmem);
$readmemh("jmp_opsd.vm", wrmem);
wait (PAT_DONE);

resettask;
CMP_ERR_L = 16'h0000;
PAT_CNT   = 4'h6;
$readmemh("blank_xx.vm", rdmem);
$readmemh("blank_xx.vm", wrmem);
$readmemh("io_ops.vm", rdmem);
$readmemh("io_opsd.vm", wrmem);
wait (PAT_DONE);
```

Listing 7-15. top_levl.v running the test pattern in the normal case.

Once the simulation completes without the `CMP_ERR_L` variable ever being incremented the design has passed the simulation, and I'm done.

8. It's Finally Done. Now what?

Introduction

Once the simulation is okay, the design can be reduced to practice. At the very least this requires a logic synthesis tool, perhaps a static timing analysis (STA) tool, and a place and route (P&R) tool. Most FPGA vendors provide graphical front-ends for these tools, but each vendor is different, so I will not attempt to cover all of the different possibilities here. But all Electronic Design Automation (EDA) tools that I am aware of can be controlled using Tool Control Language (TCL) scripts, so that is how I will present the information here.

The Details

With a design this simple, logic synthesis is almost a simple push of a button. The CPU is fully synchronous with a single clock, and all of the outputs come directly from the outputs of flip-flops. That means that the only constraint that you really need to give to the logic synthesis tool is the desired clock period. Here is what is required to tell the synthesis tool to try for a 25MHz clock:

```
create_clock -name CLKC [get_ports clkc] -period 40 -waveform {0 20}
```

More complex designs will require more constraint information, and it can get really messy with multiple clock domains. If you have to use multiple clock domains try to make the interfaces across clock domain boundaries as simple as possible.

Static timing analysis attempts to examine every possible logic path in the design to verify that timing constraints are being met. The critical phrase here is "every possible logic path". Even with a design this simple there are a lot of possible paths that will never be relevant to this analysis.

As a simple example, any path that starts with the A register and goes into the Temporary register is never used. So I don't want the STA tool wasting time trying to meet timing for this false path. This means that I need to tell the STA tool to ignore this possible path. The complication here is that the STA tools works on the output of the logic synthesis tool rather than the Verilog source, so I need to specify the physical cells involved. This makes the TCL commands a little complex:

```
set_false_path -from [get_cells DATAPATH/*_aa_reg*] -to [get_cells DATAPATH/tmp_reg*]
```

Since the Temporary register is used primarily to hold address information most of the other CPU registers will need to be similarly marked for the STA tool. This quickly leads to a lot of typing. I never attempt to identify all of the false paths before running the STA tool. I will mark the obvious paths and then run the tool to find the paths that I have forgotten about. After all, not every false path will lead to a timing violation anyway. You will be surprised at the false paths through the logic that the STA tool will find.

There is another type of path that can give the STA tool (and designers trying to identify these paths) fits. These are called multi-cycle paths, and they occur when the path from output of a flip-flop is not required to be valid on the next clock cycle at the input of another flip-flop.

The easiest way to illustrate this type of path is with the registers that control the register banks in the CPU. Remember that the `alt_af_reg` flip-flop controls the selection of main or alternate Accumulator and Flag register. This flip-flip changes state at the end of the *if1b* clock cycle, but this state will never be needed before the end of the next *if1b* clock cycle. This makes it a multi-cycle path with a period of two clocks. The way to tell the STA tool about this path is with these two TCL commands:

```
set_multicycle_path -setup 2 -from [get_cells DATAPATH/alt*_reg] -to [get_cells DATAPATH*_reg*]
set_multicycle_path -hold 1  -from [get_cells DATAPATH/alt*_reg] -to [get_cells DATAPATH*_reg*]
```

It is inevitable that there will be a multitude of multi-cycle paths in the design, and the STA tools will find a lot of them that will not meet your timing constraints. As in the case of false paths, I usually run the STA tool multiple times, adding to the list of multi-cycle paths between each run. I have found that each run will uncover a class of paths that I hadn't previously considered.

Once the logic synthesis and timing analysis is complete it is time to place the cells and route the signals. When I started as an IC designer this was done by completely by hand, but modern P&R tools are so advanced that only the most critical circuits are now done manually. In large designs the floorplan for the individual functional blocks is still created manually, but everything else is done by machine. P&R tools are specific to the technology used to implement the design, so I won't even attempt to cover this step here.

Enhancements

The design that I have presented here is fairly basic, but still perfectly usable for many types of projects. To keep from getting bogged down in complex details I have only implemented a few optimizations, so there is still room for improvement. Here are some improvements that you may want to try:

1. The encodings in the defines.v file are not necessarily optimal. Try to find better choices.

2. The address multiplexer in the alubmux.v module uses more cases than are strictly necessary, and two of the cases can be removed by choosing a different ALU operation for a couple of instructions. Implement this.

3. Accepting a Bus Request only on an instruction boundary does have a slight performance impact. A better choice might be to accept a Bus Request after any machine cycle. Try implementing this option and weigh the cost versus benefit of each choice.

4. The uniform two-clock-cycle machine cycle also has a performance impact. Try doing the address calculation in a single clock cycle. How much does this improve the performance, and is it worth it?

5. Instead of shortening the address calculation machine cycle, take advantage of the time to pre-fetch the next instruction. This will only work if the next instruction requires more than one machine cycle. Instead of following the *if1b* state with the *dec1* state, you can proceed directly to the *dec2* state. What is the performance gain? Don't forget to implement Wait states in these pre-fetch machine cycles!

6. The Z180 added a few new instructions, including multiply, to the Z80 instruction set. Try implementing these new instructions.

7. Upgrade the testbench to include checks for timing (setup, hold, output delay) for all signals.

8. Check the test programs for fault coverage and make improvements if necessary.

I hope that I have taken some of the mystery out of how to design a microprocessor. Remember, a CPU is just a group of interconnected state machines. If you approach the problem methodically and implement one piece at a time the design of a microprocessor is a manageable task.

Index

A

B

C

D

E

F

H

I

L

M

N

O

P

R

S

T

U

V

W

X

Z

Appendix

Figures

Listings

Tables

Resources/Bibliography

1. Files to accompany the book can be found at http://www.circuitcellar.com/book/

2. OVI Verilog HDL LRM
   http://www.vlsi-design.net/wp-content/uploads/2008/01/veriloglangrefmanual.zip

3. Z80 CPU User Manual http://www.zilog.com/docs/z80/um0080.pdf

4. William Barden Jr., *The Z-80 Microcomputer Handbook*, Howard W. Sams & Co. Inc., Indianapolis, IN, 1978.

5. Adam Osborne, Jerry Kane, Russel Rector and Susanna Jacobson, *Z80 Programming for Logic Design*, Osborne & Associates, Berkeley, CA, 1978.

6. The design spreadsheet is called “execute.xls” and is in the directory called “privdoc.”

7. Z80/Z180 Assembler: http://www.softools.com/sasmzilog.htm

CPSIA information can be obtained at www.ICGtesting.com
Printed in the USA
BVOW080000130112

280396BV00002B/2/P